JUST BEING **JON**

A MEMOIR

DEDICATION

Just Being Jon *is lovingly dedicated to my mother,
Willie Mae Walker-Haggins, for her patience, love, friendship, and
support throughout the years. Through her struggles, perseverance,
and determination, she remained strong. She was the root, trunk, and
branch of the tree, I was only a leaf. And my grandad, Richard Walker,
who inspired me during my early years. He told me that
anything is possible — all you have to have is a dream. Mother and
Grandad were my angels. They allowed me to spread my wings.
I would also like to honor the countless and faceless unknown
Forefathers and Foremothers who endured and stood strong.*

Just Being Jon *is also lovingly dedicated to:
Katherine Stephens, Laurel Van Horn, and Lorraine Curry
believed in my dream and inspired me throughout my adult years.*

AUTHOR'S OTHER BOOKS

The African American Travel Guide

Yes I Can — A Memoir of an African American Family

Chasing Wild ASS — Travel Book

Jon Haggins the GlobeTrotter TV — Travel Book

Contributed short stories to Eric Copage's *Soul Food Book*

TABLE OF CONTENTS

INTRODUCTION

Just Being Jon is a memoir of an African American family through seven generations. *Just Being Jon* addresses anyone who wants to live their life as fully and freely as possible. It is my great hope for some part of my story — my family's story — will serve as the impetus, and inspiration to help you discover how special we are to live in this moment; having not lived in the past. It allows you to address the internal fire within you, that wants to live life as fully and freely as possible.

I want the reader to see how much we have gained mentally and spiritually, to achieve all things possible, whether it is material or mental. Through the struggles of our parents and grandparents, we can understand our family's history, what we are made of and how their struggles made a better life for us.

The idea that curiosity and exploration are vital to the human spirit, was relayed during the early years that I spent with my grandfather. We traveled up and down the coast of Florida, visiting relatives. It was from his pivotal advice and loving influence that I began to travel. My first international trip was to Rio de Janeiro, Brazil for Carnival, when I was 23 years old. My first trip where I found my center — was to the Ivory Coast, West Africa, where I saw many Black business owners and entrepreneurs. They walked with great stride and pride. I returned home with newfound confidence and center.

As a descendant of slavery, I come from a line of people who spent their lives in oppression, restricted of opportunities to make life choices, which we sometimes take for granted —where to plant roots, how to raise children, what to think and how to be in the world. Through their struggles, our ancestors and family members have made a better life possible for us. It is through my life of travel that I pay homage to those before me, who were not afforded this opportunity.

To acknowledge how special this moment in time is for us, having not lived with oppression imposed upon us, is to grasp our opportunity to think independently and be free to do whatever we choose. Life is meant to be lived, enjoyed, and experienced in all aspects. To fully live life is an adventure unto itself. It helps me to remember life's fragility and beauty at the same time.

I wrote *Just Being Jon*, to inspire everyone to live out their dreams. I came to New York, from a small segregated town in Central Florida in 1953. Arriving in New York City, the Big Apple, was a culture shock that knocked my socks off. I entered the fashion business shortly after graduating from the Fashion Institute of Technology in 1964, during the Black Revolution, without realizing the turmoil of our country. I knew what I wanted to do from an early age. I wanted to be a Fashion Designer. It was a time when Blacks were relegated to the back room of the fashion houses. The Seventh Avenue designers were designing little stiff dresses.

Without having any contacts in the industry, but I did have Chutzpah, I made my path. I called editors and showed my soft drapey fashions. *Vogue* and *WWD* were the first to recognize my talent. A variety of national stores and publications followed suit. It was not an easy road, but I stuck with it. I became a fashion designer in 1966 and the darling of all the fashion editors in the mid-sixties and early seventies, for a short while, as everything in fashion is short-lived. I also had a fairy tale wedding at the end of one of my fashion shows. After closing my fashion design company in 1972, I did a little soul searching. I became a cabaret singer in NY. There were a lot of ups and downs in the cabaret. I couldn't wait to return to designing again. I opened another design studio in 1981. It was a very exciting time because several celebrities rushed in a bought my fashions. The Schomburg Center for Research in Black Culture (part of the NY Public Library) has 16 boxes of editorials and photographs from my fashion career.

After several years of being under-capitalized, I closed my design business in 1984 and decided to take a little time out to discover other things I could do. I became a stylist, a motivational speaker, a tour operator, a food and travel writer, and the producer and host of *GlobeTrotter TV*. *GlobeTrotter TV* has taken me around the world. The best part is, that I met incredible people who have inspired and helped me celebrate life. It's been a bumpy road, but through it all, I have survived, because of my perseverance and determination. Hopefully, this book will inspire you to reach for the stars and live out your dream. Remember there is no such word as 'No', because there are no limitations in life, you can do anything you desire.

While travel plays a vital role in my life, it isn't my only source of understanding of the preciousness of life and all the gifts it has to offer. I cherish the time spent in the latter years of my mother's life when we traveled together. That was before dementia set in. It was a deeper reminder of the most precious, beautiful, and miraculous gifts of life have to be savored.

It is my great hope for some part of my story — my family's story — to serve as the impetus, the inspiration to help you remember the opportunity it is to be alive at this moment in time; to address the internal fire within you that wants to live life as fully and freely as possible. *Just Being Jon* is about how special we are to live in this moment; having not lived in the past.

In writing this book, my intention is for you, to think about what you are made of, and what was given to you by your ancestors, and family members to help you live your life to the fullest. When we know who we are and where we come from, it informs the decisions we make in our lives. It helps to clarify our values, what is important and what message our life will give. To see how much we have gained mentally and spiritually to achieve all things possible, whether it is material or mental. We each have been given all we need to live the life closest to our hearts. Through the struggles of our great-grandparents, grandparents, and parents, we can understand our family's history, what we are made of and how their struggles made a better life for us. *Just Being Jon* is not just my family's story, but it's a story of many people of color. I would like to honor the countless, faceless, and unknown Forefathers and Foremothers who endured and stood strong. *Just Being Jon* is about discovery and Freedom.

CHAPTER ONE

The Beginning

I was standing next to the 'Door of No Return', at The Slave House on Goree Island in Dakar, Senegal, West Africa. The door opens onto the Atlantic Ocean. As I looked out, I reflected on the Middle Passage. It was the door that my ancestors were herded off like cattle, except they were bound with shackles and chains, to board a slave ship headed to the Americas. The Africans would never return to their culture, language, religion, tradition, or family.

I began to reflect on my family and their struggles, and how they survived in America. Therefore, I wanted to know what I was made of, so I began to follow my family's path from their humble beginnings, to what I have become. I was a fashion designer, then a Cabaret entertainer, a Tour Operator, a Food and Travel Writer, and finally the TV producer and host of *GlobeTrotter TV*.

My family is responsible for me being who I am. I am a part of them and they are a part of me. Their lives were similar to other families of color. They persevered through their struggles and survived. It proved to me that anything is possible, all you have to have is a dream.

William Walker, my great grandfather was born in South Carolina several years after the Civil War and shortly after Lincoln freed the slaves. As a wedding gift, William's Irish father-in-law, McQueen, decided to bequeath each of his seven children a portion of his 40 acres in northern Florida. He was one of the few Black men who received land. William and his wife, Alice McQueen-Walker, left South Carolina to plant roots of their own in the countryside of Monticello, which is located in the Panhandle North Western tip of Florida. McQueen's decision to bequeath land proved to be pivotal for my family lineage. It was their opportunity to establish themselves; an opportunity many Blacks did not receive.

A row of tall oak trees with Spanish moss dangling from its branches created a willowy canopy that shaded a long, long, winding dirt road that lead to Walker's farm. With Alice by my great grandfather's side, he built a home made from logs, known as a log cabin house. The open window shutters allowed light and fresh air to filter throughout the house.

Alice, my great grandmother, was of Blackfoot Indian and of Irish descent. Blackfoot Indians were native to the Northern Great Plains and prevalent at that time. Her hair was long and black, she kept it neatly coiffed in a traditional braid.

William Walker and Alice McQueen-Walker bore three sons, Richard, William, and James, and a daughter, Rebecca, on the farm. Richard Walker, my grandad was born on September 13th, 1898; the man who would "plant seeds" in my mind and show me anything is possible if you have a dream.

William and Alice understood the importance of teaching their children to think independently and to become unhindered from the harmful messages and conditioning placed upon Blacks. With persistent guidance from his parents, Grandad learned that independent thinkers strive to make a difference not only for themselves but also for others. In their striving, they inspire others to try different things. He and his siblings couldn't venture far from the family farm, because Whites were out to torment Blacks just for their amusement.

William and Alice were always looking out for their family's safety and health. They wanted their children to think for themselves, make good decisions and protect themselves. It was a risk to teach a Black child to have confidence, to hold his or her head up high, and be proud of what he or she did, but my great grandparents believed it was a risk worth taking. They wanted their children to understand the difference between following rules and being a conformist.

Accustomed to the laborious life of living and working in the countryside, like other farmers and sharecroppers. The countryside was peaceful, calm, and simplistic and it meant family and neighbors were always nearby. Grandad, as a young black man didn't like the tainted limits of not being able to move about freely, because of this, his internal "fire" couldn't be extinguished.

My folks weren't free, they were sharecroppers during Jim Crow. It was one more thing to endure while working for the white man. They also had to learn to crawl before they walked. However, they were self-sufficient, because they grew their crops and raised hogs and chicken for consumption. They ate fresh kill. Not the kind of food that's pumped with steroids that we eat today.

The farm didn't have electricity or refrigeration. My Great Grandad built a Smokehouse, where he smoked meat. Smoking the meat was a way to preserve it by drawing out the moisture, and making it difficult for bacteria to spoil the meat. He also smoked tobacco leaves in the Smokehouse.

Men chopped down trees, and cut them into smaller pieces, then stacked them close to the house for easy retrieval. The wood was used for the wood-burning stove.

Flour was the only thing they purchased from the General Store. It was used for making those hot, fluffy, flaky, homemade Southern biscuits. Great Grandma rose early to prepare the meals. She had to fire up the wood-burning stove. Then prepared a hearty breakfast of grits, eggs, thick slices of bacon or ham from the smokehouse, and of course those hot, fluffy, flaky, homemade biscuits. Everyone was awakened by the aroma of the hot biscuits that were baking in the wood-burning stove oven.

Preparing a meal was laborious because spices such as nutmeg, cinnamon, seasonings, and salt and pepper had to be ground. Men worked all day in the fields beneath the hot sun. They dug deep into the fertile soil to plant rows and rows of collard and mustard greens, corn, spinach, potatoes, beans, peas, red delicious tomatoes, and other vegetables. They reaped the fruits of their labor as their harvest came to fruition.

They also milked cows for fresh milk. A delicious thick white cream floated on top. The cream was used to make butter. Naturally, homegrown food was fresh and plentiful and a hot supper was always waiting on the table when the men returned from the fields. Dinner was eaten in the early afternoon. It always included fresh vegetables and meat from cows, pigs, or whatever they caught and killed, such as a possum. Exhausted from a hard day's work, a small meal was eaten under the light of a kerosene lantern in the early evening.

After everyone finished dinner and the dishes were washed, William and Alice sat in their wooden rocking chairs on the front porch and slowly rocked back and forth. Grandad, grandma, and his siblings sat on the steps. They talked about the goings-on in the countryside.

The tobacco from the smokehouse was compressed into small compact portions, then it was tightly packed inside the mouth, between the bottom lip and gum, then chewed for several hours. A commonality not foreign to the South, chewing tobacco was as much a part of daily life as cooking, cleaning, and working. Chewing tobacco created excess saliva that turned into a dark liquid. It also prevented the mouth from becoming dry. The liquid was typically spat onto the ground or suddenly there was the 'ping' sound when it abruptly hit the side of a tin can placed nearby. As the day drew to an end, the moon illuminated the farm. The farm was peacefully quiet, except for the sound of crickets and frogs.

Despite the physical and mental rigors of living a life of subsistence, the natural offerings were bountiful. The lush vegetation of the countryside was unparalleled. Pecans dangled from tree branches, before dropping on the ground for easy picking, and succulent peaches blossomed and ripened on the tree with a sweet bouquet and a fruitful flavor. Mulberry bushes were filled with dark purple berries. The berries were picked and made into delicious jams. The orange flower blossoms, bloomed into ripe, juicy sweet oranges with seeds, while the large, green plump watermelons lay on the ground attached to vines. When the watermelons were sliced, black seeds dotted the interior. Each sweet bite of that lush, red interior was memorable. The delicious juices dripped down onto their homemade clothes. Whatever fruit that wasn't eaten was canned and preserved for the winter.

A Water Well was located next to the house. Water was retrieved by tying a rope to a bucket, then lowering it into a Well. Water was then heated on the old wood-burning stove. Hot water was used for washing dishes and poured into a large galvanized tub for bathing. The toilet was an outhouse in the backyard, so there was no such thing as flushing the toilet. It was common to see something crawling around while you "handled your business."

Whenever my great-grandmother wasn't helping deliver babies, she tended to domestic work like all the other women. She made lye soap, which was used for the laundry. After placing the dirty clothes in a large galvanized tin tub, she scrubbed them with an up and down motion on a washboard, which was made from a ridged sheet of galvanized tin, it had a wooded frame. Once the clothes were washed and rinsed, she stretched them out and hung them over a clothesline. The clothesline was constructed with a rope that was suspended between two poles in the backyard. She used wooden clothes pins to anchor the clothes. The clothes were left to dry in the hot sun. Once dry, the fresh smell of flowers and country air lingered on the clothes.

Families in the backwoods of the countryside were very close and protective of one another. My great grandparents were close to one family in particular, the Proctors, who lived on the other side of a small pond that separated the farms. The pond was shaded by rows of tall oak trees. Fresh spring water slowly and gently flowed downstream.

A small wooden bridge allowed everyone to cross to the other side, where they gathered, worked, and checked on each other. Both families lead a simple and peaceful life of daily chores. The Proctors often gathered on Walker's porch in the evenings. The vast fields offered a sense of serenity. In the ebb and flow of laughter and conversation, timelessness lingered on. The vast fields offered a sense of serenity in the evenings. The Proctors had one daughter, Viola, whom Grandad was smitten with. After his chores were done on the weekend, he made a point of spending time with her. Viola was five feet six inches tall. Her smooth, brown skin glowed with pride. Grandad stood six feet tall and walked with perfect posture and a powerful stride. And his skin was smooth, olive-brown. His handsome face bore chiseled features with high cheekbones.

Grandad often spoke of the fish they caught and the days spent swimming and how freely the fresh water flowed. To this day, the stream remains vivid in my mind from my many visits to the farm when I was a little boy.

Grandad was a bold and brazen young man who wasn't afraid to take chances. After several years of courting, he asked Viola for her hand in marriage. Following the good start set in motion by his grandparents and parents, he would also plant roots in Monticello, Florida.

Grandad didn't have a formal education, because he had to help with chores on the farm. He learned carpentry by watching his family build homes. He quickly became a very skilled carpenter. He built his first log cabin home, for his new bride, in preparation to start a family of their own. The house was constructed with two rooms. Two beds and a dining table in the front room and the second room was furnished with two additional beds and a make-shift kitchen with a wood-burning stove. Grandad also added a front and back porch. The open window shutters allowed light and fresh air to filter throughout the house.

The house rested on a farm with a garden. The garden was dotted with magnolia trees. Magnolias blossom into six to twelve showy large white petals with a waxy texture. This striking evergreen, with full, dark green leaves bore sweet and fresh fragrant white flowers. Magnolias can smell like sweet candy, spicy verbena, tart lemon, citrus honey or dusty violets. A silent, sweet breeze gently brushed against the swaying branches creating a whisper of silence and calling out its southern beauty. Magnolia trees offered a symbol of strength and stability near the home where three generations of my family would live.

They were blessed with four children, my mother Willie Mae Walker was the first born on September 21, 1925, then Rebecca, Jackie, and Robert.

Mother was the third generation of my family in Monticello. Grandad's parents were proud of him and their grandchildren. In light of the strenuousness of circumstances in the countryside, Blacks were drawn to each other. The spirit of comradery kept them optimistic. They knew that whatever happened, someone would be there for support. There was constantly a looming physical threat. Even though the KKK remained prevalent and was relentless in their mission to purge the area of Blacks. Grandad never personally encountered the KKK, but certainly was aware of their activities.

Black children in the countryside didn't have fancy toys to play with such as Atari games, iPads, or computers. They used their imagination. When siblings weren't playing with each other, they played with cousins, neighbors, or animals. With plenty of open space to run, they chased whichever pig, chicken, or hen was left over after a slaughter. When there wasn't an animal available to ride, one of them got down on the ground onto their knees and pretended to be a mule. Little ones climbed onto the back of the "mule" and yelled out routine "commands" overheard by adults. They also climbed tall oak trees in hope of seeing something new, or at other times just sat and looked out as far as their eyes could see. They picked berries and knew to stay away from anything poisonous. And there was fishing. It seemed there was nothing more exciting than a fish biting the worm at the end of the fishing line. They grinned proudly and ignored the pull of the fish to get away, then abruptly yanked it out of the water. Fresh fish was always a welcomed dish.

Grandad was thirty-one at the start of The Great Depression in 1929. It was similar to Reconstruction following the Civil War, Retrenchment — budget cutbacks during the Depression — rendered a disproportionately negative impact on Blacks. The Great Depression affected rural Black areas more because their school budgets were already minimal. The average Black family income, already very low, decreased dramatically.

By the time my mother was seven-years-old, the effects of the Depression overshadowed all aspects of urban society. Many people face unemployment or severely reduced incomes. The value of farm land plummeted, and they could no longer pay their property taxes that supported schools. The most Blacks could contribute to maintaining their schools was labor.

Black students — facing racism, poverty, and neglect — were once again severely impacted. They received far less financial support than White schools. Black schools had fewer books and supplies were virtually nonexistent. The schoolhouse was one large room where all grades were taught. The buildings were in bad condition. Cutbacks resulted in reductions in school hours, increased class sizes, and decreases in teachers' salaries. Some Black schools could not pay for heat and White school boards were more reluctant than ever to fund Black schools. Many Whites did not want Blacks to become educated, fearing they would challenge White Supremacy and not be content with jobs working in the fields or domestic service.

There were no school buses or transportation in Monticello. Black children, who still attended school, walked barefoot for miles along, long dusty, dirt roads. They remained cautiously mindful of Whites driving down the road. Whenever Black children saw a car filled with Whites coming down the dirt road, they were taught to stay out of sight. To avoid being seen, taunted, tormented, or even killed. They quickly raced to hide in a ditch or behind a tree.

Considering pervasive racism failed to diminish with the Civil War, by the 1890s. With the ever-worsening economic conditions in the early 1930s, the Black population shifted dramatically, as thousands migrated from the rural South to the urban North in search of better economic, social, and political opportunities. For those in the southern countryside, there remained a lingering threat of violence against Black families. They were alone, amongst themselves with little protection from authorities. Black families understood the importance of looking out for one another and the community was tight.

When inciting or inflicting violence, Klan members wore white cloaks with a pointed hood that only exposed their eyes and hands. The purpose of the cloak was two-fold: to conceal identity and to intimidate. To exert social, political, and economic power over Blacks, the KKK utilized violence to injure, threaten, and murder Blacks.

The KKK made it difficult for Black families living in the backwoods of the Panhandle region of Florida. In the late 1800s, the KKK was formed to prevent Blacks from having equal rights, privileges, and opportunities as Whites in the south. Even though the Civil War and the 13th Amendment granted Blacks freedom, the KKK made sure their freedom came at a price.

While the KKK's presence was heavily felt throughout the region, they didn't hesitate to oppose all forward movements in the Black population. They burned crosses in front of Black families' homes. They hanged or killed a Black person just for the fun of it. While all Whites were not members of the Ku Klux Klan, Blacks couldn't be sure what an interaction with Whites would yield.

Lynching postcards were popular amongst whites. The first time I saw Lynching postcards was in 2001 at the King Center in Atlanta. The postcard bore a photograph of lynching — a vigilante murder usually motivated by racial hatred — intended to be distributed, collected, or kept as a souvenir. Often a lynching postcard would be inscribed with racist text or poems. In a typical lynching postcard, the victim is displayed prominently at the center of the shot, while smiling spectators, often including children, crowd the margins of the frame, posing for the camera to prove their presence. Facial expressions suggesting remorse, guilt, shame, or regret are rare. Often the photographer was one of the killers. Lynching postcards were in widespread production for more than fifty years in the United States; although their distribution through the United States Postal Service was banned in 1908.

The song, *Strange Fruit* was written by Abel Meeropol and performed by many artists (but most notably, Billie Holiday and Nina Simone,). It is a dark and profound song about the lynching of Blacks in the Southern United States during the Jim Crow Era. In the lyrics, Black victims are portrayed as "strange fruit," as they hung from trees, rotting in the sun, blowing in the wind, and becoming food for crows.

It was a protest song that Billie Holiday very bravely performed under grave threats and at high personal cost.

(Verse 1)
Southern trees bear a strange fruit
Blood on the leaves and blood at the root
Black bodies swinging in the southern breeze
Strange fruit hanging from the poplar trees

[Verse 2]
Pastoral scene of the gallant south
The bulging eyes and the twisted mouth
Scent of magnolias, sweet and fresh
Then the sudden smell of burning flesh

[Verse 3]
Here is a fruit for the crows to pluck
For the rain to gather, for the wind to suck
For the sun to rot, for the trees to drop
Here is a strange and bitter crop

Consistent with inhumane treatment carried over from slavery, Blacks were forced to speak and behave in a submissive demonstration of "knowing their place" to avoid racist confrontations. When confronted, they didn't dare argue, raise their voice or "speak out of turn." The appropriate response to any question from a White person was simply, "Yes," or "No Ma'am," or "Sir." However, acquiescence wasn't enough. With the mounting number of Blacks killed by the Klan, it seemed only death would satiate a heart consumed with hate.

Slavery and racism took a staggering toll on the mindset of Blacks. It shaped the attitudes and opinions they would pass from generation to generation. Among the many devastating physicals, mental and emotional effects of slavery and racism, one of the most debilitating were the psychological conditioning ingrained in Blacks. Considering freedom is a birthright for every human being, it was a birthright denied to Blacks physically and mentally. Similar to my great grandparents born free at the end of the Civil War, many children who were born free to enslaved parents subconsciously carried on the mentality that sought to keep them enslaved. While land ownership was a good start and played a pivotal role in changing the trajectory of my great grandparents' lives, it would take more than land to change the mindset of Blacks to cultivate mental freedom.

To free themselves of the mental restrictions, which sought to keep Blacks bound by submissive ways of thinking, behaving, living, and being in the world, would require great courage. It would also require endurance, persistence, the will to "plant new seeds" in the family lineage, and the foresight to utilize obstacles they faced beneficially. Blacks would have to teach and show their children a life beyond what they could see as possible.

Years passed in the countryside, but racial tension did not. Segregation tightened and racial oppression escalated across the United States. During the Great Migration (1910–1920), many Blacks left the countryside and poured into industrial cities to find work. They filled labor shortages created by World War I, such as working in factories, slaughterhouses, and foundries, where working conditions were arduous and sometimes dangerous. Female migrants had a harder time finding work, spurring heated competition for domestic labor positions.

That was not something my great-grandparents wanted to do. Knowing they lived during a hostile time when Blacks were still viewed as inferior, freedom tenuous and laws mandated separation, whether you were a Black in the city or the rural area they were all in a similar situation. There was continued discrimination in employment, as well as segregated schools and public accommodations. However, the war and migration bolstered a heightened self-confidence in blacks that manifested in the New Negro Movement of the 1920s. Evoking the "New Negro," the NAACP — the National Association for the Advancement of Colored People — whose goals were the abolition of segregation, discrimination, disenfranchisement, and racial violence, and particularly lynching, lobbied aggressively for a federal anti-lynching law.

I recently visited Galway, Ireland, Liam Silke, a guide, shared the origin of the word 'Lynch'. In 1492, Stephen Lynch, the father, idolized his son, Walter. Walter was mad about a lovely girl called Sarah, so to be true to each other, they were going to get married. Stephen Lynch was a very successful merchant and also the mayor of Galway and a high court judge. He did great business with a family called Gomez in Spain. Gomez had a son who came over as an exchange student. In those days you came for a year or two, not for a week or two like today. So, he and Walter became great pals. However, nature took its course, and Sarah, Walter's fiancée had eyes for the Spaniard. The Spaniard was tall and very handsome. Sarah sent Walter packing and he was not happy. One night Walter was on his way home and spotted Gomez coming out of Sarah's house. Gomez was there because he wanted Sarah to translate a letter to send to his father to say what a fantastic city Galway was. Walter had had a few drinks and was quite mad, Gomez saw it in Walter's eyes. Walter also had a large knife. Gomez didn't wait around, he ran down one of the alleyways and fell. Walter caught up with him and put a knife in Gomez's back and killed him.

Walter threw Gomez's body in the estuary that took his body out to sea and six hours later the tide washed the body back to the shore. The police found Gomez's body with Walter's knife in him. They arrested Walter. Walter being a gentleman admitted to the crime. Walter was found guilty of murder by the jury. His father was the judge. One year before this, the judge's best friend's son had committed murder and he begged for clemency for his son. Lynch said no! Justice must be done. He hanged his best friend's son. What goes around comes around. He had no choice but to find his son guilty of murder. Walter was brought to the gallows, the hangman refused to hang Walter because he was the judge's son and feared repercussions to his family from the judge. So, Stephen Lynch brought his son to a window and put a noose around his son's neck, tied his hands behind his back, then caressed his son and told him how much he loved him, then threw him out the window. He was lynched. That is where the term 'Lynching' comes from.

Despite rapid changes taking place in industrial areas, it was not enough. The Jim Crow laws of the Segregation Era (1900–1939) continued to mandate the separation of the races in practically every aspect of public life. Water fountains, restaurants, theaters, hotels, restrooms, stores, buses, trains, workplaces, and other public facilities were typically designated with "White Only" and "Colored Only" signs.

No matter where you were, in the countryside or the city, racism, restriction and the absence of true freedom were pervasive.

My grand and great-grandparents also had to learn to crawl before they walked. However, they stood strong and survived those difficult times, so that I can tell my family's story. And to think that I have the freedom today to do whatever I like. I am an independent thinker and doer.

My great grandparents, William and Alice, lived to see some changes take place in their world and society; some good and some bad. They also lived to see their grandchildren. They died at an early age on the land they knew and loved.

With the ever-worsening economic conditions in the early 1930s, many rural Blacks moved into the cities. However, it was also at this time Blacks found an opening and pushed for equality. The epicenter of this opening was in Harlem, New York. Harlem was originally developed for White workers who didn't want to commute to the city. It was abandoned by the White middle class in the early 1900s'. The neighborhood of Harlem was revitalized and became a haven for those who escaped the south during the Great Migration (1910-1930). It became a destination for Black immigrants, Black intellectuals, artists, and entrepreneurs, and years later a destination for Mother. Black performers could entertain in downtown clubs and hotels, but couldn't stay there. They had to go back uptown to the Teresa Hotel on 125th Street in Harlem. The Teresa Hotel was their 'Waldorf Astoria'. Sammy Davis wasn't allowed to see his friend Frank Sinatra perform at the Copa until Frank made a stink, then they allowed Sammy in.

Langston Hughes and Zora Neale Hurston began their careers in Harlem's vibrant literary community. Duke Ellington, Bessie Smith, and Louis Armstrong performed in Harlem's jazz clubs where clubgoers first created swing dance. The area soon became known as the "Capital of Black America", during what was also known as a "spiritual coming of age."

The massive migration of Blacks into new areas led to more tension and race riots. Irreconcilable differences increased not only between Blacks, Whites, and social classes but also between Grandad and Viola.

Younger Grandad

Young Grandad in hat

Grandad was six feet tall and physically fit. His olive-brown skin was smooth and his handsome face bore chiseled features with high cheekbones. He was also a playboy. While infidelity meant different things to different people, to Viola it meant the end of their marriage. She would not tolerate his philandering, so they separated in 1932 before Mother turned seven years old. Unfortunately, their marriage only lasted eight years.

After they separated, Grandad left Monticello and moved to Sanford, a small town in central Florida. He was the first in his family to leave the countryside. He rented a single-room house for $2.00 per week from Miss Sneed, the property owner. Miss Sneed was an elderly and graceful lady. Her property and house were kept clean, simple, and quiet just the way she liked it. The little house that Grandad rented did not have finished interior walls. He was crafty with imagination and knew he would need more space when his children visited. He asked Miss Sneed for permission to add another room. She agreed. In addition to the extra room, Grandad added a front and back porch. When he sat on the front porch in the evenings, it was very calming. It reminded him of evenings with his parents and siblings on the farm.

Viola also wanted a new start. She uprooted herself and settled in a new home in Fort Pierce, Florida, a two-hour drive from Sanford. She quickly found work as an elementary school teacher. She was at a calm place in her life, because she was working on something she had a passion for, and found a new social circle.

Education was important to grandma. She wanted the best for her children, even if they started school late, due to the effects of the Depression. Mother entered the school and split her weekends with Grandad. Life in a new city and a new school was a difficult adjustment for my mother. It was also difficult adjusting to two homes and two cities. Everything and everyone was new and different. The days spent carelessly swimming in the stream in the countryside were long lost. Those days were distant memories, figments of a world left behind.

It wasn't long before Viola met and married Willie Lee Jones, but the adjustment to a new father figure didn't go well for my mother. There were numerous conflicts between her and Mr. Jones. He insisted that she drop out of school. He wanted her to work and contribute to the household expenses. Mother adamantly opposed that. She was not a happy camper. She didn't want to walk an uneducated path like so many blacks were forced onto. She was eager to learn and wanted to stay in school, but Mr. Jones' demanding presence made it difficult for her. So, she dropped out of school in the middle of her ninth grade. She knew she couldn't stay under the same roof with Mr. Jones.

Several years later, something remarkable and unexpected happened. Viola introduced my mother to a young man named John from Statesboro, Georgia. John had recently settled in Tampa, a new area in Florida for my mother. In an unusually short courtship, eclipsed by the fact that she was more than ready to be out of her stepfather's house. Mother ran off at 17 years old and married John Wesley Hagins. Then she moved to Tampa, a two-hour drive from both Grandad and Viola. They lived in Ybor, the Black section of town, near Central Avenue. It was close to the hub of the city, known as the "Harlem of the South." Similar to Harlem, New York, where clubs in that area hosted a national array of black entertainers. Within a year of marriage, my mother was almost 18 years old when she was admitted to Tampa

Mother holding me

Negro Hospital, where I was born on September 5th, 1943. weighing in at nine and a half pounds.

No one historic event can be said to have been the origin of World War II (1939-1945), but as preparations for war accelerated, minority groups hoped they would benefit as much as the rest of the country from the new jobs in military production. Conversely, black workers were often shut out of defense plant jobs, and when they could find work it was often in the most menial, dangerous, and low-paying jobs. Although blacks had mixed feelings about supporting the war effort when their own country did not offer them the freedom America was fighting for overseas, many enlisted to fight, and my father was one of them. When he registered in the Army, his last name, Hagins, was misspelled with an extra 'G'. Mother was afraid if anything happened to him in the line of duty, she wouldn't be able to prove she was legally his spouse, to receive military benefits. Being diligent and not willing to take any chance on the potential effects of an administrative error, she changed our family surname to "Haggins" to correspond with the Army's misspelling.

In 1944, one year before the suicide of Adolf Hitler and Germany's unconditional surrender on May 7th, 1945, my father was discharged from the Army. Until the formal surrender of Japan on September 2nd, 1945. There was an average of 27,000 people killed each day, making World War II the most destructive war in human history. The primary combatants were Germany, Italy, Japan, Great Britain, The Soviet Union, and the United States.

Relieved he was not physically injured and home with his family, they celebrated on many occasions in their special way. My mother soon discovered she was pregnant again. However, she later had a miscarriage. Having been away from her husband for so long made it difficult to imagine his return home would be anything less than wonderful, but that was not the case. When Dad returned home after deployment, he also brought with him disturbing thoughts, feelings, and trauma-related symptoms. The war had changed him. He was paranoid, abusive, and shoved my mother around. He was no longer the same man he was one year prior. Mother occasionally visited her in-laws, he accused her of cheating with another man. No explanation of her absence would suffice. She realized there was nothing she could do to convince him otherwise, and his rage wouldn't stop. Mother packed a suitcase one afternoon, bundled me up, and boarded a bus to Sanford, where we stayed with Grandad. The room she once slept in felt too new and too foreign, but now brought comfort and solace when she needed it the most.

Several months after her arrival in Sanford, she made a lost attempt with my father to sustain martial stability and a home of her own, she began dating a young man. Things went well, so well that within their short time together he promised to marry her. To her surprise, she suddenly began to notice consistent feelings of nausea and the inability to keep food down. She was pregnant. Once the young man found out about the pregnancy he left town. My sister, Carolyn, was born in Sanford on January 30th, 1946. Mother was now a single mother of two small children. She did not take the relationship losses well. First, her parents separated, then the realization that she couldn't stay with the man she loved, and now the betrayal of Carolyn's father. She knew she had no other option than to move forward; to continue going on without completely closing her heart.

She needed space to clear her head, which was difficult to do in Sanford because everyone in town knew her story. She uprooted herself with Carolyn and me and moved to Jacksonville where she stayed with her aunt Rebecca. She became gainfully employed as a maid at the Ponte Vedra Resort, just outside of Jacksonville. Domestic work wasn't her first choice of work, but the income would feed her and her kids and keep a roof over our heads, or so she hoped. Many years later, I was a guest at that very Resort. A funny thing happened when I entered the restaurant for breakfast, a Black waiter leaned over and quietly asked if I was a guest. He was surprised that I was. When I arrive for breakfast the next morning, the same waiter addressed me as, "Mr. Haggins." Funny how things have changed, and yet they haven't.

Work at the resort was laborious and more demanding than she anticipated. It was too much to work, cook, clean the house, and care for a one and three-year-old. Underneath the weight of financial concerns and the inability to see her way forward, she had persistent chronic migraines and her health began to decline. Mother was mentally, physically exhausted, and overwhelmed. The last thing she wanted to do was call her father, not because she was embarrassed, but because she knew what the call would mean. She would have to ask for something she never anticipated. He was sympathetic to the situation, due to his separation from Viola when his children were young,

A few hours later, Grandad, got in his big Buick and drove to Jacksonville to discuss the possibility of taking me 'for a while. At the time, neither of them anticipated that "a while" would turn into six and a half years.

Because he often worked in different towns as a freelance carpenter, he told her he couldn't manage both children. There were no provisions to accommodate a little girl. "I'll return within two weeks and take the boy." I didn't want to wait, I wanted to go......then. When I heard that, I jumped up and down on the front porch and cried my eyes out as he drove off in his big Buick and vanished into the horizon as the sun was setting. I remembered an earlier brief stay with him, and how patient he was and I didn't want to wait. As promised, he returned in two weeks.

Mother asked several members of the family if they would assume temporary responsibility for caring for my sister, Carolyn. No one wanted that responsibility. With no other alternative she felt she had no other choice, but to place her in a foster home.

Despite ample financial resources held by the resort to pay employees a good wage, Black women were placed in domestic service positions with little pay and no opportunity for advancement. Those conditions served as a powerful incentive for Black southerners to look for other opportunities elsewhere; hence the Second Great Migration. The Second Great Migration began in 1940 when more than five million African Americans from the South moved to the Northeast, Midwest, and West and it continued throughout World War II and lasted until 1970.

Like the first Great Migration, blacks were motivated to move based on economic concerns. As long as she remained employed at the resort, Mother's path to self-sustenance, stability, and any semblance of upward mobility was non-existent. Overshadowed by a complex combination of distress, despair, and hope, despite health concerns, she considered the opportunities in the "Capital of Black America." One of her relatives told her about a cousin in New York who thought she could stay with her. She took the little money she had and bought a Greyhound bus ticket to New York. Several days later she boarded a bus and walked to the back of the bus to find a seat. Riding in the back of the bus was part of the Jim Crow era and that's what blacks did in the 40s.

Upon arriving in New York, she quickly understood the name 'Big Apple.' It was the first time she was surrounded by so many people in one place and saw many tall buildings. She felt displaced. Her cousin welcomed her, and they shared an apartment in Harlem. Albeit by her hand, she was once again in a new place, far from the home she once knew.

Several months after my mother arrived, she was infected with a fungus that caused pneumonia. She was rushed to New York Hospital, where the doctors rushed in and gave her antibiotics and oxygen to help her breathe. The pneumonia was so severe that her prognosis wasn't favorable. She remained in the hospital for one month. Several doctors said she would not recover. However, her being a religious woman, faith and her belief in God prevailed. She told the doctors and nurses, "I have to live because I have two small children." By some unknown miracle, she regained her strength and recovered. The doctors were amazed.

CHAPTER TWO

Sanford

Sanford was a typical small town, located in Central Florida at the southern tip of the St. John River. The river is approximately three miles wide. The Nile in Egypt, the St. John River in Canada, and the St. John River in Sanford are the three rivers that flow from south to north. Sanford is also the last stop for the auto train.

Sanford was also a slow-paced town where everyone knew each other. It was a conservative southern town where residents took great pride in their homes and respected their neighbors. It was also known for its lush vegetation of celery crops, slightly akin to Monticello. A bouquet of celery permeated the air on any given day.

While Grandad was building a new home, he left me in the car, when I was very young. Periodically, he brought me food or toys to play with. Whenever I cried, he'd come to change my clothes and then go back to work. Once the shell or frame of the house was completed, he would come and take me in, and allow me to crawl around the floor, and boy that was fun.

Walker, the family surname, suited Grandad perfectly. He had a slim build and walked with great strides and perfect posture. I found it difficult to keep up with his pace due to my small size.

Grandad's home was situated on the back lot of Miss Sneed's two-story, white clapboard house, which was located on the corner of Locust Avenue and Tenth Street. A row of banana trees stood gracefully between Grandad's and Miss Sneed's house. The banana bushes produced bunches of tiny, sweet, yellow bananas that I loved and devoured. Several orange trees bore a flavorful, sweet citrus fruit. Whenever my fruit tooth had a craving, I readily plucked bunches of oranges from the tree. Several Mulberry bushes also stood in the backyard. The bushes bore plentiful dark purple and delicious berries. The neighboring ladies often ask me to pick a bunch of berries, so they could make succulent mulberry jam.

A group of black men dressed in black and white stripe outfits with chains around their ankles was repairing the road near my house. They were from the chain gang, also known as free labor. Guards with guns and nightsticks watched over them as they worked. I was about 6 years old and not afraid. I walked out and gave them a bunch of sweet bananas. To me, they were just unfortunate men, forced into a situation and treated badly.

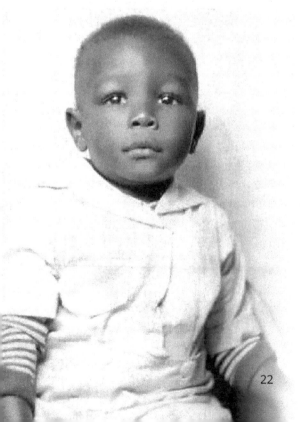

Jon at age 3

I was quite comfortable in my new environment at Grandad's home with one exception. The outhouse. It was something I could not and did not use. I simply refused. I was too afraid of snakes, bugs, or whatever else could crawl into some forbidden area of my body. Against Grandad's instructions, I decided to use a pail to 'handle my business. I alone decided that would be the extent of my relationship with the outhouse.

Miss Sneed's home was rather large. The top floor featured four bedrooms. I often thought of Miss Sneed's home as my second home. I spent quite a bit of time with her because she was my guardian when Grandad was away working as an independent carpenter. Miss Sneed treated me kindly. I felt welcomed as if I lived in that big house. When she was busy with housework or cooking, I would run through the house and entertain myself. The front porch had a wooden slat swing, where I sat and ate the center of juicy, ripe watermelons with black seeds, not the kind we buy in the supermarket today. A large watermelon only cost 50 cents at that time. During those blistering hot summer days, I slowly quenched my thirst with a glass of cold, freshly squeezed lemonade that was poured over lots of ice.

A gigantic oak tree stood in the front yard and shaded the open veranda. I marveled at the strong limbs of the oak tree and fantasized about building a tree house, but never did. That was the tree I climbed, it was a magical place of solace. I look out into the distance to see all the things I couldn't see from below and dream of places I would like to go.

Grandad always invited me to accompany him as he drove around town visiting his friends. He was popular amongst his peers and knew everyone in the neighborhood. After all, Sanford was a small town. His friends called him, "Big Man." They often reminisced about the 'Good Old Days.' They were keenly interested in the up-to-date gossip, mutual friends, work, the news, and the upcoming Friday night fish fry (freshly fried fish sandwich on white Wonder Bread). The fish fry was held on the corner of Locust and Tenth. The fish fry permeated the air from half a block away.

Grandad was keen on hearing the latest news, unfortunately, he couldn't read. Grandad was 'book illiterate', because, when he was young, he didn't have the luxury of attending school. He had to help his family with chores on the farm. He asked Miss Sneed to read the newspaper. He often asked, was a white or colored person. If the news was about a white person, he wasn't interested, but If it was about a Colored person, he was always interested.

While letters might have passed by Grandad, he learned basic math that was necessary for his craft. Despite not having a formal education, he thought education was the most important thing in life. With an education "one can achieve anything one desires." He said, "If I had an education, I would have been an engineer, instead of a carpenter. You shouldn't ever allow yourself to feel limited as I was. Having an education will afford you many opportunities for a broader, more productive, and fulfilling life." He wanted more out of life and relayed it to his four children. He wanted them to receive a good education. Although he couldn't afford to fulfill all of his dreams, he continued to try. One of his dreams was to send all of his children to college. However, he achieved part of his goal when he sent his youngest son, Robert, to The University of California. That was a proud moment in his life. He was very proud of his son and his achievement. He wanted all of his children to dream and achieve whatever they aspired to do.

He taught me how to use my imagination to draw images. I frequently thumbed through Sears Roebuck Catalogs and cut out pictures of the fashions of the day. I had an innate interest in fashion.

Grandad treated me with the utmost respect. He was my Guardian Angel. He protected me. But he couldn't protect me from a secret that I never shared with him. I was seduced by a pedophile before I was seven. The pedophile rented a room on the top floor in Miss Sneed's house. He enticed me to his room by promising to buy me toys, which he never did. I don't think I was the only boy in the neighborhood that he seduced.

Everyone often gathered on Miss Sneed's porch after dinner to catch up on the events of the day. The pedophile also joins the group. He wanted me to sit next to him on the swing and I refused because I didn't want anyone to know what had happened between us.

Friday was also grocery shopping day. I loved to shop with Grandad. The highlight of my day was a stop at a bakery shop, where the donuts were freshly baked with a sugary, sweet glaze. Grandad always bought one dozen. When we returned home, I'd place the box of donuts on the dining table. I couldn't wait to sink my teeth into them. As I bit down into the soft glazed donut, the sweetness was everywhere. I couldn't tell what I loved more, the taste of the donut, Grandad, or both. With every bite, it seemed nothing could be better than that.

Whenever Grandad wanted fresh chicken, he would kill one from the backyard. First, he would catch the chicken and wring its neck and then allow it to run around the yard until it finally dropped dead, or he simply chopped the head off. I always thought that was cruel. Then he dropped the chicken in hot water to loosen its feathers, then pluck them.

Surprisingly, Grandad knew his way around the kitchen. He was a fantastic cook. He brought some of the traditions from the country to the city, for example: cooking our meals on a wood-burning stove. His timing was impeccable for homemade, baked, fluffy biscuits and cornbread, just like his mother used to make. I loved watching him flip pancakes in an iron skillet. He flipped them with precision. He also boiled chitterlings ('chitlins'). Chitlins' are the small intestines of a pig. When the 'chitlins' were boiling on the stove, the vile odor permeated the entire house. I wondered how something that smelled so bad could taste so good. I knew it would be the best dish of the day. He also made the most delicious pumpkin bread. I tried his recipe during my adult years and discovered I couldn't mimic his magic touch. Instead of my bread rising to the top of the pan, it went under. Cooking, pots, and pans were never my thing, but I truly enjoy the pleasure of eating. He had an Ice Box Metal Refrigerator, that kept the food chilled. An Ice Box is a pre-refrigerator. The ice man delivered a large block of ice on alternating days.

Grandad also fermented apples in sugar in a large pan of water for several weeks. It became brewed into a pungent drink that knocked my socks off. One could become inebriated with just a few sips. He would occasionally have a drink, but never exceed his limit or get totally wasted.

We amused each other and found delight in each other's company. I enjoyed listening to colorful stories of his life on the farm. One story he often told, was about an incident at a country fair. He successfully threw a hoop over a glass bottle and won a prize, but the vendor refused to honor it. Grandad naturally got upset. A gang of young White boys suddenly appeared, as if they were summoned. They surrounded Grandad and shoved him back and forth. To defend himself, he pulled a switchblade from his pocket, lunged, and swung at one of the boys, but quickly realized he was outnumbered. Before things took a turn for the worse, as they often did in those days. He was quick on his feet, and did an about-face and ran. The boys shouted profanities and racial slurs as they chased him. He ran as fast as he could, then turns to look back, that's when he crashed into a wire fence. Grandad yelled, "Oh! They got me! They got me!" My eyes opened wide and my ears were fixated on his every word. He went on, "I bounced off that wire fence and continued to run until I found a safe place to catch my breath!"

Young White boys consistently sought to intimidate young Blacks. Intimidating Blacks was recreation for them. Upon the next confrontation, Grandad didn't take a risk. When he saw them approaching, he quickly turned his back, got into his car, and drove away in the dark, without turning on the headlights to prevent them from following him. Some of his stories were funny, others were too horrible to comprehend.

During my childhood, just before the Civil Rights Movement, prejudice and racism were not something we sat around thinking about. It was a part of our life; not something we liked or ever fully got used to, but tolerated like a festering wound that wouldn't heal. Because of many injustices, Blacks were treated as sub-humans, and Grandad viewed Whites as enemies. He resented the fact that he raised his voice an octave, whenever he spoke to a White person. Raising his voice was a submissive demonstration of "knowing his place." Grandad didn't consider himself submissive, but he played the role. He tried to avoid any racist confrontation, but in the event, it was unavoidable, Grandad was prepared with a pistol tucked on his hip for protection.

Packing a gun was how Grandad and his family protected themselves in Monticello. He brought a gun to Sanford and knew how to use it. Fortunately, he never had to. He was level-headed and tried to figure things out in a logical way. He wanted the same for me. When he talked with me, he was stern and authoritative. And when he said something, I had better listen. Although Grandad was 48 years older, he respected me. I felt safe and protected by his concern for my well-being. He was a good role model. He wanted the best for me and in the absence of my father, that was exactly what I needed. I couldn't imagine life without him.

Grandad thought perhaps my father might try to take me away from him during one of his infrequent, brief visits, without advance notice. It was difficult for me to remember him from one visit to the next. He was inconsistent. I didn't feel as comfortable with him as I did with Grandad, because I didn't know him. On one occasion, he did try to take me from Grandad. Grandad didn't like my father anyway and grimly said, "There he is. See if you're man enough to take him." He knew Grandad was packing a .45 strapped under his jacket and that put an end to his attempt. Each time he visited, it was as if it was our first meeting. Curiously enough he gave me a Brownie box camera. It was the only thing he ever gifted me. It was a special memento that I fondly kept for many years.

Grandad was a fine quality carpenter, he built homes all over Florida for Blacks and Whites. Whenever Grandad was offered an assignment in another part of Florida, his first consideration: was whether I was permitted to come along, if not, Grandad simply refused the job. He was a remarkable artist and spent countless evenings sketching the interior and exterior of proposed homes. I guess I was inspired to be an artist by observing him. One of Grandad's carpentry jobs took us to Southern Florida for a few months.

I recall Grandad driving along a long, long highway, and on the side of the road was a pipe that protruded from the ground. The pipe shot the coldest, cleanest, purest spring water, you'd ever want to taste. There were no 'Colored' or 'White' signs over the pipe, thank God. Those signs were quite common in the Southern States. We stopped just for the sheer taste of it.

On another occasion, Grandad was driving to a campsite in Southern Florida, where he was contracted to build several homes. Our car climbed to the top of a hill. Hills are very rare in Florida, and as we were declining, suddenly my door flung open. I held on for dear life. Grandad quickly stopped the car and pulled me back in from what could have been a serious accident or death.

After we arrived at the campsite and settled in, Grandad asked me to find a few pieces of wood and sticks to build a fire. I found several and placed them in an array on the barren ground. Then Grandad struck a match and PUFF, there was an instant flame. Once the yellow and orange flame flared up and got hot, Grandad knew it was time to prepare our dinner. Our dinner consisted of chicken, which was roasted over the fire. He also boiled kernels of corn. And a can of baked beans and several large sweet potatoes were thrown in the fire. They

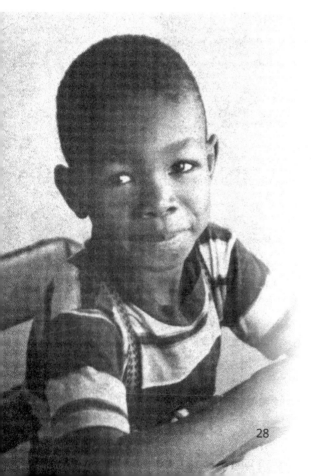

Jon at 6 years best

were the tastiest and sweetest potatoes I ever had. The fresh aroma of food cooking in the yard permeated the camp. I sank my teeth into a kernel of corn and its juices popped in my mouth with the sweet taste of freshness. Nothing taste as sweet as the corn on the cob. It was sooooo delicious. It was like a grand picnic in the open yard. The crackling of the fire brought warmth to the cool evenings. I loved those camp side hot dinners, because, it was just the two of us.

When we returned home for the weekend, Bozo, my black and white dog had been taken away by the city dog catchers. Bozo was a Mutt and I was very fond of him. My heart was broken. I was so disappointed. I never wanted another dog after that. Bozo was a friendly dog, that I romped with and had the best time running through the streets. I will never forget Bozo.

My life was blissful until I started school at the tender age of six. The bliss was broken because I didn't want to be separated from Grandad. I didn't want to go. He promised to buy me a present if I stayed in school all day. I stayed just for the present. I don't remember what the gift was, but I loved the idea of receiving something special.

My first four years at school were spent in an all-Black school due to segregation at that time. All of my friends were from the neighborhood. The two-story, wooden schoolhouse was located two blocks from our home. Teachers were allowed to smack our hands with a ruler if we misbehaved. After being smacked, we had to say, "Thank you, Ma'am," as if to show gratitude for the discipline.

One day, I got down and dirty during playtime in the schoolyard. Miss Young, my first-grade teacher said, "Go home to your mamma and change your clothes!" All the kids snickered because they knew I didn't have a Mom at home. I was so humiliated. When I arrived home, Miss Geneva, one of our neighbors, saw that I was upset. She told me to stop crying and come inside, so she could wash me up and clean my clothes. Then she rushed me back to school. It takes a village to raise a child, and that's what happened in our neighborhood.

I was attracted to a little girl from the neighborhood, her name was Joan Robinson. I thought of her as my girlfriend. She was playful and awfully pretty, with a 'high yalla' completion. She passed my house each day on her way to school and sometimes I'd walk her home.

Joan lived with her mother and grandmother on Eighth Street in a single-family home. I often visited her. Her family was the first in the neighborhood to have a television. I recall watching one of the first TV commercials for Pabst Blue Ribbon. "Whata ya have Pabst Blue Ribbon," and thought, that was magic, what fun.

My friends took piano lessons after school. I wanted to join them, just to learn church chords. I'm not sure if Grandad didn't think I was serious or if he couldn't afford it. We were poor, but I didn't know it, because I had everything I needed, except piano lessons. Later in life, when I began singing in cabarets around Manhattan, I bought a Baby Grand and took private lessons. The lessons were extremely boring, so I didn't continue. My dream was shattered.

Grandad had a weekend side business; a homemade barber shop business. He placed a chair on the front porch and was ready for business, only $0.50 per haircut. The money was stored in a large jar on a shelf. I was highly mistaken when I thought I could outsmart Grandad. I took the liberty of taking a little change from the jar each day to buy candy that I shared with friends. Grandad finally took note, and patiently waited for me to return from school. Well, I got the whooping of my life. It wasn't until later that, I understood the punishment wasn't about the money; it was for being dishonest. Well, I never did that again.

Miss Fields lived in a white clapboard house across the street from our house. She watched everything and reported to Grandad if I did anything out of order. Grandad didn't hesitate to hand out a whooping when I did something or if the neighbor didn't approve of something. He'd tell me, "Get the strap." Black kids knew that meant business. That was the advantage and disadvantage of small-town life; everyone knew each other and someone was always watching.

Grandad arranged for me to have credit at a store around the corner from our house, in case I needed something, while he was at work. I recall buying fresh bottled milk. I couldn't wait to get home to dip my fingers in and scoop off the frosty cream that floated on top of the milk. Those were the days.

As Christmas rolled around, Grandad bought gifts and placed them on the top shelf in the closet. He told me it was too hot for snow in

Florida; therefore, Santa came in a Jeep. My gifts were practical things I needed, and a few toys for fun like the Lionel Train set. I cherished that train set and never let on that I knew the truth about Santa and the Jeep.

I always wanted a new bicycle, but never got one. I learned to ride on an old rickety bike left from Uncle Robert's childhood. The bike was much too big for my little frame, but I rode it anyway. I watched with envy while all the other kids in the neighborhood rode brand-new, shiny bicycles. I can still hear the wheels turn and glide. The wind rushed against my face as I sped up-and-down those long, lonely, dirt roads. Of course I rode the bike within the Colored section of town.

There were clearly defined 'Colored' and 'White' sections in town. Whenever I felt like a daredevil, I'd walk on the wild side, through the White section of town. I didn't do that often, because I knew that wasn't the place to be. I wanted to see for myself what it was like. Their open porches were trimmed with beautiful fretwork. White ladies sat in large, rattan swings and casually swung back and forth while they idly chatted. They cool themselves from the sweltering heat with paper hand fans while sipping cold freshly made, sweet iced tea or lemonade.

The Colored section was socially similar to the White. The tempo of the town was set by little old ladies sitting in their rocking chairs on their front porch, while they slowly sipped ice-cold fresh-squeezed lemonade and rendered an

Uncle Robert Walker, 1950

31

opinion on any and everything. Ladies gossiped and minded other people's business as they watched the time go by, much like the white ladies on the other side of town. Sanford was so still, usually, the only sound to disrupt the silence was an occasional car driving by or children playing on the dirt roads.

Neighbors were friendly and respected each other. They shared a wave, a smile, and a greeting as they passed. It didn't matter if you knew the person or not. It was a Southern thing to do. People also referred to each other as "Mr.", "Ma'am", or "Miss". For example, a child or younger person could use the adult's first name, but they had to put a "Miss" or "Mr." before the first name. The dirt roads in the colored section of town were lined with weeping willow trees, except the large oak tree that stood at Locust and Tenth Street in front of Miss Sneed's house.

We played stickball on the open dusty, dirt road. The road appeared as a boulevard when I was a kid. The hibiscus hedges on both sides of the road were used as first and third bases. Our ball never bounced beyond our block. It was always eventful whenever the circus came to town. It was also a time when colored performers couldn't stay in motels in town, so they rented rooms in my favorite big, white house on the corner. I don't know if they referred to the Green Book (a book with a listing of where Coloreds could stay), but somehow, they always landed at Miss Sneed's house. The performers were very friendly and generous. They gave me free passes to the circus to see their performance under the Big Top. I loved the clowns, games, and naturally the cotton candy. One of the most spectacular things for me was a motorcyclist running his bike around the walls. That was fascinating. The circus livened up the sleepy town. Everyone loved the Ferris wheel and exploring other rides.

There was only one movie theatre in Sanford, and it was also segregated. Admission was 0.10 cents, but I frequently received free admission passes. Whites sat downstairs in the orchestra and Blacks sat in the balcony. For once, the seats for Blacks were the best in the house. It's from where I casually dropped popcorn. I could see the entire theatre from the balcony. The movie screen stretched from one wall to another. I loved going to the movies because they helped to expand my perspective on life. I fantasized along with the actors and momentarily stepped into another world.

Beyond school, stickball, the movie theater, and the circus, there was church. The church was an enormous influence in the community. Everything revolved around the church. Miss Sneed volunteered as a church usher. She often asked me to accompany her to pour grape juice into small glasses and sort the saltine crackers that were to be passed out for the First Sunday Communion. The juice represented the blood of Christ and the crackers represented the body. The portions were so small, that it stimulated my appetite.

Going to a Sanctified Baptist Church was a social experience for me. I loved to watch the ladies sashay into the church in their floral, cotton dresses accented with large, picture hats and short wrist-length, white gloves. Little girls wore freshly starched, crisp, white, cotton, Sunday school dresses that could have only been starched and pressed by a Southern mom. There were always a few women who jumped out of their seats, screamed, danced, shouted, and levitated, then fainted on cue when the preacher gave his usual spirited sermon. Several ushers rushed over to fan the ladies back to consciousness. I recalled one lady got a little carried away with the spirit, she threw her head back and her wig fell off, then threw her head forward and her false teeth fell out of her mouth. Now, that was funny. The performances were well worth my 0.10 cents contribution.

The choir, on the other hand, and the beautiful songs they sang were nothing less than celestial. I got a special tingling sensation when the choir sang, it kind of moved throughout my body and uplifted me to what I imagined heaven would be. It wasn't a religious experience, but instead the sheer joy of hearing such beauty and love in their voices. Although Grandad was deeply religious, he never accompanied me to church, because he had his intimate way of believing in God. He lowered himself onto his knees and prayed at home.

Blacks were relegated to the back of the city bus during Jim Crow. However, I didn't experience that because Grandad always drove his car where ever we wanted to go. I loved watching him with one hand on the steering wheel and his left arm resting on the window ledge. He was quite a sport. He also parked the car without any effort.

I was always excited about seeing the next year's motor cars. That's when cars were designed, and I immediately recognized each brand. They were distinguished by their fish tail or other ornate design. The American Cadillac was the most prestigious car at that time. If you owned a Cadillac, you had arrived. Several newspaper articles projected a future flying car. Well, we still haven't seen that yet.

The Wilson Funeral Home was located on Locust Avenue and Ninth Street. It was only a block away from our home. I often dropped by to see the latest victim. The funeral home was also located across the street from the Juke Joint, where locals hung out for a good time on the weekends. The proximity of death and a good time seemed too close for comfort. Grandad didn't have a telephone. Mother often called the funeral home to get in touch with us. Whenever she called, an employee from the funeral home would come to our home to tell us there was a call.

Mother was almost a phantom, someone I wrote letters to and talked with on the phone, but had not seen in years. I often thought about her; what did she do in the big city and wondered if she missed me. I was constantly growing, so Grandad would place a piece of paper on the floor, then take a pencil to trace around my feet, then mail the paper to her, so she could buy the correct shoe size. Christmas and Easter were always exciting times because Mother sent boxes of clothes, shoes, and all kinds of goodies. She always had an interest in fashion and that was her way of showing off.

I got the travel bug early in life because we often visited relatives in Lake City, Monticello, Orlando, Fort Pierce, and other parts of Florida. Grandad was very close to our family. He cared deeply about his relatives and made a consistent effort to stay in touch. We frequently visited the farm in Monticello where Grandad's brother, Uncle William, (we called him Cot) and sister-in-law Aunt Sally lived. A long winding dirt road leads to the farm. The road was shaded by a canopy of tall oak trees with Spanish moss dangling from its branches. I loved the farm because I could ride horses and run through the fields and play with my cousins. The farm was home for Grandad, it was comfort and a place to share with family. Grandad was raised on that farm and it's where my mother and her siblings were born back in the mid-1920s. That was the first house Grandad built, so he had a special fondness for the surroundings.

Grandad asked me to go into the watermelon field when I was about five-years-old. He asked me to select a ripe melon. I walked amongst the crop and chopped into every melon until I found a perfect one. I had literally ruined the crop. When he discovered what I had done, well, I received a memorable whooping.

Grandad and I occasionally visited Carolyn, my little sister, at Miss Dobby's Foster Home in Jacksonville. Miss Dobby Foster Home was a home for several boys and girls. On one occasion, I gave Carolyn 0.10 cents as a present, because I thought it was a big deal. That was a lot of money for me in 1950!

Back in Sanford, Grandad was repairing the interior of an old bus, when a photographer appeared to take his picture, I quickly ran in from playing in the yard and upstaged Grandad by posing on the side with my right hand on my hip. It's my favorite picture and the only picture I have of Grandad and me.

Grandad and me, 1949

On another occasion, Grandad and I were having a day in the park. There were two signs posted over the water fountains that read, 'Colored only' and 'White only.' I read the sign 'White only,' but that didn't stop me. I was curious as to how the White water tasted. I turned the faucet on and gulped a few sips. Surprisingly, it tastes the same as the Colored water. I simply didn't get it. It was also against the law for Coloreds to vote during the 1940s and early 1950s. But at my age, I wasn't concerned about voting.

I often visited an elderly lady, who lived around the corner from our house. She was disabled and housebound. I was mesmerized by an oil painting of Venice on her living room wall. Venice was so different from Sanford. I asked her to share some of her worldly adventures. The painting clearly showed Venice surrounded by water and the only means of transportation was by Gondolas. Gondoliers rowed the boats along the canal using one long oar. I wondered where Venice was because I thought Venice was somewhere on another planet like New York, from where Mother sent seasonal gifts. Somehow everything and anything beyond Florida seemed as if it were on another planet.

Carolyn at age 3

I patiently listened as the neighbor shared her many colorful stories. She inspired me to use my imagination and to dream that I'd travel someday to all those faraway places. Grandad also constantly encouraged me to stretch. I began to dream more and more of that other planet, New York.

Grandad was my guardian angel. He filled the parentless void. The thing I cherished most was spending precious, private time with him. Even though I was born in Tampa, I think of Sanford as my home. The strong Black community ties provided the comfort of knowing I was part of an extended family. My own family was what I called broken — a father nowhere to be found, a mother in New York struggling as a maid to make a better living, my younger sister in a foster home in Jacksonville, Florida, and me with Grandad.

I often thought how wonderful it would have been to have Carolyn, my little sister live with us and how much she would have liked Grandad. But to be honest, considering the many things I liked most about my life with Grandad, was that I had him all to myself. During those years with him, I learned what I consider to be the basic principles of life:

- Never take what doesn't belong to you.
- Don't make promises you can't keep.
- If you can't help someone, you shouldn't hurt them.
- If a situation isn't working, find a way to change it and make it work for you.

And the most inspirational thing he said: "Go out there and take a chance on life. Go for the brass ring. Shoot for the moon and always have a dream."

My first defining moment was at the age of nine when I realized there was a bigger world beyond Sanford, Florida. I wanted to get the hell out of town, to discover the world. Life was too limited in Sanford; I just knew I had to make a change. I had heard that New York was free and integrated. I wanted to go there. I wanted to be there.

I knew all about the small towns and small minds that surrounded my town and the evil, prejudiced son-of-a-guns in the South. There were frequent cross burning on Colored people's front lawns. The KKK was a mean group of Crackers that executed Black people for the slightest reason. God forbid if a black man looked at a white woman. Colored people were being disregarded and not respected for their attributes. There were frequent hangings even if we were just suspected of getting out of line. White people had imposed a line that was not to be reckoned with. They made sure we knew our place.

The neighborhoods were segregated. Colored people were ordered to sit in the back of the bus. And if a White person got on the bus and couldn't find a seat, the Colored person had to relinquish his or her seat. Bus stations, trains, schools, and hospitals were also segregated. White folks were small people with narrow minds.

After spending six years with Grandad, I wrote a letter to my mother in 1953 and asked if Carolyn and I could come and live with her for a while. I wasn't dissatisfied with Grandad. I just thought it would be nice to spend some time with her. She immediately replied and confirmed that she would come down at the end of the school year. The year couldn't end fast enough. I was finishing fourth grade and Carolyn was finishing first.

At the end of the school year, mother kept her promise. She boarded a bus from New York to Jacksonville to collect Carolyn from the foster home. Carolyn was quite disoriented. She cried and didn't want to leave the family she had known for six years. They arrived in Sanford on the hottest day of the year. Mother stood proudly at five feet-eight inches. I will never forget the outfit she wore. It was a fashionable black and white, cotton gingham, two-piece sleeveless dress. I was so proud to have a mother. I showed her off to anyone passing. She extended her visit for a week because she wanted to gather her thoughts before returning to New York. She cleaned Grandad's house because he was a pack rat. He never threw anything away. Mother and I also spent a little time getting acquainted.

At the end of the week, mother packed our luggage and stuffed them in the trunk of Grandad's car. We were going to Jacksonville to visit his sister, Rebecca. Shortly after arriving, an

Aunt Rebecca, Jacksonville, FL

argument erupted between Mother, Grandad, and Aunt Rebecca. It was regarding something Mother said in the past. I was nine and three-quarters, but I knew what was going on. The tension was thick, so I kept my distance. Mother was beyond frustrated. She called for a taxi to take us to the bus station.

Most colored folks migrated from the south to the north by bus in the 1940s and 1950s. While sitting and waiting in the bus station for what seemed like a lifetime, it occurred to me that Mother and Grandad were no longer on speaking terms, and I might never see him again. I worshipped that man and missed him, already. Suddenly, I began to cry.

"What's wrong? Why are you crying?" she asked.

"I'm hungry," I quickly responded.

"Why didn't you simply say so?"

That was my first lie. That was the first time in my life that I felt I couldn't express my true feelings to a stranger because that's what she was to me.

I knew everything was about to change forever, as I left my small comfortable world. We boarded a Greyhound bus on June 18, 1953. Then rushed to the back, because that was where people of color were relegated to sit during Jim Crow. The bus made several bathroom stops along the way and again we were directed to the Colored bathrooms in the South. It was a very long ride, and not very comfortable. We must have been on the road for two days before we finally arrived in New York City.

CHAPTER THREE

Transition

M other, Carolyn, and I arrived in New York City on Saturday, June 20th, 1953, it was nothing less than a traumatic transition. Everything was unfamiliar, from the weather to the landscape, language, food, clothes, social roles, people, and mother. Everything I was accustomed to was no longer in place. I was nine-and-three-quarter years old when I left that small, quiet town of Sanford for the fast-paced, unstoppable city of New York — the Big Apple. It was a culture shock that knocked my socks off. It would become my new world and it was both frightening and liberating.

The bus station was located on West 34th Street between Seventh and Eighth Avenues, diagonally across from Macy's department store. As we stepped off the bus, I looked up at what appeared to be the tallest building in the world, 450 Seventh Avenue, in the heart of the Garment District. I didn't realize if I had turned a little to the right, I would have seen the Empire State Building, which was the tallest building at that time. The tallest building in Sanford was a mere four stories! Although I couldn't have known then, that many years later, yards away from where I stepped off the bus, in 1953, would become the threshold of my future career as a fashion designer.

Mother walked us to the Subway at eighth avenue and thirty-fourth street. I had never heard of going underground for anything. The subway fare had just been increased from $0.10 to 0.15 cents. Mother insisted that we duck underneath the turnstile, even though we were both somewhat tall for our age. I guess 0.15 cents made a difference in her budget. The 'A' train platform was hot and crowded. When the train arrived, it was filled. Our first subway experience felt like a joy ride at an amusement park. I looked up from my seat and stared at the unfamiliar faces and wondered,

"Where are all these people going?"

People stood and held onto the overhead bar, some sat and read quietly while others stared straight ahead in a quiet daze. The train rattled with a lot of noise as it made its way to Brooklyn.

The adjustment to the Big Apple was difficult, not only for me but for my mother and Carolyn. We lived in a studio apartment at 149 St. James Place in the Clinton Section of Brooklyn. Three of us slept in a large bed. That was an enormous adjustment because Carolyn and I lived in a house with a yard, lots of trees, and friends to play with on the dirt roads.

Unlike Sanford, where I was only exposed to Colored and White people, I was suddenly introduced to Puerto Ricans, who lived on the block. They spoke Spanish, a language I had never heard before. When they addressed each other, it sound as if everyone had the same name — every sentence began with 'Mira.'

I was taught to respectfully address my elders as "Ma'am." Suddenly, I had to learn to say, "Yes, Mother," or "No, Mother." It felt so strange to call her "Mother." Grandad was the only parent that I had known up until that time in my life. Mother was the voice I heard several times a year on the telephone at the funeral home. Now, even though we were together, there remained a distance between us. It took me forty years before I truly felt comfortable addressing her as 'Mother.'

One afternoon, we were off to the subway station. As we were walking down into the station, suddenly out of nowhere a group of ladies raced up the stairs. I was so startled, that I didn't wait around to find out what happened. I took off and ran down the street.

Mother yelled, "You'd better get back here! Where do you think you're going?"

The very idea of going underground was unimaginable. Folks in Sanford would only run if their house was on fire! So, I thought there must be a fire.

Mother had lived alone and single for six years and now had two young children. She wasn't used to the rambunctiousness that accompanies the presence of children. She often lost her patience and yelled at us. That was always a surprise and not a pleasant one. No one ever yelled at me in Sanford. As a result of not knowing what would upset her, Carolyn and I became nervous wrecks. Mother yelled, sometimes during dinner, and it startled us. We jumped and more often

Mother, 1952

than not, end up with our food or drink spilled over the table. I assume her impatience was due to the grand expectations she had for us.

That first summer prolonged the transition for Carolyn and I because we were locked in the apartment during the day, while Mother worked as a maid at the Essex House Hotel. We were used to our freedom in Florida, but Mother's rules were different. We sat countless hours gazing out the window, wishing we were outdoors with the other kids. We were bored out of our skulls, with plenty of time on our hands, so we became creative with silly games. For example, we created flying saucers with the cold cuts that were set aside for our lunch. We used them to attack neighbors seated across the way in their gardens. On another occasion, we took a roll of toilet paper and a pail of water and made spitballs that we tossed and plastered the entire ceiling. Later that day while we were having dinner, vibration from a slammed door in the building released one of the spitballs from the ceiling. Carolyn and I watched in horror as a spitball landed on Mother's plate. She looked up and saw the entire ceiling was plastered with spitballs. Boy did we get whopping!

Mother bought several books for us, but I never liked her choice for me, because it was all about science. I was never interested in science. She was very particular about our appearance. She washed and scrubbed our clothes to make sure we looked our very best at all times. We were allowed outside after she returned from work. She applied Noxzema to our faces, so we wouldn't appear ashy. Ashy is a grey cast on the skin. You could have the best outfit on, but if your skin was ashy, it was all for naught! She dressed us in our Sunday best and sent us out to sit on the stoop. We dared not move. We were so jealous of the other kids as they freely played on the block.

Carolyn and I met Ethel Proctor Rolle, my mother's cousin shortly after we arrived in New York. They spent their early years in Monticello, Florida. She was one year younger than Mother. Ethel had chiseled facial features and dark brown skin that glowed. She also had southern manners and a zest for life. I liked her right away. Carolyn and I 'adopted' her as our Aunt Ethel. Ethel treated us to our first New York show at the world-renowned Apollo Theatre, where Peg Leg Bates and Moms Mabley performed. Peg Leg Bates tap-danced on a wooden leg. Moms Mabley, a comedian, was an old lady with false teeth and a gravelly voice. She dressed as a bag woman.

One of her most memorable jokes was:

"The only thang an old man can do for me is to brang me a young man."

Ethel was married to Jerry Rolle and they lived in the Bronx. Carolyn and I often spent weekends with them. Their apartment was a terrific escape from our normal environment. They exposed us to new places and events. I loved to watch them dance the Lindy to rock 'n' roll music. They started with a count, 'Ah one, ah two,' and then on three they touched knees. They were the best dancers in my mind. Unfortunately, Ethel had a miscarriage several months after we arrived. I think she would have been a wonderful mother. I also think she adored us because we filled the gap of her not having children of her own.

At the end of the summer, and the beginning of our new school year, I entered fifth grade. The new school, PS 11, was just around the corner from our apartment. However, the harsh mental effect of the big city transition reared itself in a myriad of ways. For example, at the beginning of the school year, for the life of me, I couldn't remember

Jon at age 10

whether I wrote with my left or right hand. Fortunately, with a little patience from myself and the teacher, I began to write with my left hand again.

I recall my first winter: while sitting in class, I looked out the window, as beautiful, fluffy, white snow began to flutter to the ground. I was mesmerized because I thought snow came from under the ground. School in the north was very different from that of the south. Teachers were not permitted to reprimand students. However, my fifth-grade teacher verbally threatened me and I told my mother. She confronted the teacher and oddly enough I was immediately transferred to a slower-paced class. That was a miserable time for me. I was very unhappy but endured.

In a way, Brooklyn was kind of like Sanford in the sense that a lady who owned a dry cleaner on the corner, looked after us after school, until our mother returned from work. It reminded me of 'it takes a village' as in Sanford. There was always someone to look after us.

Sometime during my first winter in New York, I received news that Miss Sneed had died of old age. I was deeply upset to learn of her death because she was instrumental in taking care of me in my youth. Soon after her death, Grandad bought four lots in another part of town and built his very own three-bedroom brick home with indoor plumbing. He was very relaxed and enjoyed his newfound home.

Eight months after our arrival in New York, my mother was offered a spacious new two-bedroom apartment in a public housing development in Coney Island. Mother was always looking for a better life for us. We lived on the sixth floor. It was a mixed-race floor with Jews, Italians, Whites, and African-Americans. Everyone left their front door open to allow neighbors to visit.

One sunny afternoon, I was wrestling in the grass, with an Italian neighbor's boy and he asked, "Why don't you take a bath, so we can be the same color."

I was delighted about the transfer to a new school. I spent the last few months of my fifth grade at P.S. 188 in Coney Island. My report card grades weren't up to snuff. I was embarrassed to show my mom, so I'd forge her signature. Fortunately, her signature was easy to copy.

Mother occasionally suffered from migraine headaches, so we had the impossible task of remaining quiet while she rested. Do you know how difficult that was for a ten and seven-year-old? We were creative and quietly designed games that kept us occupied. Mother never complained, regardless of how difficult things were for her. I'm sure she often reflected on her newfound responsibility of taking care of us and wondered how the hell she was going to make it through the next day.

Uncle Bill and Aunt Betty from my father's side of the family lived in East Harlem in Manhattan. Bill and Betty were in their late teens, but had a sense of family and loved staying in touch. They often visited us and it was always a great pleasure seeing and spending a little time with them. It was always a pleasure to see any guests. Uncle Bill often said we were the quietest kids, he had ever met. Mother trained us well. Bill and Betty also gave us a little money upon departure. That was always a treat.

Carolyn and I spent a couple of summer weekends with them at Grandad and Grandma's apartment in Harlem and that was a fun time because we could play outside without restrictions.

Life was simple for me in the 1950s, because, I was a little boy with no worries. It was a time when my mother could fill a grocery cart for $50.00.

I recall the day the ice cream truck arrived in front of our building with those dreadful chimes. Carolyn and I desperately wanted to go out to buy an ice cream. Mother asked us to make our beds before going for ice cream. We didn't know how to make a bed, so she showed us. I sketched the making of the bed, so we would never forget, and it would ensure us we could go for ice cream the next time the truck came around. Despite mother being so strict, we could see she tried to do her very best.

We had a telephone party line because it was cheaper. A party line is a shared phone line with several homes. When a call rang for us, there was a special ring, and so forth. Those were the days when you could dial 'O' for the operator and 411 for directory assistance. Mother couldn't initially afford to buy a TV, but when she did, it became family entertainment. Like kids in a candy store, we watched, You Are There, Lassie, and The Ed Sullivan Show religiously.

Every Sunday, Carolyn and I walked around the corner, to the candy store to purchase the Sunday papers. There were seven daily newspapers in the 1950s: *The Daily News,* the *New York Mirror,* the *Journal-American,* the *World-Telegram & Sun,* the *Herald Tribune,* the *New York Post,* and *The New York Times.* The Sunday *New York Times* only cost .50 cents. It was the thickest newspaper. You got a lot for your money. I often complained that I needed a donkey to carry it home. The Times was not like the thin expensive paper we know today. Carolyn would pick up the Sunday New York Daily News because she loved the comics. I never liked comics, because I believe in the real world.

Mother insisted that we return home directly after school, with no stops, no playing. She bought a record player as it was referred to in those days. I loved playing recordings of Broadway Musicals and listening to the popular music of that time. Alan Freed was a popular host of a TV dance show on Channel 5. Carolyn and I would rush home to watch the show. We also learned to dance the Lindy to the Rock 'N Roll music by watching the show. Carolyn and I were quite a team. We danced up a storm in the living room.

Mother arranged for us to spend the summer of 1955 with Grandma, Viola Jones, in Fort Pierce. We couldn't wait until the end of the school year. Once the school year had finished, Mother packed one large suitcase with lots of summer clothes. She also packed another trunk with canned and non-perishable food. She was as excited as we were to spend the summer with Grandma.

We took a taxi to the original Pennsylvania Station in Manhattan. Pennsylvania Station was originally constructed in the Beaux Arts style between 1905 and 1910, by the Pennsylvania Railroad. It was a majestic architectural wonder, a masterpiece with Doric columns that were embellished with fluted pink granite marble. Eagles boldly stood at the base. Eighth Avenue between 31st and 33rd Street was known as the Avenue of Columns because the General Post Office on the opposite side of the avenue was also adorned with columns. The main waiting room was inspired by the Roman Baths of Caracalla. It was the largest indoor space in the city, expanding over an avenue long and two-blocks wide. The vaulted glass windows soared 150 feet over a sun-drenched chamber. Sunlight streamed through the window and reminded me of a Vermeer painting. When it was time to board the train, "All Aboard," echoed throughout the station.

Grandma Viola

Mother escorted us onto the train. It appeared to be the longest train in the world. We were not big on hugs and kisses and telling each other that we love them, but deep inside we knew we were loved. She gave us a big hug and a large lunch box filled with fried chicken, biscuits, and other goodies. She also instructed the conductor not to allow anyone to remove us from the train until we arrived in Fort Pierce. That was our first experience on an interstate train. By the time the train rolled into Savannah, Georgia, we had eaten everything in the lunch box. Against Mother's instructions, we ventured into the dining car for breakfast. That was a big deal for us.

Ft. Pierce was a typical Southern town where colored and white neighborhoods were separated. Actually, all of the south was separated at that time. Ft. Pierce was a quiet town as I remember, with not much going on. Grandma lived in single-family homes on a quiet street. My mother's youngest half-brother Willie Lee lived with Grandma. He was three years older than I. Aunt Bea, her sister, lived around the corner and her brother lived a few blocks away. She had a close-knit family that cared and looked out for each other. They lead a simple life of daily chores and of course, church on Sundays. Several cousins lived down the street. They were closer to our age, so we had a lot in common. We often visited each other that summer.

Although that was our first lengthy stay with Grandmother Viola, it was the second time I'd visited her. The first time I saw Grandma was in 1949, at Uncle Jackie's funeral, mother's younger brother. Uncle Jackie's car accidentally missed the bridge crossing and crashed into the river. He drowned while trying to rescue his girlfriend. He was only 19 years old. It was a great loss for the family. Mother flew down from New York for the funeral. I vividly remember her fainting as she walked down the aisle to her seat. Grandad was very distraught over Jackie's death. He was very anxious for us to arrive on time for the funeral. We forgot to take our dress clothes for the funeral. Jackie's car had been retrieved from the river and aunt Rebecca was driving it around Fort Pierce.

When we returned home, our suitcases were resting on the hood of another car in the front yard. Grandad was devastated and never fully recovered from the loss of his son. We all were. For several weeks after the funeral, I'd wake up in the middle of the night in a cold sweat. I had nightmares, where I had fallen into a deep hole and each time I tried to climb out, the sand buried me again and again.

Now back to that summer. It was early, one Sunday morning when Grandad drove down to Grandma Viola's house. I heard his wonderful baritone voice call out, "Viola Jones!" as he approached the front porch. I was barely awake and still in my pajamas, but that didn't matter. He didn't have a chance to step onto the porch. I rushed outside and leaped into his arms and hugged him for what seemed like forever. I missed him and it was clear to me that he missed me too. For me to see Grandad again was the happiest day of my life. I loved him and he knew it. Once I calmed down, we sat and talked for hours. I wasn't the only one who had changed. He had a change of his own, he brought his new wife, Miss Leslie, with him. She remained in the car, so I walked out and introduced myself. I talked with her and was impressed because she was genuinely a nice lady. It was good to see him with a special person in his life, someone who cared about him. Later, as he drove off, into the sunset, I knew I couldn't wait as long to see him again.

That was the summer Carolyn learned to ride a bicycle and I turned twelve years old. Mother had to pay full fare for my return trip.

Grandma packed a boxed lunch with fried chicken, biscuits, soda, and of course napkins. A typical Southern picnic basket. Our return train trip from Florida took place during the Jim Crow era and before the Pre-Civil Rights. Blacks were relegated to occupy the first coach of the train behind the steam engine. Carolyn and I were content. Sitting behind the steam engine didn't matter to us. We were looking forward to returning home safely.

By the 1950s, the Civil Rights Movement gained momentum. August 1955, while spending the summer with relatives in Money, Mississippi. Bryant's husband Roy and his half-brother J.W. Milam were armed when they went to Till's great-uncle's house and abducted Emmett. They took him away. Till had been badly beaten, one of his eyes was gouged out, before shooting him in the head and sinking his body in the Tallahatchie River. Till was killed for allegedly having wolf-whistled at a white woman in a store. The visceral response to his mother's decision to have an open-casket funeral mobilized the black community throughout the United States. That sparked public outrage about the injustice that was done to Emmett Till, a 14-year-old boy from Chicago.

One hundred days after Emmett Till's murder. Rosa Parks helped initiate the Civil Rights movement in the United States, when she refused to give up her seat in the front of a segregated bus to a white man in Montgomery, Alabama on December 1, 1955. That set off a successful boycott of the city buses that lasted more than a year. The boycott put the bus companies out of business, resulting eventually in a U.S. Supreme Court ruling that segregated buses were unconstitutional. It's also successfully launched nationwide efforts to end racial segregation of public facilities.

Upon returning home, I entered the seventh grade at Mark Twain Junior High School. The school was located at the end of Gravesend Park. Mark Twain was an integrated school with Italian, Jews, and Puerto Ricans and six students of color. That's where I first encountered racism. I was one of two Negro students in my seventh-grade class. Negro was first used in the census in 1900 and was the most common way of referring to Black Americans through most of the early 20th century. 'Negro' itself took the place of 'Colored.' Starting with the 1960s Civil Rights Movement, Black activists began to reject the 'Negro' label and came to identify themselves as 'Black' or 'African-American.' To call someone 'Black' when I was in the seventh grade, provoked a fight because it was considered derogatory.

That was a time when most Americans didn't know much about the continent of Africa or anything about the history of Blacks. What most White people knew or thought they knew wasn't positive.

Lena Horne once said, "The only thing Hollywood knew about us, was what Tarzan told them and he was not the bright one in the group. Heck, Cheetah taught him how to read and write and put his clothes on."

The White boys in my class often teased me by calling me a "Mau Mau." They had read about Mau Mau in the Junior Scholastic book, and that was the only reference they had for people of color. It was extremely unsettling to go through my adolescence being referred to as a Mau Mau, with pimples all over my face, missing Grandad, and dealing with racism. It was by far the worst period of my life.

The Mau Mau Uprising (1952–1960), also known as the Mau Mau Rebellion, the Kenya Emergency, and the Mau Mau Revolt, was a war in the British Kenya Colony between the Kenya Land and Freedom Army, also known as Mau Mau, and the British Colonists. Junior High School, on the other hand, was not a pleasant experience.

I wanted to join the music class, just to learn to play the piano. But I was rejected because I didn't have an ear for it. So, I join the Glee Club, where I succeeded. One of my fun experiences was as a soloist, where I sang one of Gilbert and Sullivan's little ditties with a cockney accent. Mother and Carolyn attended each performance.

I had a crush on my seventh-grade teacher, Miss Diamond. She was young and very pretty. She wore circular flared felt skirts that were adorned with an image of poodles. The fashion of the day was a crinoline under the skirt. She also wore a pretty crisp white blouse. All the boys in my class were going through puberty, we groped each other in the hallways, just for the fun of it. I never knew where the grope was coming from, it was always a surprise.

Gravesend Park was located across the street from our apartment building, next to Gravesend Bay. The park had a racing track, Charlie Heichman was the only person that could run faster than I. There was also a handball court, a set of swings, and a basketball court. I wanted to join the basketball team, but the boys wouldn't let me participate. I felt like an outcast.

To pass the time on weekends, I fished for mackerel and caged crabs from Gravesend Bay. I was always amazed when I caught a fish. I snapped it up and quickly put it in the bucket to bring home for my mother to prepare for dinner. Mackerel fish is an oily fish, as I remember, but it was a refreshing change, compared to some of the other dishes she prepared.

Mother was very strict, she insisted that we ate everything on our dinner plate. We were also not allowed to talk at the dinner table; therefore, Carolyn and I learned to communicate with our eyes. Mother prepared food on Sunday for the entire week, and we had to eat it until everything was finished. It's one of the reasons, I don't like leftovers. Whenever we told Mother we liked a dish, she would make it often, so we learned not to tell her. For instance, her pineapple upside-down cake was the best, and we loved it, but not all the time. I never liked tripe, because it was like chewing bubble gum, and it seem to never end. One of my favorite meals was collard greens, macaroni and cheese, fried chicken, and one of her tasty cakes.

Fresh bottled milk was delivered daily. It reminded me of the milk I drank in Sanford with the cream floating on top. Sunday was also the day Mother cleaned the apartment and washed and ironed our clothes for the week. She also pressed Carolyn's hair with a hot comb to prepare her for school. The mother often sang or hummed a tune while working around the apartment. She instilled in me an appreciation for a well-ordered home. All of that was in addition to her working 40 hours per week at her job. She rarely stopped working even at home. She was like the Ever Ready Battery. I observed my mother's work ethic from an early age and how determined she was to accomplish her goals. I called her the busy bumble bee. I take a quote from '*In Living Color TV*,' one of the characters said, "You only have one job, you lazy lima bean."

I credit Mother for my walking style because she washed and polished our floors until they were shiny and slippery. I walked carefully with small steps, so I wouldn't slip. Carolyn and I often ran through the apartment and grabbed the walls to avoid falling. Our hand prints were left on the walls. Mother made us wash the walls from top to bottom with Ajax and a sponge. That is specifically why I don't touch walls today.

Carolyn and I were playing in the living room when we accidentally broke one of the figurine lamps. I knew our behinds "belonged" to mother. When Mother returned from work and saw what we had done. It was the beating of a lifetime. Now, as I look back, I think she thought, my God, I worked so hard to buy nice things and provide for these kids and now look what they have done.

We were locked in our apartment while our mother was at work. Similar to our old studio apartment in Clinton Hills, Brooklyn. We used our imagination and always kept ourselves busy while Mother was at work. One day, she left some eggs for our after-school snack. We opened a cookbook for a cake recipe and combined the eggs with other ingredients then whipped up a cake. It turned out to be a golden-brown baked masterpiece. We ate the entire cake before Mother returned home! We didn't dare share it with her, because we weren't allowed to use the oven. Fortunately, the oven cooled before she returned home. We were very thorough and didn't leave a crumb of evidence.

Carolyn and I often snuck out of the apartment during the day to play in the park. Mother had no knowledge of our escape. Thank goodness the neighbors didn't tell like the neighbors in Sanford. We knew approximately when she would return home, so we rushed back and pretended we were inside all day. Then she would send us out to play. Our timing was impeccable because we had a sense of when to return for dinner.

I worked as a Good Humor Ice Cream guy on Coney Island Beach one summer, during my early teen years. I hated the job because my friends were enjoying the summer, while I worked. I would have preferred relaxing on the beach with them. Coney

Carolyn and me at age 15

Island amusements were extensive at that time. I loved going to the Steeplechase Amusement Park. That was a very special destination. It was self-contained with everything I could wish for. Similar to a mini Disney Land. I rode on the Cyclone, the Wonder Wheel, and the Bumper cars. Those were my favorite rides. The haunted house was also a favorite, where something always popped up and surprised me. I only wished I could've experienced the Parachute. I thought about it but didn't want to spend fifty cents for the ride.

After mother quit her job as a maid at the Essex House Hotel, she routinely looked ahead for a better work opportunity and better pay. She studied and became a nurse's aide at the New York Hospital. Traveling to the NY Hospital was inconvenient because she had to spend hours on public transportation to-and-from work. The days were long and tiresome.

Mother found gainful employment at the Coney Island Hospital, which was closer to home. Mother learned to drive, when she was thirty-four years-old, then bought a car. It was stolen from the parking lot, but that didn't stop her, she bought another. While working at Coney Island Hospital, a friend told her that Creedmoor Hospital, for the Mentally Ill, was looking for workers, so she transferred for a salary increase.

Somehow Mother managed to be fashionable on a meager salary. She was a 'fashion plate.' She inspired me to become interested in fashion because she loved to dress in fine attire for evening events. She was so beautiful and happy when she dressed up. I loved to see her smile and proudly don her outfit. She was 'fauched' (dressed to the nines) in those swish-swish taffeta crinoline skirt dresses. I loved hearing the sound of taffeta as it swished and she sashayed in the apartment while preparing to depart for a formal event. Occasionally, Carolyn and I accompanied her.

We always knew when she was returning from a formal evening because she had a distinctive step that we could hear from our sixth-floor apartment. She walked with a step-step-da-rum-drag rhythm.

Mother, formal night out

Carolyn and I watched television in the living room until we heard our mother's steps. By the time she turned the key to unlock the door, I was underneath the covers of my pull-out sofa bed in the living room and Carolyn had run to her room.

Mother had an impeccable fashion sense, except for the old man's hat she bought for me to wear to school. For some reason, she considered that hat the fashion of the day and insisted I wear it. I felt foolish and embarrassed

Family formal affair with friends

because all the neighbors laughed at me. Yet, I wore it anyway. That's probably why I'm not fond of hats to this day.

Mother hadn't spoken to Grandad for three years, since the incident in Jacksonville. I still missed Grandad. I secretly wrote to him with the assistance of our cousin, Ethel. She read his replies over the phone. After several letters, I asked if we could spend the summer of 1956 with him. He immediately replied, "Yes," directly to Mother. She was delighted to hear from him. That patched everything up between them. Carolyn and I were anxious and couldn't wait for our summer break. He sent two roundtrip train tickets at the end of the school year. Once school was out for the summer break, we were off to Penn Station again to board an interstate train. It took 21 hours before we arrived in Sanford.

Grandad's home was located on the outskirts of town. That's where I discovered local creatures that I had never encountered before, for instance: a scorpion was entering his home at the same time as I. I didn't know what a scorpion was, however, grandma told me they were dangerous, then I freaked. The next adventure was a flying cock roach. I was running around the living room trying to get away from it when suddenly the roach lifted its wings and began to fly. Well, I knew I couldn't fly, so I fainted. That was the first time I saw a flying roach. What a surprise.

My childhood memories and the time spent with Grandad felt like old times again. I made the mistake of calling him Granddaddy instead of, Grandad. Ms. Leslie reminded me that he preferred, being called Grandad as I had called him when I was a little boy.

He had planted several orange trees next to his home and raised chickens in the backyard. One day, he asked if I'd like chicken for dinner.

"Not one of those from the backyard," I remarked.

I insisted that he purchase a chicken from the grocery store. Because that was what I was now used to. After all, I had moved to the big city and grown accustomed to life in the city, I was not used to freshly killed chickens. With the many changes I experienced in life, I had changed.

Carolyn and I spent several summers with Grandad. Each summer was different because we were growing and becoming more independent. I recall Carolyn and I were having dinner at the table and bouncing in our seats.

"Of course, now I see why your appetite is so bountiful," Grandad said.

We got to know the neighboring kids, who were our age and often shared games, such as stickball.

One afternoon, Carolyn and I had just finished playing with the neighbor's kids in the backyard. Suddenly I ran in the house and a man who was talking with Grandad, grabbed my arm and asked, "Do you know who I am?"

"The Insurance Man," I replied.

"No, I'm your dad."

I sat down and we talked for a while. It had been years since I saw him, so there was no way I'd remember him.

I was thirteen years old that summer and Aunt Sally died on the farm in Monticello. Grandad drove us to her funeral. It was a solemn occasion where everyone was dressed in black. As I looked in the casket, Aunt Sally lay peacefully in her best dress. Being that I was mischievous, I sang, "Little Sally Walker lying in her coffin, rise Sally, RISE!" We returned to the farm after the funeral for the repass. There was a variety of food choices and homemade drinks. Everyone sat around and reminisced about Aunt Sally's life on the farm. All I wanted to do was to walk outside and smell the fresh country air.

The open fields were still peaceful and idyllic. Luckily, some things never change. I meandered through the fields that bore fresh fruits and vegetables, while the entire family of brothers, sisters, in-laws, and cousins gathered inside. As sweet as it was to return, life in the countryside also meant we ate fresh kill. Dinner was lit by a kerosene lantern. There was no electricity. I didn't feel calm. I was skeptical because I couldn't see what was on my plate. The atmosphere certainly wasn't romantic. Actually, it was scary!

I slept in the car that night, I didn't feel comfortable because Aunt Sally had died in the house. I woke up the next morning and discovered I'd been devoured by those vicious mosquitoes. There was no proper bathroom to freshen up, so I filled a basin and sponge-bathed myself. After I freshened up, I took a walk with one of my cousins. We walked along a long, long winding dirt road that was shaded by a canopy of oak trees with Spanish moss dangling from its branches, as it had been for many years. As we walked and talked, I discovered we had a lot in common. It was terrific to meet so many relatives that I didn't know.

After we returned to Sanford, I was walking two blocks from Grandad's home to Mr. Henry's Motel (Grandad's good friend). While quietly walking and reading, suddenly I heard a strange noise. I quickly looked down at my feet and there was an enormous black snake. I must have jumped five feet in the air. Frightened out of my mind. A family across the road was sitting on their porch and saw what happened, they began to laugh. I didn't think it was funny. It was not an encounter that I wished for.

Mr. Henry hired me that summer, as a receptionist for his contracting company. I think he paid me 0.10 cents an hour. Grandad wanted me to share my earnings with Carolyn. I refused since I had worked so hard for the money. My punishment was to wash and dry all the dishes by myself. I didn't mind, because I had plans for the money. At the end of the summer, I had earned enough to buy a red shirt and red pants. It was a time in our history when department stores did not allow Coloreds to try on clothes in the store and there were no returns.

When we returned home at the end of the summer. Mother saw the red outfit and said, "No son of mine is wearing a red outfit." She quickly threw the pants and the shirt in the incinerator. My heart was broken because I had worked the entire summer just to purchase that outfit. Later in life, as an adult, I bought six pairs of red pants just to prove her wrong.

That was the year Elvis Presley was the rage, and rock and roll was everywhere on jukeboxes, radios, and records. It was a happy time when a slice of pizza and a soda only cost .25 cents.

Mother was very generous and invited her sister Rebecca from Miami to stay with us for a while. I recall Aunt Beck, (that's what we called her), at dinner, she told mother that she couldn't eat another

Mother and Carol socializing, 1959

bite. Then she asked, "What can I do with it?" I was only thirteen when I suggested she put it in her pocket. That was the first time I was outspoken.

I met Pat Davis in our eighth-grade class and immediately had a crush on her, I also had a little competition from my best friend, Alonzo Settles. Thank God, I won out. She was my first kiss. Pat's parents moved to another neighborhood, which meant Pat transferred to another school at the end of that year, but we stayed in touch.

I sketched a ladies' fashion for my Junior High School yearbook at the end of the ninth grade. I was inspired by my younger years of observing Grandad, as he brilliantly sketched a horse from his recall of living on the farm. After graduating from Mark Twain Junior High, I entered Lincoln High School, which was the catalyst for a major awakening. I walked into the illustration class one afternoon and said, "I can do that," and immediately signed up. I aspired to be a fashion designer or an artist of some kind. I had a talent for drawing ladies' fashions and wanted to know more about the nine heads, it's the fundamental starting point for fashion drawings. I was also eager to learn about garment construction, such as, what a sleeve looks like and so on. The guidance counselor suggested I transfer to the High School of Fashion Industries in Manhattan.

I heeded the counselor's advice and transferred. I was unhappy at the High School of Fashion Industries during my first semester and it was reflected in my grades. The guidance counselor suggested I try a course in shoemaking or tailoring, anything but fashion design. That was my wake-up call and the advice I definitely would not take heed to. My mother's fashion sense inspired my decision to follow my dream and interest in design. I wanted to be a fashion designer, PERIOD!

The strangest thing was, the lunch room was divided into three sections, one for girls and another for boys and there was one section for everyone. I found that peculiar, so I sat in the everyone section. I made an enormous improvement during the following semesters. I received all 'A's,' but still hated the school. However, I became fond of one teacher, in particular, Miss Katherine Scarpa. She was a screamer but cared about her students and I learned a lot from her. I also joined Miss Goodman's Glee Club. We performed Christmas Carols in

Grand Central Station and other public spaces. Paula Baldwin (James Baldwin's sister) was one of my classmates. Myrna Stephen was also in my class and I quickly became fond of Myrna. I occasionally accompanied her on the subway to her home in the Bronx and then turned around and rode to Coney Island, where I lived.

I knew I had the drive, perseverance, and determination it would take to pursue my dream. I submitted one of my designs to the annual fashion show. Mother was my model. She wore my black, brocade, keyhole dress with a dolman cardigan jacket. It was a way for her to get another outfit. I loved the fact that that outfit became one of her favorites and she saved it for many years.

One of my High School pals asked, "Where do you live?"

"Coney Island," I responded.

Then he asked, "Do you live in the freak house?"

"No, I live in an apartment."

My old flame Pat was my date at the high school prom. I designed and made a hand-tucked yellow silk chiffon dress for the occasion. I arrived at her door the night of the prom and presented her with a white orchid corsage. I was dressed in a white dinner jacket with black formal trousers. My cousin Josh Davidson chauffeured us to the Hawaii Kai Restaurant on Broadway at 51st Street in Manhattan. That was a big deal to us. We danced the night away. Several friends hung out at my apartment after the prom. Fortunately, Mother was on vacation in Florida.

Just before graduating from the High School of Fashion Industries, the placement office informed me that the Fashion Institute of Technology bookstore was looking for a part-time worker. That was perfect! I could attend classes and work part-time and earn a little money. The best part was, as an employee, my tuition was paid for by the school as long as I continued to work at the bookstore. While working at the bookstore, I interacted with everyone who came into the store. I recall Antonio Lopez, the illustrator needed art supplies but didn't have any money, so I told him he could pay later. However, he returned within a few days to pay and approached Ms. Guedenet, the store manager, he told her that I had allowed him to take the supplies without paying and he was returning to pay for the supplies.

High school graduation, 1961

I was reprimanded for that incident. Actually, he should have come to me to ring it in the register.

The Snack Bar was next door to the Bookstore. The jukebox played the best rock 'n roll music. On any given day and time, you could find me dancing to the "The Boston Stomp" or "Peppermint Twist" or some other hot tune. Charlotte Guedenet often came to the Snack Bar and pulled me off the dance floor to finish ringing up a sale.

I had no interest in science and the science teacher realized it. I couldn't see the point of it. He took precious time out of his schedule to tutor me to make sure I passed the course. I frankly couldn't see how it would apply to my life as a designer.

FIT was a colorful and explosive part of my life, it's where I blossomed. I was truly in my element; my talent was energized. For the first time in my life, I became popular, found my niche, and thus began the most inspiring years of my life.

I loved fashion, actually, I was a true fashion victim. I stayed up many nights sewing a new outfit for the next day. I kept a chart, so I wouldn't repeat an outfit within the month. I designed a variety of

Carolyn – high school graduation, 1962

original jackets and pants. For instance, I doubled layered muslin cloth shirt and my favorite cardigan tweed double-breasted jacket with one button.

I also participated in the theatre group at FIT. The director asked me to sing 'Day O.' I told her I hated that song, but she insisted I sing it anyway. On the day of my performance, I sang "Day O, Day O, come Mr. Tally Mon" and at that point lost the words, so I instantly ad-libbed with, "Show me your banana." The audience started with a slow roar of laughter and continued into a crescendo for 20 minutes! The curtain dropped and the show was stopped. It was the first time in my life that I improvised and got everyone's attention. Several boys teased me in the gym shower by showing me their "bananas." I was teased for the duration of my tenure, but I didn't care. That was the best time of my life. It was also the first time I had sex .... with someone else.

I was in class on November 22, 1963, when an announcement came over the speaker that said, President John F. Kennedy was shot. The school closed immediately and so did all of New York. The boardwalk in Coney Island and the amusement park closed as well. It was a sad and isolating day for the entire country. However, things got back to normal within a few days. I realized the world does not stop for one person. No matter what, life goes on.

Mother and I attended Carolyn's High School graduation at Brooklyn College. Naturally, mother got fauched for the occasion.

FIT held a dance at the Essex House Hotel. Mother didn't want Carolyn to go with me, but we went anyway and we won a trophy for being the best damn dancers. We had the best time together. But when we returned home, Mother had locked us out. I called Richard Smith, a friend I had met on the beach the previous summer. I asked if we could spend the night at his place. Carolyn wore a long black, spaghetti-strapped gown to the dance. I didn't want her to look

Mother at Carol's graduation, 1964

ridiculous walking down the street in a formal gown, so we pulled it up to street length and used the belt to hold it in place. Then we took the subway to Richard's apartment where we spent a quiet, restful end of a beautiful night.

Mother was still upset when we returned home the next day. I knew my days were numbered. I was coming of age and wanted to be totally independent. It was time to move on.

CHAPTER FOUR

Independence

S hortly after graduating from FIT in 1964, I landed my first real job as an assistant patternmaker for a men's wear jacket company. I was so excited to get the job, but to my absolute surprise, it was boring beyond belief. I didn't like the idea that I had to clock in and clock out. I felt confined and without autonomy. I knew what I wanted to do: I wanted to design. I liked the idea of being independent and now finally having enough money to move away from home. I gave Mother a two-week notice. She was disappointed, about my decision, because I guess she thought I would finally contribute money to the household. She refused to speak to me for the duration of my stay. Mother was so strict in so many ways that I couldn't wait to get the hell out of her home.

I was twenty years old and the banks would not allow me to open an account until I became twenty-one. Meanwhile, I asked Richard Smith, a friend, who lived in downtown Brooklyn, if I could share his apartment and expenses. I moved in and we became lovers after a short time.

Moving from my mother's home gave me a sense of independence. I called Mother several times after I settled in, but she didn't want anything to do with me, so I stopped calling. Carolyn worked as a clerk at the Metropolitan Life Insurance Company. I stayed in touch with her as best I could.

My job as an assistant patternmaker lasted for four months. It wasn't creative, so I quit. I made an appointment at The New York State Employment Office. They recommended me for a job as a blouse designer. So, I became gainfully employed as a blouse designer. I knew nothing about blouses, so I ventured into Macy's during my lunch break, to discover what the hell a blouse was. My first experience of designing a blouse left a lot to the imagination. I forgot to add seam allowance to the pattern. When the sample maker sewed the blouse, it became two sizes too small. I was fired within a day and a half because nothing fit. I never forgot to add seam allowance after that experience.

I managed to get hired and fired from several companies. I felt displaced for a short time. Finally, I stumbled into a position as an assistant sportswear designer. Richard asked me to pay my share of the expenses during the first week of employment. I asked if he could wait one more week until I received a check. He was very impatient; he refused and suggested I move. Well, that was a rude awakening. The wind was knocked out of me. I felt very insecure especially after having moved away from my family. I knew I couldn't go home again. I was at a low point, two weeks later I moved out.

I was a very proud young man. I had to start over again, so I packed my belongings and moved to Manhattan, and shared a studio apartment with Renee Selver. Her apartment was small but comfortable. I lived with her for a month, until her mother got wind of our arrangement. Her mother discovered that a young Black man was living with her young Jewish daughter. I had to move again. I did a lot of moving during the next few months.

I was very close to my cousin Ethel and spent many evenings with her. She was always in great spirit, and she was my anchor. I thought of her as my second mother I was unemployed for a short while and penniless. I commented, "I'm grateful for a box of cookies." Ethel and I shared precious time. I recall having dinner with her in a restaurant when suddenly several people at the next table asked us to join them. At the end of the evening, they invited us to their apartment for a drink. Ethel was adventurous and a free spirit. That was one of the things I loved about her. She also invited me to several Broadway shows to lift my spirit. I adored her.

One morning, I woke up and thought, "Why don't I get my apartment and make my own rules. It will be cheaper and make my life less hectic."

A friend told me about an apartment he was renting, but not living in. The apartment was located on First Avenue, between first and second street in the East Village. I gave him a month's rent and a month's security. I took the apartment, sight unseen, only to stay one night. I hated the apartment, the neighborhood, and everything it represented. I called him to reimburse me, but he refused. I took him to court and he still wouldn't refund my money. It was a lesson well learned.

Shortly after that, I found my very first real apartment at 110 Sullivan Street, in the heart of Little Italy. I borrowed the money for a month's rent and the security deposit from my friend, Pat Davis. I knew I'd be able to pay her back within two weeks because I had begun working at McCall's Pattern Company.

I was one of the layout artists, who figured out the fabric yardage for each garment. That information was listed on the back of each pattern. McCall's Co. had stupid rules, such as we had to arrive at 9 am to have a fifteen-minute breakfast break. I'd arrive at nine-fifteen instead because I already had breakfast. That didn't sit well with my supervisor.

One day, I was returning late from lunch, and the boss man was waiting as I stepped out of the elevator.

"Mr. Haggins, do you know what time it is?"

"No, but perhaps you can tell me."

Obviously, I knew, but wouldn't give him the satisfaction.

Another thing I didn't like about McCall's Company: everyone had to line up at four-thirty, to wait for the five o'clock dismissal bell. I felt like I was still in school, it was ridiculous and so pedestrian. I hated the job and everything it represented. I only stayed one month.

Shortly after that, I managed to break the record of getting three jobs in a week. I also asked for more money for each. The next potential employer called a previous employer for references, while I was sitting in her office. Fortunately, she answered the questions instead of asking. The former employer agreed to whatever she said. I was hired on the spot. Imagine if the situation had not turned out in my favor? I would have said, "So, I lied, I wanted the job."

I lived in the studio apartment on Sullivan Street, for four months until a group of Italian boys saw a group of young, gorgeous model types visiting me. They were jealous and decided to throw raw eggs at my windows. I encouraged the girls to return the favor. Well, all hell broke loose; there was a war on Sullivan Street. I thought they were going to murder us. Those were the rough and ready guys that were just waiting for something to set them off. We waited two days to allow everything to cool down, before leaving the building. We feared for our lives. I couldn't believe that this was their real world and we weren't going to be in it much longer.

After reviewing the situation, I called the landlord and told him that I was going to move at the end of the month. I suggested he keep the security deposit because I wanted out. He was very happy and I was happy to get the hell out of the neighborhood ALIVE.

In a frantic search for an apartment, I visited a new building on 14th Street, between Fifth Avenue and University Place. Two days later, the rental office called to tell me I couldn't have the apartment because I was Black. I was so SHOCKED, that I didn't know how to react. I only had two days left before I agreed to move. Ironically, I returned to 16 West 16th Street, the building where I shared Renee's studio apartment. Her apartment was available. It was familiar, so I signed the lease and lived there for two happy years. The apartment building was conveniently located in the center of most of my activities. The traffic on Madison and Fifth Avenue changed in 1965 to a single direction.

The 1960s was a time when anything goes, especially after the Kennedy assassination in 1963. The Civil Rights Movement began to gather momentum. I have a vivid recollection of visiting Sanford, Florida, for summer vacations, where blacks and whites were segregated in toilets, buses, restaurants, public spaces, and neighborhoods. Coloreds were not allowed to try on clothes before purchasing them and we certainly could not return them after they were purchased. It was an awful period in American history. There were vile lynching and cross burnings throughout the South. It was a time in our lives when people of color were fighting for equality and justice.

Our country was in serious shock with the Civil Rights Movement, Vietnam War, youth movement, and the assassinations of John Kennedy, Robert Kennedy, Malcolm X, and Martin Luther King. I was relaxing in my apartment when I heard Bobby Kennedy that was shot. Out of disbelief, I was thinking about what was the world coming to, so much hatred and despair. Where was the peace and love especially during Wood Stock, Martin Luther King, Bobby Kennedy, and Malcolm X in the 1960s?

While our country was in turmoil, with the Black revolution, Rock & roll, drugs, and sex. No drugs for me, but I had my share of Rock & Roll and sex. I was creating fabulous fashions. My eye was on the ball. I knew I wanted to be a designer from my early teenage years.

CHAPTER FIVE

Style Born in a Disco

Grandad was an independent carpenter and he worked for himself. He was the most inspiring person in my life. I soon realized that I also wanted to work for myself, to be free to express myself with my designs. So, did other young designers, as the restlessness of the 1960s began to reach all of us.

My Mother had a terrific fashion sense that fueled my decision to follow my early interest in designing. It was a crazy time, as I look back. Blacks were largely invisible members of the backroom staff in fashion houses during the 1960s. I continued to hunt, but never found a satisfying spot in the fashion industry. I must have had twenty jobs within two years; getting hired and fired came easily to me. At first, it was disappointing and frustrating, but I knew I had the talent and a dream to pursue. My last employer sent a telegram informing me that I was fired. "Oh well, Next!" became my expression and attitude. None of those jobs were satisfying, because I knew what I wanted to be. I wanted to be a fashion designer. I recalled Grandad saying, "Follow your dream."

I soon realized that I wanted to work for myself, to be free to express myself with my designs. So, did other young designers, as the restlessness of the 1960s began to reach all of us. There was an "anything goes" mood. Thank goodness I had several jobs that didn't last because that prompted me to create my own fashions.

Sybil Burton divorced Richard Burton in 1963. Fortunately, she opened 'Arthur', a nightclub in 1965. Every celebrity of that time frequented the club. Sybil became fond of our little group, which consisted of Myrna Stephens, Jane Friedman, Joey Jessic and me. She invited us to all the parties at the club and we also appeared on Arthur's TV special. You could find us in the club six nights a week. I was so exhausted by Wednesday that I couldn't get out of bed. I was having the best time of my life. I robbed my piggy banks for taxi fares, just to get to the club, knowing that once we arrived,

Myrna and I, 1966

someone would treat us to drinks. You could often find us congregated around the bar in the zebra-striped banquet back room or on the dance floor where a live band was interspersed with vinyl records.

Myrna was my favorite dance partner. I designed and made a dress per day for her to show off at the club. We'd arrive with her wearing one of my new gowns and I wore jeans, very informal. She tested the dress of the day: if her bosom popped out of the tiny top while dancing the Boogaloo, it meant I had to go back to the cutting board and add another half-inch under the bosom to perfect the garment. One of my designs was a beautiful polka dot palazzo jumpsuit. I hadn't gotten to the stage of understanding the female anatomy, especially when it came to making clothes that would allow a woman to easily undress in the ladies' room. But I quickly learned what was practical.

Many celebrities who frequented the club approved of my designs. That gave me the courage to charge forward. On any given night you could find Jack Nicholson, Sidney Poitier, Paul Newman, Judy Garland, Shirley MacLaine, Geraldine Paige, Arthur Mitchell, Warren Beatty, Liza Minnelli, and Leslie Uggams. That would never have happened if I still lived in Sanford, Florida. Nothing was going on in Sanford except the leaves being blown by the wind. That's how still the town was. Even as a child, Grandad gave me the gift of using my imagination for bigger things, things he couldn't have while he was going up.

I saw Judy Garland three times in Arthur's. The first time, she was sitting at a center table in the private bar room. She looked radiant in a baby blue silk peau de soie dress, her face was framed with a portrait collar. The second time, she arrived after her show at the Palace Theatre, wearing a glittering, bugle-beaded pants suit that she wore during her performance. She was radiant and danced the night away. The last time I saw her, she entered the main room with her husband, Mickey Deans. Then sat quietly next to me with a large bouquet of red roses. She appeared very thin. A few weeks later, I read that she had died in London. It was the end of the road for a fabulous star.

Jackie Kennedy also danced at Arthur, but she was not much of a dancer: I guess her interest was elsewhere. Arthur was a Mecca for celebrities. Imagine dancing on the floor next to Judy Garland or Jackie Kennedy.

Another night in the club, I was sitting next to Geraldine Paige, who had just completed her Broadway engagement of 'The Great Indoors.' I turned to her and said, "Watta ya wanna go dere fur, dere's that new bunch...the Porter Ric-i-ans?" She burst into a thunderous laugher, because that was one of her lines from her show. Unfortunately, the show only lasted a week. I was the only one in the audience who laughed at that line. My friends Jane Friedman, Myrna Stephens, Beverly Silver, Peaches Brewer (Mrs. Edgar Bronfman Jr.), and Joey Jessic loved to dance. Tiger Morse designed and wore an electric dress that she turned on and it appeared as a dancing Christmas tree. Some of the other clubs that we frequented were The Dom, Ondines, Cheetah, Tamberlane, Charade, and Nepentha.

When I started out in the mid-60s as a fashion designer, it was not easy for a young man to make it in the garment business, if he didn't have relatives or others to turn to for guidance. It was a crazy time, as I look back.

The '60s, despite all the social turmoil, were good times for me. The mid-sixties were a unique period when it was possible to launch a new company with very little money, as inflation hadn't yet started to roar. But at twenty-two, I had the drive of youth, the will and desire to pursue my dream and be my own man. I applied all the things that I had learned, from typing to additions, and used them in my business. That was the beginning of Jon Haggins, Inc., my very own design company. Initially, I couldn't get credit from fabric mills. I had to pay cash to establish a working relationship before the mills would establish a line of credit for me.

I was discovering all kinds of fabrics that worked best for my designs. My dresses were designed with no zippers or buttons. I managed to design twelve gorgeous garments in just two weeks.

I said to myself, "Oh, my God! I've got a collection."

I didn't know anyone in the fashion business at that time. I had no idea of how to attract buyers and editors, but I did have the instinct to buy several magazines and newspapers and looked at the masthead for names of the fashion editors. I called several editors and told them I had the most fabulous designs in the world. That stirred their curiosity. They were very enthusiastic and set up appointments to

Myrna Stephens models my fashions

1966

1967

1967

view my collection. Joanne Jenkins from *Women's Wear Daily* was the first editor to view my collection. My image of a fashion editor was that of an international dame, wrapped in an enormous stole, with a very long, lean cigarette holder in one hand and a pencil in the other. When I opened my apartment door, I stood at six feet one inch tall, and looked straight ahead and thought, "Where is she?" Then a little voice from below called out, "Hello, I'm Joanne Jenkins, from *Women's Wear Daily.*" Joanne stood approximately five feet with no cigarette holder and no wrapped stole. She walked in, sat down, and loved the entire collection.

An editor from her office, later told me, that when Joanne returned to the office, she announced that she had just discovered a tall, 'ebony,' a young man with the most inspirational new fashions. I couldn't sleep the night before my first editorial appeared in *Women's Wear Daily*. I was so excited to see my name in print. I felt I had arrived.

I was also producing the samples and stock. Irene Allen and Sandy Cole of Allen and Cole Boutique and Splendiferous boutique were the first to buy some of my original designs. Those were two of the most creative and adventurous local shops with pizzazz. Those shops had razzle, dazzle, and glitz.

I ran around town showing my collection to several editors on my list. Randy Mersel at *Glamour* magazine suggested that my designs were too sophisticated for her magazine, she thought perhaps I should call several editors at *Vogue* magazine. I followed suit and secured an appointment with Margaret Ingersol, Carrie Donavan, Cathy di Montezemolo, and Caterine Milinaire. They loved my enthusiasm and spirit and also my collection. Cathy di Montezemolo rushed down to my apartment and asked me to design two dresses using a Tom Isbels' geometric print on Enkalure fabric.

My first *Vogue* editorial featured Marisa Berenson wearing two of my asymmetric fashions in a double-page spread, in January 1967. The dresses were photographed in the sugar cane fields on the Island of Mauritius, Africa. Several local ladies accompanied her through the fields. They wore colorful saris draped around their waist and tossed over their shoulders. Stalks of sugarcane weighted their heads as they walked brazenly through the fields. *Vogue* magazine was the first

Marisa Berenson in Vogue, 1967, on the Island of Mauritius

national publication to feature my designs. Many years later, I visited the Island of Mauritius and walked through the sugar cane fields where *Vogue* photographed Marisa.

Diana Vreeland was the Editor-in-Chief at *Vogue* and quite a character in her own right. She was *VOGUE*. Miss Vreeland allowed designers to be very creative. She took chances with new designers and models. Caterine Milinaire walked me into Ms. Vreeland's little cherry red office in the Grey Bar Building and introduced me. I thanked Ms. Vreeland for featuring my designs in her magazine. Talk about excitement, I was out of this world. I was in another stratosphere and was so impressed to be working with the best.

The editors at *Vogue* also introduced me to Geraldine Stutz, president of Henri Bendel. Miss Stutz invited me to her executive office for high tea. She also called Margaret Bronson, (her buyer), to view my collection. Myrna modeled a polka dot palazzo jumpsuit, a short jumpsuit with a contrasting floral pattern, a Banlon dress with a tiny solid top with a chevron printed pleated skirt, and several other styles. Margaret bought everything on the spot.

Cathy di Montizemolo also arranged another appointment with Barbara Leary, the buyer for Bonwit Teller's Safari Room. Barbara also loved and bought my collection. Meeting Barbara Leary was another feather in my cap. That was my ticket to two of the world's most prestigious stores. I thought I had died and gone to heaven. I also thought I'd make millions. That was the beginning of my fashion career. I had a good start, with the best stores in my pocket.

I also carried my designs to *Harper's, Cosmopolitan, Town & Country,* and *Look* and received equal acceptance. Then a thrust of other national fashion magazines and newspapers followed, such as *The Daily News, Mc Calls, Life, Ebony,* and *The New York Times.* Actually, I called Charlotte Curtis, head of the fashion magazine section of *The New York Times,* and suggested they feature my designs and they did. My first editorial in *The New York Times* Sunday magazine was a full page featuring a long white matte jersey wrap gown photographed on a beach. It was the simplest design, with no buttons and no zipper. The gown just wrapped perfectly around the body. My fashions always had a look of ease and felt great without a lot of construction or fuss. For a magazine to feature my designs, I had to sell the dresses to several national stores to make them available to the public. It's called "merchandising."

I lived in a new building where the lobby was embellished with floor-to-ceiling mirrors. I frequently used mirrors for fashion fittings. The hallways were so narrow, that you had to be thin or walk sideways. I called them "Hooker Hallways." Everyone who lived in the building was in his or her twenties and thin. The building was more like a dormitory than an apartment building.

Fashionable editors charged into my Smart Little Studio and featured my fashions on the covers and interior pages of their publications. My fashions were worn by the hottest model at that time. I just knew I was on my way.

Mai Britt Davis, was my first celebrity client. I called her home to confirm our appointment and Sammy Davis Jr, her husband, answered the phone. It was the first and last time I spoke with him. Eugenia

Shepperd from *Herald Tribune* newspaper featured Mai Britt in two of my designs: a white pique two-piece pants suit and a horizontal striped jersey gown with long sleeves.

My apartment was so small, that whenever the doorman rang the intercom, it reminded me of my next appointment. I'd rush to throw the garbage in the oven and close the kitchen door. When guests entered the apartment, it was impeccably organized. Of course, I couldn't open any door until they left.

George, the doorman had a great sense of humor. As editors arrived, he automatically commented:

Mai Britt, 1966

"You must be going to 12ES."

"How do you know?"

"Because everyone that looks like you go to 12ES."

They had the LOOK. Can't explain it, it's just a LOOK. I like to think it was because they were dressed so fashionably!

Talk about excitement, I was out of this world. I was in another stratosphere. I was so impressed because I was working with the best. I became the darling of the fashion editors in the mid-1960s.

Another glorious experience was cruising on a yacht up the Hudson River, sipping champagne and sharing hor d'oeuvres. It was a perfect day for cruising, because the sky was totally blue, not a cloud in the sky. I presented a fashion show before we arrived at a boutique in Nyack, NY. I also recall waking up the next morning and opening my door, reaching for *The New York Times*. To my surprise, I was featured on the cover of *The New York Times*, with one of my models on the Hudson River cruise.

My clothes were drapey and seductive at a time when seventh avenue designers were creating constructed hard-edge clothes. I used chiffons, jerseys, and silks to enhance the female figure. My fashions were like lovers: you never lend them out.

The response to my designs was so favorable that it encouraged me to continue to pursue my dream of designing. My designs were indeed soft, drapey, and glamorous.

Dancing was the one thing that I cared about. Bernadine Morris from *The New York Times* once wrote,

"His Fashions Were Born in a Disco." And another article was titled: "Made Dresses by Day and Danced by Night."

Exhibit at FIT, NYC

In 1966, Jon Haggins defied the popular trend for structural clothes, founding his company in soft, sinuous designs that foresaw the disco era. The response to my designs was so favorable that it encouraged me to continue to pursue my dream of designing. My designs were indeed soft, drapey, and glamorous. I designed a one-seam horizontal striped pants, that I shared with friends. We wore them out in the evenings to various events. I recall stepping out of a taxi one evening and a gentleman yelled, "Oh, my God! They're coming in their pajamas!"

FIT Black Designer Exhibit

The country was in turmoil during the sixties and yet, it was an exciting time for me. New York City had the first blackout on Tuesday, November 9, 1965. The entire city was blacked out. I was fortunate to be resting in my apartment when the lights went out. Then I decided to walk down to Tad's Steak House on Sixth Avenue, in the Village for dinner. I carried a candelabra that I had pinched from the Plaza Hotel. I placed it on the table, then ordered a medium-rare steak, and thoroughly enjoyed the experience. My neighbors were sitting in the lobby of the building, when I returned with the candelabra, they commented, "That must be Jon Haggins."

Talking about having a hoot of fun, someone told me about a warehouse that sold old fur coats. I escorted Margaret Mazzarraco and several other editors from *Women's Wear Daily* to the warehouse. That's where I found a fantastic black longhaired bear midi-length coat with a brown and white cow skin collar. The shop owner wanted $15.00. I told him I only make $12.00 a day. He sold it for $12.00 and made me very happy. The coat was a smasharoo.

Vogue magazine photographed me on Fifty-Seventh Street wearing the coat. Baron de Gunsberg at *Vogue* suggested I shorten the coat and use the bottom for the collar. "Who's the designer?" I responded. I wore that coat while visiting the Safari Room at Bonwit Teller. Later, I was told that several security men had

Fur coat on 57th Street, 1967

followed me around until my buyer identified me. I knew then that I truly had a following.

My first editorial in *Harper's Bazaar* was a two-piece wrap red and purple bathing suit made of Stretchnit Enkalure fabric. That editorial garnished the attention of Clarence Ross who owned Stretchnit Fabrics. The red top wrapped around the body and the bottom was a purple brief; it was the simplest design that worked on so many bodies. It was pretty amazing for that time. I loved Mr. Ross's soft drapey modern knitted fabrics because they complimented my designs. Several major fashion magazines featured a variety of my designs in Stretchnit fabrics. That worked for both of us, because we received free editorials.

I always called him Mr. Ross, although others in the industry referred to him as "Clanky." He befriended me and his company was the first to extend me a credit line. That was particularly important for a young designer starting out with very little capital. In the apparel business, you need as many friends as you can get.

During the years that followed, Mr. Ross introduced me to his entire family, including his wife Ethel, daughter Katherine, son-in-law Norman Kaufman, who was the VP of the company, and his grandchildren Stephen, Peter, and Katherine. His family became my extended family. No matter how busy he was, he always found time to share a moment with me. We often discuss the problems of running a business. And he shared fabrics that he was developing. I looked up to him as the Pop that I never had. He was a great friend and advisor. He was my mentor. His daughter Katherine Stephens and I are still long-time friends (not old friends).

I didn't know about cash flow but quickly learned. I wish I had taken some business courses at FIT, before graduating. Whenever my cash flow was interrupted, I'd ask buyers to rush the payments. I needed the receivables to purchase more fabrics to complete orders. On one occasion, Barbara Leary at Bonwit Teller, actually purchased fabric for me, to receive her order in a timely fashion. Several other stores were also very cooperative by paying promptly, which made life on the fashion front much easier.

The orders and re-orders were stacking up and becoming unmanageable. I called the New York State Office for a seamstress. Minnie Turner filled the request. I liked her right away and hired her on the spot. We became close friends over the years.

The sixties were a time to re-invent the English language with words such as Lovie-Poo, Smasharoo, Groovy, Pizzazz, Boogaloo, Peppermint Twist, Way-Out, Far-Out, Razzle-Dazzle, Glitz, etc. Those words reflected a time when women wore ridiculous, big hair-dos and low-cut, funky, hip-hugging bell bottoms with their belly buttons exposed.

Myrna Stephens, my friend from High School, and Naomi Sims were working as illustrator models at Macy's, and that's where I met Naomi

*Naomi Sims,
Myrna Stephens,
Bob VanOsten and I
at the Paper Ball in
Hartford, CT, 1966*

85

Sims. The sixties was also the time for new inventive fashions, such as Paper fashions. Paper was the rage. Paper was supposed to replace the fabric. I was invited to the Paper Ball in Hartford, Connecticut, in 1966.

Naomi and Myrna wore my paper fashions. I was the first designer to hire Naomi and the rest is history. Myrna's paper strap broke during the event and I quickly scotch-taped her together again. Everyone from the social world was in attendance including Rebecca Harkness, the philanthropist, and Ethel Scull, the art collector. Particular attention was paid to my designs because they were asymmetric and different and worn by two stunning models. Naomi Sims was later chosen as the Paper Ball Queen on the '*To Tell The Truth*' TV Show and Myrna was featured in Carrie Donavan's Boutique column in *Vogue*.

My first in-store fashion presentation appearance was at De Pinna Specialty Store on Fifth Avenue at 52nd Street, in 1966. Bill Cunningham walked over and introduced himself:

"Hi, I'm Bill Cunningham from the *Chicago Tribune*."

I will never forget our first meeting. He was a gentle soul. Bill has photographed me several times at a variety of social events for *The New York Times*. We remained friends throughout the years. I also recalled running into him at Stephen Burrows exhibit at the Museum of the City of New York. He walked over and asked, if I remember my fashion show at Walter Reade's home in 1969, then he commented, "You have always been an elegant man." The last time I saw Bill was at Norma Jean Darden's Miss Mamie's Spoonbread Restaurant, where Norma and I hosted a Memorial party for Andrea Skinner, a former *New York Times* editor. He featured the Memorial in his weekly social column. Bill passed away two months after attending our event. He is truly missed.

Carolyn, my sister worked at the Metropolitan Life Insurance Company on East 23rd Street and Madison Avenue, which was several blocks from my apartment. I stopped by occasionally, to borrow money from her. Her co-worker would say, "Here comes your brother."

A year after getting settled in my apartment, Carolyn ran away from home to stay with me. She was pregnant, Mother was embarrassed and quite upset. She didn't want Carolyn to experience the same hardships that she endured. Mother found my phone number, then called to ask if I knew where Carolyn was? "Yes, she's with me." That calmed her down. She asked me to escort Carolyn home and I agreed but told her it would have to be the next evening. That was the first time Mother had spoken to me in two years. Carolyn and I partied that night with several friends at the Eighth Wonder disco in Greenwich Village. I'm sure Carolyn had the

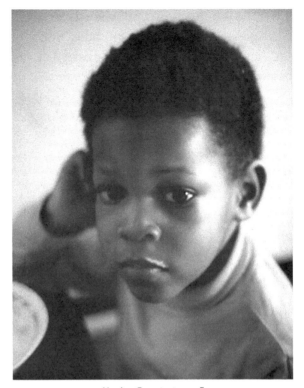

Xavier Grant at age 5

best time of her life, away from our very strict mother.

After Carolyn returned home, she ran away again several months later and stayed with the mother of the boy who impregnated her. Carolyn refused to return home. Mother disapproved, but couldn't do anything about it. Carolyn eventually got married and moved to Passaic, New Jersey where she bore three children: Xavier, Carolyn Jr., and Kelly.

After Mother re-connected with me, she was very supportive and helped me financially with my fashion business.

During Carolyn's early days in Passaic, Mother brought gallons of milk and food for the kids. Somehow that has been forgotten. Carolyn has a chip on her shoulder and complained that nobody ever helped her with the kids. I know for sure that I invited her three kids over for several weekends. I recall Kelly once did something I didn't like, so I put her on top of the refrigerator.

"Uncle Jon, get me down!" she screamed.

I waved my index finger and said, "Not until you're a good girl, will I get you down." That left an impression on her and was better than a spanking.

CHAPTER SIX

Rio de Janeiro, Brazil

I was walking down the street in Manhattan in 1967, when I ran into a friend, who told me about a trip to Rio for Carnival for only, $365.00. The trip included airfare, a hotel, and a transfer. I didn't know what a transfer was, however, I called forty friends and they joined me for the trip of a lifetime. I thought I was going to Reno, Nevada, but no, it was Rio de Janeiro, Brazil. The flight was nine hours, and I thought we'd never land. That was also my first international trip. After all, Grandad told me to spread my wings and reach for the stars.

Brazil is below the equator in the southern hemisphere, therefore the month of February is in the middle of their summer, and it's really hot. Once we landed and exited the airport, I saw the most beautiful people, who spoke Portuguese, a language I had never heard before. I also saw men wearing clunky high heels. That was long before heels were fashionable in New York. We stayed at a hotel on Avenida Presidente Vargas. Lucky us, because that was the avenue of the carnival. Carnival is celebrated five days preceding Ash Wednesday, which is the start of Lent in the Catholic calendar. Samba is the heart of the Carnival and a perfect illustration of the Afro-European blend that defines Brazilian culture. The Carnival is colorful with endless parades of Samba School floats and music. The Samba schools parade in outrageous, elaborate costumes. Each Samba School competes for the best music and costume. Carnival is designed for voyeurs. It was the most festive and original experience I had ever encountered at that point in my life.

The first evening was equally exciting because a group of Americans and Brazilians gathered in one of the Carnival dance halls. Americans remained glued to the wall because the floor wasn't stable. The Brazilians were brazen and danced the samba with all vigor in the middle of the floor. Finally, the Americans drummed up enough courage to bobbed up, while the Brazilians dipped. It was quite a sight to see.

The next morning, I dressed in the shirt from the previous night and trotted down to the grand avenue to catch more of the Carnival parade. While standing and observing the parade, a funky urine odor seems to be too close. As I moved away, the odor followed me. After the fifth move, I check my underarms and discovered the funky odor was coming from the polyester shirt that I wore and sweated in the previous night. That experience cured me of ever wearing polyester again.

I fell in love with Rio and its free-spirited people. Brazilians are like feijoada (a Brazilian stew), a melting pot of many cultures and people. They are a mix or blend of African, Indian, and European people. Brazilians are beautiful people, after all, they invented the floss bikini. So, what if they sound like steam heat when they speak Portuguese. It's also a terrific time to party on the beach and that's exactly what we did. That's where we met Nina Simone and invited her to one of our parties.

Hot Hot! Hot! As the temperature climbed, I wore the briefest bathing suit and relaxed on Copacabana beach. The beach embraced the edge of the city. That's where all the beautiful people hung out, played Brazilian futbol, and drank caipirinhas, a traditional Brazilian drink made with cachaca, lime, sugar, and lots of ice.

The boulevards are lined with outdoor cafes from where I watched the tall and tan, and young lovelies sashay along the undulating, mosaic tile sidewalks that accentuate the esplanade that framed the city.

I could not visit Rio without visiting Sugar Loaf mountain, where cable cars pass each other in opposite directions. It was a thrilling ride that took me to the top of Sugar Loaf Mountain for the best view of the city and its beaches. The other highlight was Christ de Redeemer, who stands on top of Corcovado mountain. It is listed as one of the Seven Wonder of the World. A special tram, the Corcovado Rack Railway travels through the beautiful, lush Tijuca Forrest, (a national park) and up 2,300 feet to the feet of Christ de Redeemer. Christ looks out and over the beautiful city of Rio. Once at the pinnacle of the mountain, I saw a hang glider flying another 2,300 feet above Christ de Redeemer. Amazing!

On another occasion, I had the magical experience of flying in a helicopter. The helicopter was pitched forward, slightly tilted down, so I had the best view of the beaches and the city. Not a comforting experience. However, the most thrilling experience of the day was flying up and around Christ de Redeemer. That was an experience, I will never forget.

I returned to Rio in 1969, for another Carnival. Just before I entered the hotel, suddenly out of blue, someone yelled my name. I turned around and it was Elsa Peretti yelling from a taxi. She invited me to join her, to pick up Naomi Sims at the airport. I immediately hopped in the taxi. Once we arrived at the airport, low and behold Naomi was at the baggage conveyor waiting for her 15 pieces of luggage. Once she collected her bags, we discovered one of her suitcases was filled with just makeup.

Once they settled in their hotels, we made a date for dinner and took Kenneth Jay Lane with us. He was staying at the Grand Copacabana Palace, which was around the corner from my hotel. I suggested a stop at Zum Zum, after dinner. It was a local disco that my friend Roberto owned. That was another fantastic evening in Rio.

Roberto wanted to throw a party for us, but we turned him down. We wanted to experience a game in the Maracana Stadium. Brazilians are passionate about Soccer, they call it Futbol. Maracana is a very large arena, perfect for futbol. That evening, the Brazilians played against the Russians. Pele was the star player on the Brazilian team. He is regarded as one of the greatest players of all time. He is among the most successful and popular sports figures of the 20th century. During his playing days, Pelé was for a period the highest-paid athlete in the world.

The Russian won that game one to 0. The Brazilian were so upset, that they lit fire to the stadium. That's how passionate they are about the game. We departed the stadium at the end of the game and I had the bright idea that we could hail a taxi right away.

Well, no such luck. We must have walked several miles before finally hailing a taxi. As the Brazilians always say, "No problem."

I was so inspired by my Carnival experience, that I returned to New York and created a collection of colorful, soft and carefree fashions. Visiting Rio also inspired me to travel to many other exotic destinations around the world.

Grandad

After having such a fantastic cultural experience in Rio, I wanted to visit Grandad and share my experience. So, I booked a flight to Orlando, the nearest airport to Sanford. Grandad picked me up and was delighted to see me. I noticed that his reflexes weren't as sharp as I remembered, so I asked,

"What will you do when you stop driving?"

"I will get a bicycle," he quickly responded.

That's the thing I loved about Grandad, he never gave up and always thought positively. He was the beam and shining light in my life.

The first thing he asked about my trip to Brazil,

"How much did my trip to Brazil cost?"

I reluctantly told him.

"You could have come here for nothing," he suggested.

He didn't understand why I chose to go to Brazil. I explained having the experiences of the fantastic beaches, different cuisine, and the mix of African, Indian, and European cultures. Then he understood why I chose Rio. He got it. I stayed with him for the weekend. He asked, why I couldn't stay longer and I'd explain that I had a business that required my attention.

Then he'd ask. "Is there anything or anyone that I would like to see?"

"No. I only came down to see you."

I walked into the bedroom at the end of the day and pulled back the top sheet and to my surprise, there lay a long black snake. I was startled and ran out and called Grandad. He walked in and quickly grabbed the snake by its neck and threw it out the front door. I was so freaked after seeing that snake, that I wrapped the top sheet tightly around my body to not to allow anything to enter. I also keep the light on, just in case another creature showed up. I laid there like a mummy. It took a while before I doze off to sleep. That was an experience I never anticipated.

Sanford is a sleepy little town with not much going on. Grandad drove me around town to show off some of his carpentry work. As I stated earlier, he was a fantastic artist and craftsman. The purpose of my brief visit was just to see him. I loved listening to stories of his younger life on the farm.

While touring the town, at first nothing seemed to have changed, but in the late '60s, like a shattering mirror, my old world disappeared. I returned to the dirt road where I once played stickball and discovered the had been paved. The house I lived in was no longer there. I felt I had lost my history....I felt empty. The kids that I spent my former years playing with were adults and their interest was totally different from mine. They weren't exposed to all the things I had encountered around the world and in New York City. Obviously, there was nothing there for me except Grandad.

I called Grandad during the summer of 1969, a neighbor answered the phone and told me he had been taken to the hospital. I call mother and told her we have to go to Sanford to check on him. Mother immediately requested time off from work. She prepared a large box of delicious food, to avoid any Jim Crow segregation in the south. The lunch box included delicious fried chicken, and southern potato salad, made from sweet pickles, eggs, mayo, mustard, onions, black pepper, and salt. Mother, Carolyn, and I packed our luggage in the trunk of the car and began our journey down Interstate Highway 95.

Mother was the only driver, so she occasionally stopped to rest. We had no knowledge of the Green Book, which was the Bible for Negros. The Green Book was the travel guide during Jim Crow. Mr. Victor Green created the Green book for Black people. It listed motels, homes, and restaurants where blacks were welcome. It was a testament that blacks are people like you, and we deserve equal treatment. I recall the day my mother stopped to use the bathroom at a motel and was turned away.

After a long, long, long drive, we finally arrived in Sanford. I felt as if I had left my butt in the car. It was my longest ride ever, in a car. We dropped off our suitcases at Grandad's house and dashed to the hospital. I became very emotional when I entered his room and saw him lying in bed. I turned around and stepped into the hallway because I didn't want Grandad to see how upset I was. I understood his needs were being taken care of, and the hospital was the best place for him, but it was just painful to see him lying there.

I stayed a few days, then returned to New York by plane because I could not endure another long haul. Mother and Carol stayed on for a week and Thank God, Grandad did recover.

Looking back over the years, I wish I had visited him more often. He was my angel.

CHAPTER SEVEN

The Smart Little Studio

I opened my second Smart Little Studio at 37 West 39th Street in 1967, with a staff of four. A lot of funny things happened in 'The Smart Little Studio.' One day a young man appeared at the studio and asked,

"Is your boss in?"

"No," I quickly responded.

Then I closed the door. I guess he figured I was too young to be a boss.

My studio was too small to present my collection, so I asked Mr. Ross if we could present the show in his showroom. That was my first formal presentation. Carrie Donovan from *Vogue* and Sybil Burton were in attendance. Myrna had an embarrassing moment as one of her breasts was exposed as she modeled one of my dresses. She quickly tucked her breast in and rushed off stage. That was another lesson on how to construct a dress that fits properly. I was the first designer to exclusively use black models such as Naomi Sims for my fashion shows. Those young ladies had pizzazz and could move and wear my fashion down the runway like nobody else. They sashayed like women of experience. I worked on a barter system: exchanged clothes for service, because I simply couldn't afford to pay them cash.

The press didn't write about my fabulous Black models until the White Seventh Avenue designer began using them. Then Black models became the rage. Bernadine Morris from *The New York Times* featured Pauline Trigere, "The designer making a stab at using a black model, Beverly Valdez."

It was a time when Seventh Avenue designers were designing stiff little dresses and suits with pillbox hats; a la Jackie Kennedy and Audrey Hepburn. My clothes were always soft and drapey and women loved them. I was one of the leading designers that set the fashion revolution in the mid-sixties.

In 1968, Bernadine Morris of *The New York Times* wrote, "He's gaining recognition for the right reasons — his designs not his race" (though his race did not go without saying).

Florence de Santis from United Media once said, "Jon's clothes are not hard edge like rock music, they are drapey and soft like jazz."

The wild sixties, as they were called meant a lot to young talents, especially Black talents, because we were seen for the first time commercially. Nineteen hundred and sixty-six was the beginning of the "Black is Beautiful" revolution. Black people began to take pride in their heritage and whites began to acknowledge our buying power.

Young portraits, 1969

Somehow, fashion people can predict a trend before it happens. Seventh Avenue manufacturers were alarmed because British Mod fashions had filtered into the market; therefore, they started seeking out young designers. African-American designers such as Scott Barrie, Stephen Burrows, Willi Smith and I were beginning to appear on the fashion scene. The reception to our work was enthusiastic and well-received. People began paying attention to us, because we were featured in editorials in all the major publications. Each designer had a different fashion sense and point of view.

Stephen Burrows was born September 15, 1943, in Newark, NJ. He attended the Philadelphia Museum College of Art and FIT, in New York City. We were at FIT at the same time. His first job as a designer was for Weber Originals. He began making colorful little jersey T-shirts on the side. They were designed with zigzag stitching on the edges, which was called the "Lettuce" stitch. That changed the concept of dress production throughout the world. All of his friends wore those smart little T-shirts out in the Pines on Fire Island. Jimmy Valcus recognized his talent and sense of humor and decided to back him with a boutique called "O Boutique." Stephen created patched appliqué dresses in leather and jersey. Some of his designs had a playful suggestion of phallic symbols decorating the front. They were terribly amusing "O Boutique" closed after a year. Roz Rubenstein rescued Stephen when she introduced him to Bendel's and the store installed a Stephen Burrows Boutique. Stephen became the first house designer with his own boutique. Shortly after winning many accolades including the prestigious Coty American Fashion Critic's Award in 1973, he moved to Seventh Avenue where Seventh Avenue's "Angel," Ben Shaw, financially backed him. Stephen was also one of the five American designers invited with several European designers to the historic Versailles fashion show in Paris. He also received a special Coty award in 1974 for lingerie and loungewear.

Stephen's Seventh Avenue operation was short-lived. He returned to Bendel's where Pat Tennant and Geraldine Stutz were not pleased because he had deserted them for his Seventh Avenue venture. After all, they had built him up and stood behind him in the early years. After a short time, they also gave him the boot.

On August 10, 1993, an editorial appeared in *The New York Times*, "The Return of an American Original." He was back on his stomping grounds with new management and owners. He's creating what he likes best, soft easy dressing. The Metropolitan Museum of Art also exhibited his wares from the 1973 Versailles Show.

Scott Barrie was born on January 16, 1941, in Philadelphia. He studied at the Philadelphia Museum College of Art and the Mayer School of Fashion in New York City. Scott designed for several New York firms, before starting his label. I met Scott at Allen & Cole boutique while he was selling his beautiful clingy jersey dresses.

Scott was very lucky early in his career because he hooked up with the right backers and stayed with them until 1980 when they decided they wanted out of the garment business. Scott worked with another firm for a short while, before departing to Italy to design for Krizia. Unfortunately, Scott passed away in Italy in June 1993.

Willi Smith was born on February 29, 1948. He also studied at the Philadelphia Museum College of Art. He arrived in New York with two scholarships to Parsons School of Design. But, was very anxious to get started, so he dropped out of school and freelanced for two years, and then became the designer for Glenora. Digits' was formed in 1969, and hired Willi as the designer. Laurie Mallet and Willi formed Willi Wear in January 1974. He worked very closely with his sister Toukie, who was his muse. Willi was financially the most successful of all the African/American designers. Willi Wear produced affordable, fun, colorful, sportive, funky streetwear in India. He was generous with his friends, he even sent Toukie to my studio to purchase an evening gown. His company was doing a cool 25 million dollars at the time of his untimely death in the late 80s.

The fashion industry had changed drastically since my first entry into the business in the 60s. A new generation had arrived with new thoughts on how to conduct business. Black talent was no longer a novelty, and AIDS began to bash Blacks and Whites. There is no racism with that virus. Nor is success proof against it. Patrick Kelly, Scott Barrie, and Willi Smith all died of that disease.

I had the radio on when I heard the shocking news: "Designer Willi Smith is dead." I couldn't believe it. I called my friend Andrea

Skinner and told her. She couldn't believe it either. Then suggested we call Toukie, his sister, to find out if there was anything we could do. Willi's sudden death wasn't easy for anyone to accept. I began to recall those wonderful weekends we shared at his house on Fire Island in the early 70s.

Marion Etoile Watson from the McCreary Report on Channel Five invited me to talk about the life and times of Willi Smith. It was very emotional for me, it was like losing a little brother; a link in the chain was broken. We began our careers approximately the same time in the mid to late sixties. It took me several weeks before I recovered from Willi's sudden death. I only hope he has peace wherever he is because he was a very talented young man.

Bernadine Morris — *New York Times* wrote: We "means himself," Jon Haggins, Willi Smith, and Stephen Burrows, the Black designers, who along with the vibrant black models, crashed Seventh Avenue during the Glory days of the 1960s. They brought with them a brashness, vitality, and creative energy that stimulated the world of fashion.

Each designer had a different fashion point of view. There is no such thing as a group in the fashion business. Everyone made his or her own statement. It's the last bastion of individualism in business because it starts by being an art. In fact, the toughest thing about fashion is its combination of creative impulse with salability. The New York editors noticed something special about Black designers.

One day, a less sophisticated and less informed editor asked, "What is it like to be a Black designer?"

"What a stupid question," I responded. "Do you design for the Black woman?'

My favorite stupid article title appeared in a Reading, Pennsylvania newspaper:

"For Her He Designs Negro Clothes."

I always promoted an International look with my fashions. My fashions were worn by models of different races because I felt any race can wear my fashions. I never thought as that editor from a Pennsylvania newspaper in 1967 titled her article: "For her, he designs Negro clothes." I was always puzzled: "What are Negro clothes?"

Sally Kirkland, fashion editor at *Life* magazine featured Diahann Carrol wearing one of my jersey gowns and the caption read, "Negro designer Jon Haggins."

I maintain that women are women and designer clothes should enhance their bodies. My Smart Little Studio Company was mushrooming rapidly at that time and I needed a front office assistant. A friend recommended Penny Vellasarapolis for the position. She was English, married to a Greek. The contrast between her and myself was fabulous. When an appointment arrived, they didn't quite know what to make of me when I appeared. Penny added a little cachet to the office.

Jon, 1967

I met Gregory James on the dance floor at Arthur's Disco. He was working as a hairstylist for Motown. We became lovers. He introduced me to Mary Wilson from The Supremes and Martha Reeves from Martha Reeves and the Vandellas. I designed special dresses for them. They invited me to their performances in the Copacabana Club and the Royal Box in the Americana Hotel. New York was a hot spot for the performers. Eartha Kitt performed in the Persian Room at the Plaza Hotel. She invited me to her suite after her show. I couldn't resist inviting her to My Smart Little Studio the next day.

I called Ky Hackney at *WWD* to photograph Eartha wearing my fashions. Eartha arrived with her daughter Kitt. Eartha wore several outfits for the photos. Unfortunately, *WWD* didn't publish them, because Eartha had had a confrontation with Lady Bird Johnson. Lady Bird Johnson had invited Miss Kitt to her 'Women Doers' Luncheon on January 28, 1968, for a discussion of what women could do to help eradicate crime on the streets. Toward the end of the luncheon, Lady Bird asked the room of fifty women, from groups such as the Association of Colored Women's Club and League of Women Voters, including a few governor's wives for their comments.

Miss Kitt raised her hand and told the first lady of the United States exactly what she thought. She said juvenile crime was in part a pushback against being drafted to serve in the Vietnam War. "Boys I know across the nations feel it doesn't pay to be a good guy," Kitt said. "They figure with a record they don't have to go off to Vietnam. You send the best of this country off to be shot and maimed. They rebel in the street. They will take pot and get high. They don't want to go to school, because they're going to be snatched off from their mothers to be shot in Vietnam." Kitt continued, "Mrs. Johnson, you are a mother too. Although you have daughters and not sons. I am a mother and I know the feeling of having a baby come out of my guts. I have a baby and then you send him off to War. No wonder the kids rebel and take pot. And, Mrs. Johnson, in case you don't understand the lingo, that's marijuana."

Her comments stunned the first lady. Some media reports erroneously stated that Lady Bird burst into tears. Women in the room ran to the microphone to defend the First Lady and were outraged at Kitt.

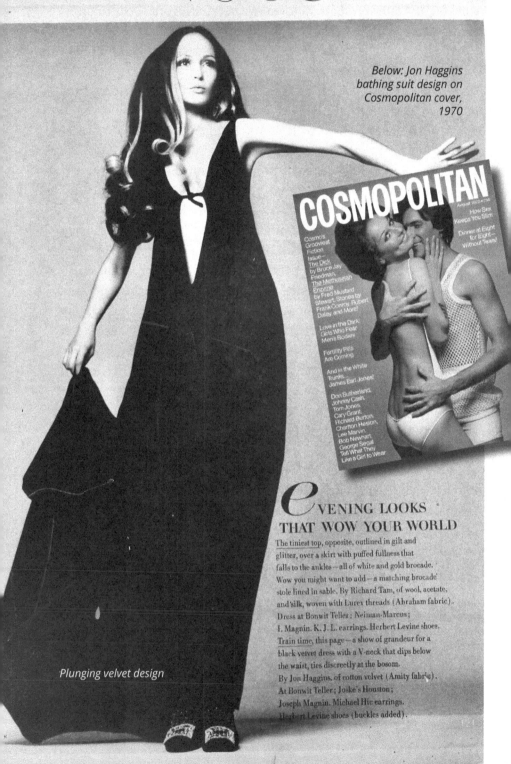

Below: Jon Haggins
bathing suit design on
Cosmopolitan cover,
1970

Plunging velvet design

*e*VENING LOOKS
THAT WOW YOUR WORLD

The tiniest top, opposite, outlined in gilt and
glitter, over a skirt with puffed fullness that
falls to the ankles—all of white and gold brocade.
Wow you might want to add—a matching brocade
stole lined in sable. By Richard Tam, of wool, acetate,
and silk, woven with Lurex threads (Abraham fabric).
Dress at Bonwit Teller; Neiman-Marcus;
I. Magnin. K.J.L. earrings. Herbert Levine shoes.
Train time, this page—a show of grandeur for a
black velvet dress with a V-neck that dips below
the waist, ties discreetly at the bosom.
By Jon Haggins, of cotton velvet (Amity fabric).
At Bonwit Teller; Joske's Houston;
Joseph Magnin. Michael Hic earrings.
Herbert Levine shoes (buckles added).

The cultural and political backlash was swift. *The Washington Post* reported that President Johnson had Kitt blacklisted. According to Broadly, Kitt alleged that the White House, which had sent a car for her, didn't arrange a car for her departure and she had to catch a cab.

After Miss Kitt expressed her views on the Vietnam War, America ostracized her for speaking out against the war. Her work in America was limited at that time. Unable to get jobs in the United States, Kitt was forced to perform in Europe, until she returned to America in 1978 to headline the Broadway musical Timbuktu! It was later unveiled by *The New York Times* that the CIA, prompted by the Secret Service in 1968, had kept a dossier on her.

"It was heartbreaking and very upsetting that her own government turned on her for something as simple as just giving an honest response to a question," said Kitt Shapiro, Eartha Kitt's daughter. "And that was really something I think, she never recovered from that disappointment."

That was a magical time in New York, when celebrities performed in a variety of hotels. Johnny Mathis performed in the Empire Room in the Waldorf Astoria. It was a most memorable up-close performance. His rendition of 'Maria' from West Side Story is unforgettable.

I designed timeless and seasonless clothes that got the attention of stores such as Allen & Cole, Splendiferous, Sakowitz, Burdines, Bullocks, Lord and Taylor, Bloomingdales, Country Club Fashions, Saks Fifth Avenue, Henri Bendel's, Bonwit Teller and B. Altman's, just to name a few.

Helen Gurley Brown, editor-in-chief of *Cosmopolitan* magazine, and Joan Shepard arrived for a private viewing of my collection. As I was presenting a three-layer, black silk chiffon, circular-skirted gown with a tiny top, Joan screamed, "Oh, baby!" Helen raised her left eyebrow and displayed a quiet smile. I guess it was her sign of approval.

Cosmopolitan magazine's most controversial cover of a backless derriere-exposed bathing suit, was also one of my designs. A female model was accompanied by a male model. It was the first and last time a male appeared on the cover. The same bathing suit was also featured in *Look, Town & Country,* and *Vogue.* The public was stunned by the derriere décolletage......then.

My classic monkey suit, which evolved into today's leotard, had long, long sleeves that extended forever. You just crush the sleeves to your desired length. *Vogue* also featured another one of my all-time creative favorites, worn by Jean Shrimpton; a burgundy-colored, long sleeve leotard with a lavender chiffon skirt complimented with a fuchsia-colored chiffon shawl accented with ruffles. The shawl wrapped around her shoulders as she sat spread eagle on a stool wearing ballerina slippers. Penelope Tree modeled a black leotard with very, very long black fringe that she showed off by extending her arms. Those were the top models of the day.

That was a very exciting time in my life. I also designed a controversial "Hug Me, Kiss Me, Fuck Me" scarf in 1969, and it was all the rage. I wrapped and tied the scarves around my models as they paraded onto the runway. The background music was Mighty Sparrow's singing, "Sell the Pussy" (referring to a cat). Some of the folks in the audience were aghast. But even so, it was a hit. Peggy Cass from 'To Tell The Truth TV' dropped by my studio and bought a dozen scarves for friends.

Next stop, I took a holiday to Mexico City and Acapulco, where I relaxed and was inspired. Shortly after I returned home, my friend Alain Chaveau called from Paris and asked, "When are you coming to visit me?"

"How about tomorrow?" I quickly responded.

I was off to Paris the next day. Once I arrived and settled in, I was free to explore the city while Alain was at work. On my first day out, I stepped into a taxi and held up both hands, and said, "Now this is the left and the other is the right. I want to go to the Left Bank." The driver was puzzled and uttered, "Ha!", he didn't understand a thing I said, until I muttered, "Le Rive Gauche." Then we were off to Rive Gauche. Upon arrival, the driver stopped to let me out. Carol LaBrie called out my name from the sidewalk. I was a happy camper because I didn't bring my phone book with me and had no idea of how to reach anyone. I was on my way to Café de Flore. Once I settled at a table, my friend Patrice Calmette arrived and we began taking photos of each other. What a fun day that was. Patrice was such a snob. He once said, "Who are zeez people, zay are nobody, I know none of zem."

I recall Alain asking if I'd like to see Montmartre. I told him I had already been there. Alain also introduced me to Bouillabaisse, a typical French seafood dish. It sort of reminded me of dirty dishwater. My first night out was at Regine's. I walked in and turned around, Alain was nowhere in sight. So, I returned to the front door and discovered they were not letting him in. He was a member of the club and I was not. Finally, they allowed him in at my request. Regine's was the place to be at that time. It's where I saw several friends. We danced the night away, and what a night that was. Paris was more fun than you can imagine. Alain took me out every night to see and explore the city.

Alain had been an excellent host for my two-week visit, so I invited him to London for the weekend. My friend John Mandell, the manager at the Lancaster Hotel invited us as his guest. John also gave me 400 pounds to spend while in London, because he was coming to New York in two weeks and I would give him the exchange. That worked for me.

As you know the British automobile drives on the opposite side of the road. I was puzzled at first. A car almost hit me on my first day out, because I wasn't paying attention to the direction of the cars, but quickly got the jest of it. Alain and I took in a show, 'Mame', starring Ginger Rogers at the Royal Drury Lane Theatre in the West End of London. We were seated in the front row. It was amazing to see Miss Rogers in person. There was only a slight "ouch" as she kicked. Of course, I recall her early performances, dancing with Fred Astaire, and other movies, but to see her in person was another magical experience.

After I returned from Europe, I decided to visit Los Angeles, where I stayed in a lovely suite at the Beverly Wilshire Hotel on Wilshire Blvd. My suite had the best view of Rodeo Drive. Rodeo Drive is where all the fashionable boutiques were located, such as Gorgio Boutique. Gorgio bought my fashions.

The *Los Angeles Times* featured me on its cover. Madame Pompidou, the French President's wife, was featured on page four. Several hotel maids were curious to see what a Black designer looked like. I guess I was a novelty at that time. I was also a guest on several TV shows during my stay. I brought along a model to show off my fashions. It was a hectic time in Los Angeles. When I returned to the airport, a porter smiled and welcomed me, "I saw you on television", then checked my bags in.

Shortly after I returned from Los Angeles, Dorcus Hardin, the owner of Dorcus Hardin Boutique in Washington, DC, arrived at my studio and bought several dresses from my fashion collection. She told me her son, Ted Hardin, was a photographer, working with *The Washington Post.*

I met Ted when he appeared at my fashion show at Walter Reade's garden in Turtle Bay. That was a time when I presented several fashion shows around town, but the show at Walter Reade's home was different and at an exciting location because Walter lived next door to Katherine Hepburn. The weather was perfect the day of the show. And the sky was blue and crystal clear, not a cloud in the sky. The show was inspired by one of my holidays in Brazil. Ted photographed my models as they parade down the outside stairs. They paraded through the garden to Brazilian music. By coincidence, *Cosmopolitan* magazine June 1969, appeared on the newsstands the same day as my fashion show. The cover featured Jane Hoffman wearing my white halter neck dress. Ted became a life-long friend, he photographed all my fashions and cabaret career.

My models paraded in large Anonymous Scarves, draped around their bodies. The dresses came alive on the models because I created fashions with movement. The most memorable moment was Naomi Sims as she danced down the stairs. She was draped in a long black

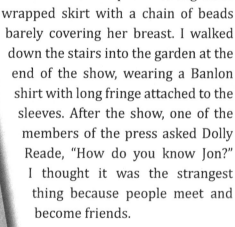

wrapped skirt with a chain of beads barely covering her breast. I walked down the stairs into the garden at the end of the show, wearing a Banlon shirt with long fringe attached to the sleeves. After the show, one of the members of the press asked Dolly Reade, "How do you know Jon?" I thought it was the strangest thing because people meet and become friends.

Jane Hoffman, 1969

106

Naomi pulls up dress at fashion show at Walter and Dolly Reade's home, 1969

Dolly Reade once told me a tale, that Katherine Hepburn sent her a note, "If you can't turn it down, then move it." She was referring to the music.

My fashion shows always had a theme that was inspired by my travel around the world. Travel had always been a vital part of my inspiration, ideas, and innovations for my fashions. I love warm destinations, especially great beaches. Travel has expanded my horizon to an enormous world of cultural differences.

I also presented a fashion show at the Fashion Institute of Technology in the president's office. Some of my best ethereal designs were shown. Sybil Burton was in the audience. I designed a black velvet gown with a deep décolletage neckline and a long train. It was my favorite gowns that closed the show. The gown was featured in *Vogue.*

Sybil Burton allowed us to use her nightclub 'Arthur' for our next fashion show. Our show had a Mexican theme. When I called to hire Mariachis, they told me it would cost $1,200 for twelve, so I asked "How much is it for nine?" Our guests sipped margaritas as they watched the show. I also designed several men's outfits for that season. The show was a smasharoo.

Several ladies from Park Avenue volunteered as dressers for the show. Backstage, when a Black model extended her arm, it meant put on a glove, and when they extended an ear, it meant an earring. Joanne Curtis from St. Louis, commented, "All of the dressers were White and all the models were Black. Imagine White women dressing as Black women. The role was reversed."

It never occurred to me that there was a race issue. I was only thinking of presenting a show. It's funny how people think. Years later she denied she said it. I have a memory like an elephant and I remember all sorts of things. So, if you don't want me to repeat it, don't say it.

I also presented a fashion show at The Sanctuary. The building was formally a church but had been converted into a disco. During the model lineup, I stopped short in my tracks in front of one of the models, she was dressed in a short white jumpsuit:

"Girl, take those black stockings off!"

"Those aren't stockings, those are my legs."

The only thing I could do was laugh and relax. The show went on without a hitch. Naomi Sims opened the show dressed as a nun wearing a black poncho with a hood and a long black wrapped skirt. Then the music hit the rafters. *WWD* raved and said it was one of my best fashion shows.

My mother frequently appeared at my fashion shows for support and always brought a neighbor to show how proud she was of my accomplishments. The fashion editors were always eager to stop her for an interview. They wanted to know more about me and my background.

There was so much going on in New York at that time. Nothing could have stopped me. Mary Wilson from the Supremes and a group of friends joined me for a night out on the town at Nepentha. Mary was a good dancer and we danced the night away. Jane Friedman and I stayed on after the Motown group departed. I got stuck with the bill. I asked the club manager to send the bill to Motown, but he didn't want to hear it. He asked me to step outside into the alley and settle the matter. I thought, "This is it…It's ovah…They're gonna kill me." We settled the bill amicably. I paid it!

Mildred Custin, president of Bonwit Teller and Barbara Leary invited me to show my Summer Collection in the S'fari Room, before the store officially opened. Those were the days when anything was possible. My collection included see through silk chiffon and other light and silky designs. The models danced to tropical music. My designs were well received by the press.

I was preparing for my summer 1970 fashion show, which was to be held at my friend, Walter Reade Jr.'s, New Zeigfeld Theatre on January 10, 1970. Gregory James told me he had discovered a model that I had to meet, her name was Norma Jean Darden. Norma arrived at my studio in December 1969 and introduced herself as Norma Jean Darden. I thought she said, Darten. She quickly corrected me by saying, "It's Darden as in Garden."

I hired her for the January 10th, 1970 show. Norma entered the stage wearing a long white flowing jersey skirt with a multicolor silk chiffon ruffle that covered her arms and breasts. She walked out on the stage and placed her hands on her hips, which accidentally exposed one of her breasts, that incident left an indelible impression. Louise Cohen was my fashion coordinator. She was very orderly; everyone was afraid of her, even me. When she said jump, you'd better jump. Clementine wore the finale gown, which was a hand-crocheted, tight see-through gown with pearls strategically placed at the intersections. Another favorite was a lavender silk chiffon rectangle shape scarf covering the model's breast, held together with a belt and a long flowing ruffled bottom silk chiffon skirt.

Dolly Reade, Walter's wife, commissioned me to design a slim, black knitted jumpsuit with long sleeves as the official hostess outfit for ninety Walter Reade movie theatres across America. That was the era of first-run feature movies, where the hostess greeted guests with a cup of fresh brewed Columbian coffee. Movie tickets cost a whopping $3.00.

Dolly often invited me to lunch at Orsini's, one of her favorite Italian restaurants. We were always ushered to the best table in the house. One day *WWD* ran an item in the 'Eye' column: "Jon Haggins was wearing a Christmas green jumpsuit and having lunch with a lady in a large hat." Orsini was a fashionable restaurant, where many celebrities dined, such as Loretta Young, Imelda Marcos, Anne Ford, Chuck Connors, Arlene Dahl, Sammy Davis Jr., and Diana Vreeland.

Julia' staring Diahann Carol and Marc Copage were revolutionary for Black people at that time from Sept. 1968 to March 1971. She was an independent mother raising a small boy. It was extremely exciting to see a lady of color with her own television show.

Norma Jean Darden rushed into my studio several months later to tell me that June Murphy, a model, was dying to meet me. June arrived for a "go-see", as it is commonly called in the industry. A go-see is an audition for models. She had the perfect body for my fashions and I was immediately attracted to her. Her long silky hair and honey-colored skin, fabulous legs and firm breasts were very appealing. For some strange reason, I paid more attention to her than to any of the other models. I said to myself, "That's the one." I hired her on the spot for my fall Fashion Show.

Kezia Keeble, a fashion editor from *Vogue* called to tell me I had to get to The Brooklyn Academy of Music to see the Alvin Ailey Dance Company. She also told me that I had to pay close attention to Judith Jamison's performance of Cry. Judith was rhythmic and sensual, and her arms and legs were eternal and extended the length of the stage. Thank God, I listened to Kezia. She was so right. Revelations, the dance, was inspired by Alvin Ailey's Southern Spiritual background and it was the finale of the show. I was so inspired, I couldn't sit still, I jumped out of my seat and stood in the back of the theatre until the end of the performance because the show was too damn marvelous.

The following night I saw Purlie on Broadway. The show featured Melba Moore, Sherman Hemsley, and Novella Nelson. Sherman played Gitlow, a role I've always wanted to portray because it's so contrary to my personality.

My Fall fashion show was presented in the Spring of 1970 in Barbara Pearlman's duplex apartment in Gramercy Park. The temperature in her apartment had reached 95 degrees and the air conditioners went kaput. It could have been a disaster, but I quickly put on my thinking cap and sent someone to the dime store to purchase several dozen Chinese paper fans, which saved the day.

The show was inspired by Alvin Ailey's dance troupe and Purlie. The models danced to the music from Purlie. Jane Hoffman and I danced arm-in-arm down the runway for the finale. The audience included Helen Gurley Brown and Nancy Benson from *Cosmopolitan*; Bill Cunningham from the *Chicago Tribune*; Ted Hardin, Dolly Reade, June Weir, and Rudi Millenorf from *Women's Wear Daily*. *Women's Wear Daily* raved about the show. It was the first time *WWD* featured my collection on page four and said it was my best collection ever. Harriet Kane, Andrea Skinner, and Bernadine Morris from *The New York Times* were also there. Bernadine gave my show favorable reviews but complained that my models had too much rhythm and movement for her photographer.

"You must keep up, my dear," I replied.

The Social Columnist, Eugenia Shepperd, from the *NY Post* and *The Daily News* also featured my show.

Norma Jean Darden,
myself and Ann Flowler

Jane Hoffman and Jon Haggins
at the finale of a fashion show, 1970

Joan Kaner, Senior VP Fashion Director of Neiman Marcus, recalled that I was the first designer to have models dance down the runway to upbeat music. Seventh Avenue designer models at that time walked like stiff little cardboard boxes, but my girls were real and alive, which only seemed natural to me.

The seventies were also a fun time when Bloomingdales and the Bethesda Fountain in Central Park were popular haunts to see and be seen. Even Yves St. Laurent strolled around the Fountain. The Bethesda also had a summer restaurant where we spent countless hours observing the crowd as they strolled by. It was a touch of Paris in New York. Another favorite thing to do in Central Park was to go row boating. That gave me a chance to flex my muscles and gently cruise on the lake, for the best view of the New York skyline.

Several months later, I was at home with a bad case of the flu. Kezia Keeble from *Vogue* called. She never asked how I was feeling. She only wanted to know when my next collection would be finished. Wow! That was a wake-up call. "Is that all I mean to those people?" I began thinking about the reality of the fashion business. "You're only as good as your next idea." I was a fashion commodity like meat hanging on a rack. I had a different perspective on the fashion business after that. Once I recovered, I began working on a new collection.

My company was expanding rapidly and we needed more space. Fortunately, there was a larger loft in the building. I signed a new lease and opened our new studio. I also garnished the attention of the press by presenting formal fashion shows with music and dancing models in my loft, which was unique at that time.

I also wrote the copy to accompany press photos (when the copy is attached to a photo it's called a slug). The press kits were mailed to the top one hundred newspapers at the beginning of each season. One of the tricks for garnishing more space in the newspaper is to photograph a model stretched out on the floor or with her arms extended, so the newspaper would have to allow two columns. Associated Press featured many articles with my copy and exposed my designs around the world.

Stuart Kreisler, my agent, partnered me with Al-Mae, a former contractor. They opened a new division in 1970. I christened it "Bymini by Jon Haggins" to honor my assistant Minnie Turner. The Bymini showroom was located in 525 Seventh Avenue, which was not a typical dress building. However, when you've got the right merchandise, buyers will cross the street. Buyers usually take their coats off in one showroom in the morning and work their way through the building until the end of the day. If you're just around the corner, you can forget about it.

I designed a less expensive collection of dresses for Bymini. The most important and successful dress was a midi-length dress made of Stretchnit Banlon Jersey. The dress was designed with long tight sleeves, a crushed collar, and a close-fitting bodice with a circular

June wearing
the Dress of
the Year, 1970

Jon Haggins Designs
Chiffon dress,
Cosmopolitan cover, 1972

skirt that was adorned with a ruffled flounce bottom. Bloomingdales advertised that dress on a full page in *The New York Times* and also opened a *Jon Haggins* boutique in its Sutton Place department. That dress was my first commercial success. Bill Cunningham featured the dress on three pages in the *Chicago Tribune*. He called it, "The Dress of the Year." The dress was the most popular selling dress in 1970.

Every major specialty department store across America bought and sold 1,000 dresses per week. Stores couldn't keep that dress in stock. Several Manufacturers copied the Dress, and added a dart, which never appeared in the original. But like Grandad's delicious pumpkin bread, there was a secret ingredient they didn't know: I never used darts in my jersey designs. That dress was phenomenal!

I also received a Montgomery Ward Award at the Waldorf Astoria in 1970. There were fifteen distinguished guests on the panel, mostly fashion people such as Bill Blass, Oscar de la Renta, Bill Smith, Eunice Johnson, and I. The moderator asked, "What do you think women should look for in the seventies?" Everyone gave serious answers. I simply stated, "The woman of the seventies should look for my label."

CHAPTER EIGHT

The Wedding

June returned to my studio several weeks after my fashion show to collect a check for modeling. I invited her to a Japanese dinner to get to know her better. I really liked what I saw and wanted to see more of her. After dinner, I escorted her to a taxi and sent her home.

I ran into June in front of Bonwit Teller, two weeks later and invited her to my apartment for pizza. We sat on the living room floor in a cozy fashion enjoying each other's company. A short while later, while standing next to my baby grand piano, she seduced me. It was very sexy being seduced by a woman. Afterward, I told her I had slept with men. "I thought so," she responded. I didn't tell her about the women I'd slept with. I had more women friends than men and had seduced most of them. Even my multiple partner sexual adventures included both sexes. I called myself a "tri-sexual", one that will try anything. But June was the woman who taught me how to make love to a woman.

June phoned me the next day and I thought, "Oh, no, so soon." Then we began spending a lot of time together, so after a month, I suggested she give up her apartment and move in with me. Fortunately, she only had very few items to move, so I hired a limo for the move.

Fresh cut flowers were delivered twice a week. I asked June to tell the florist not to include the greenery. So, when I arrived home, she had picked the leaves from the Chrysanthemums and left them bald. I took one look at the bald Chrysanthemums and quietly ordered another bunch. Then, I explained, that I meant no extra green crap that the florist includes. That was my first compromise.

I bought a bike for June, so we could share one of our favorite pastimes. Joan Shepard from the Tribune titled an article, "The family that bikes together, stays together." We loved biking around Manhattan, exploring the city, going to various markets, and just doing things together.

On one occasion, we biked from East 33rd Street all the way to Coney Island to visit my mother. That was definitely a memorable ride. As we rode through various neighborhoods, we would speed up or slow down depending on the neighborhood. Our butts were so sore when we returned home. I soaked in an Epsom salt bath to soothe my bones before taking a nap.

After several months of living together, June was very anxious for me to meet her parents in St. Louis, Missouri. I thought to myself, "Oh, my God! Do I have to?" Finally, I agreed. Her mother met us at the airport. I was a nervous wreck. I tried desperately to remember her last name, which was different from June's because she had remarried. I thought of associations such as products in the home. I knew it was something related to a household product. During my nervous introduction, I called her Mrs. Johnson, as in Johnson Wax. She told me her name was Baldwin. Suddenly, I remembered, like the piano. She told me to relax and call her June.

Her mother wouldn't allow us to sleep together in the same bedroom even though we were living together in New York. We found a way around that, by taking the car and parking near a railroad track where we made up for the lost time. It was the first time I'd done IT in a car. The windows got all steamed up and it was a real turn-on thinking somebody was going to catch us in the act. That was our little secret. We returned to the house with happy faces.

St. Louis was a slow town with not much to do. I came in like a storm and they sat there like a soft wind. I couldn't wait to get the hell out of Dodge. Fortunately, my friend Barry Pearlman from New York was living and working there. Visiting him was the only bright spot for me in St. Louis.

I returned home after the weekend, while June stayed on for a few more days. When June returned, I proposed marriage and invited Ky Hackney, from *Women's Wear Daily* to lunch. I told Ky of our engagement. She placed the item in the 'Eye', (the social column of the paper). I also called my mother and told her the good news. She was delighted and congratulated us.

The big day was going to be September 21st, 1970. The twenty-first was easy for me to remember because it was my mother's birthday. June asked me to design her wedding dress. That was the most difficult project I'd ever encountered because she wanted something totally different from anything I'd ever done. I flooded her with sketches until she finally approved one of the designs.

We rode our bikes to City Hall for the marriage license. Unfortunately, I forgot to bring my wallet, so June paid $2.00 for the license.

I asked Chadbourne Spring from the Community Church on East 35th Street in Manhattan to officiant our marriage. Then asked how much will it cost? He suggested, that perhaps I should pay a dollar for every million I think she's worth. So, I gave him 40 bucks.

June and I had only known each other for six months. She was twenty-five and I was twenty-seven years old. We talked about having kids, within the first three years. I saw a future for us of living, working, and loving together. After all, she was a fashion model and I was a fashion designer. I felt that I had met my lifelong mate. She was very special to me. It was the first time I felt I had a real relationship.

On September 20th, the night before our big wedding/fashion show, I feared the collection might be stolen, so I brought the collection home for security and delivered it to the venue the next morning.

Our real live, fairy tale wedding took place on Blair Walliser's terrace on September 21st, 1970 at 3 pm. It was a really big day in our lives. Thank God, the weather was perfect; the sky was clear and the wind stirred in the right direction. There were two hundred guests and twelve models. It was our wedding day and the most important editors in print media were there including Helen Gurley Brown

A Fashion Show With a
Surprise Ending: A Wedding

AS TOLD TO JACLYN PEISER
February 7, 2017

Fashion designer Jon Haggins married his model June Murphy at one of his fashion shows in 1970.
Bill Cunningham, far left in white jacket, was on hand to photograph the event.
JACK MANNING/THE NEW YORK TIMES

The New York Times wedding picture, 1970

(*Cosmopolitan* magazine), Sally Kirkland (*Life* magazine), Kay Thomas (Daily News), June Weir (*Women's Wear Daily*), Bill Cunningham (*Chicago Tribune*), and Nan Eckeringil (*The New York Times*), etc. Joan Shepard from WINS Radio featured a segment on her show. Our guest list was the Who's Who in New York.

We didn't hire a wedding photographer, because we knew we would receive a large selection from press photographers. Everyone was pensive trying to guess which model was going to be the bride.

I was a nervous wreck and very excited about getting married. A fairy tale wedding was the finale of the show. June and I march down the aisle holding hands. It was a glorious day. June's veil was anchored with a matching paper butterfly on the side. The bridal bouquet was designed by Ray Kahn to match her bias floral printed silk chiffon dress. A soft breeze wrapped her long streaming yellow, purple, and green floral print chiffon veil around us during the ceremony as if to say we join you in Holy Spirit. Her dress was designed with very deep armholes and the skirt of the dress had a deep dripping handkerchief hemline that floated through the air as she sashayed down the aisle. I wore a black suit that I bought in Paris, later known as my wedding suit. Gordon Barrows was my best man and June's maid of honor was her best friend from St. Louis. June refused to throw her bouquet at the end of the ceremony.

June and I walked to our apartment on East 33rd Street, after the ceremony. That's also where we held the reception. I recalled June's father commenting, "There are more people here than you can stir with a stick."

Jon and June in Look Magazine, 1971

Jon and June, 1971

119

We were the hot new couple in town and I was the fashion darling. Our wedding was featured in *WWD, The New York Times, The Daily News,* and several other papers. We received a lot of fanfare from the press and were the talk of the town. *Women's Wear Daily* followed us for weeks.

After the Wedding

June and I dined at Le Grenouille, the next day. It was one of our favorite restaurants. As we stepped out of the restaurant, *WWD* photographed us. June was carrying a lunch box that *Women's Wear Daily* featured as, "The latest craze." We were the darling couple of New York for a short while as everything is short-lived in the fashion business. My design philosophy radically changed after I got married, no more décolletage neckline. My designs became more modest, close to the neck. I didn't want my woman walking around town exposing her attributes.

We needed to get away from all the stress and the crazy pace of living and working in New York City. So, we ventured off to Quebec City for a short holiday. Québec City is located in Canada's mostly French-speaking Québec province. The city has a fortified colonial core, Vieux-Québec, and Place Royale, with stone buildings and narrow streets that date back to 1608. The towering Château Frontenac Hotel is an imposing large castle with enormous turrets that reach for the sky. The hotel also offers the best view of ships and boats sailing on the St. Lawrence River. Quebec City is a walkable city with lots to see and do. The Petit Champlain district's narrow cobblestone streets are lined with bistros and boutiques. We loved dining at the quaint petite Bistros.

Upon returning home, we made a lunch date with Nancy Benson at Le Grenouille. She arrived first and asked for Mr. Haggins' table. The Maitre d' hotel said, "Oh yes, Monsieur Haggins, Le Couturier." I later commented, "He probably thought to himself, the cheap couturier, because I never tipped him.

CHAPTER NINE

The Honeymoon

It was a hectic time, we really needed to get away and smell the whispers of life. I was looking for an unusual place to share our honeymoon. Margery Rubin from Celanese Fibers suggested Paramaribo, Surinam, South America. Our travel agent informed us that a $270.00 roundtrip ticket includes several stopovers. Our first stop was Port of Spain, Trinidad. I had previously visited the island with Gregory, a friend, and wanted very much for June to see the island. After checking in at the upside-down Hilton Hotel, we decided to tour the city.

The Alvin Ailey Dance company was performing in town. The locals thought we were a member of the Dance Company because we were wearing tight sleeveless T-shirts with elasticized pull-on pants. A large crowd followed us for a while, then suddenly gathered around us. I panicked and thought of being devoured as in the movie 'Suddenly Last Summer.' I totally freaked, then rushed to hail a taxi that took us back to the hotel. We lazed at the poolside and quietly rested for the next couple of days. I told June that I was not going out again until it was time to depart for the airport.

We departed two days later, for Paramaribo, Surinam in South America. Surinam is a Dutch Colony and Paramaribo is the Capitol city. The country was twenty percent inhabited and eighty percent unspoiled jungle. Obviously, It was not the most popular destination in the world. Paramaribo only received three hundred visitors per year. Eighty percent of its population ride bikes and never lock them. It was a safe destination. Paramaribo was refreshing and unspoiled. The best hotel in town was equivalent to a Howard Johnson. The only nightclub in town was located in our hotel and the entertainer was from Brooklyn, so we had a lot to talk about.

June and I wanted to explore the jungle, so we asked a guide to take us to the deepest and darkest part.

"What do you wear to the jungle?" I asked.

"Just wear your regular street clothes."

We departed early the next morning for what seemed like an endless ride through the inner parts of the country. I think it was the hottest day ever, when we finally arrived at the coastline, we chartered a motorized dugout boat that had been carved from an old tree trunk. Water slowly seeped in as the captain constantly scooped it up with a tin can. I thought, "In my wildest dreams...who needs so much adventure, this is it...it's ovah." As we cruised up the Marowijne River, the guide told me the river was filled with piranhas just waiting to snap up anything dangling in the water.

He said, "it's best to keep my hands in the boat."

I didn't even know what a piranha was, but I immediately folded my arms across my chest and sat very still.

We finally arrived at an Amer-Indian village. There were a collection of thatched-roof huts. We were greeted by a group of friendly ladies and children. The women were busy taking care of their children or sweeping the dirt grounds with a homemade broom.

The children were curiously asking us where we were from. They wanted to know more about us. The village lifestyle is very chauvinistic, because women remain in the village with the children, and cook, while men hunted for food in the jungle.

After a short visit, we boarded the dugout again and cruised up the river to a Bush-Negros village. The river was their only access to the world, it was their highway. I observed women washing clothes by beating them on a rock along the river banks. Traveling on the river was like watching a Tarzan movie. There was a thick brush of trees with long branches. I imagined Tarzan swinging in at any moment.

One of the ladies offered us some cassava bread, made from cassava root. It's similar to cornbread. Women in the villages adapted to two distinct cultural practices between city and bush life. They traditionally expose their breasts in the jungle but covered up while visiting the city. Our guide asked if we would like to spend the night. "Back to the hotel," I quickly responded.

I feared something strange might crawl into my bed. I would have died three deaths if I was confronted by a crawling creator. It would have been too much adventure for me. Our guide suggested we make a small offering of several coins at the end of our visit to show appreciation for their hospitality.

Once we returned to the city, I wanted to treat our guide to dinner at a private club, but the host of the club informed us that we were allowed, but not our guide. I was furious and didn't understand why we could dine, but not a local. We didn't want to be a part of that ill-treatment. I asked our guide to suggest his favorite dining spot. He took us to a smart little café where we shared a lovely evening talking, drinking, and dining.

The temperature and humidity were extremely high during the day. What the hell, it was HOT!, which caused June's hair to acquire a different texture: it became long, fluffy, and crinkly. I could only tolerate the sun for five minutes at a time. While laying on a chaise at the hotel, my only option was to jump in the pool to cool off. Paramaribo is a small town with an edge like Dodge City: it suddenly stops and the sidewalk rolls up after five- pm. I think we saw everything there was to see, so after a few days, I said, "Let's kill this town and move on."

Our next stop was Caracas, Venezuela, I'd visited Caracas once before. We stopped for a few days of exploring, and wining and dining. The most exciting thing for me was riding on the Teleferico cable car 7,500 feet through the clouds to the top of a mountain. It was the closest thing to heaven, and there was a hotel, where we dined on the best black bean soup. The temperature of Caracas varies from

June at the beach during our honeymoon, 1970

the sunny beaches to snow-capped mountains, where everyone goes ice-skating. We made reservations to see a Bull Fight, then decided to pass. I didn't want to see an animal tortured. After a few days of sightseeing, we were ready to move on to another adventure.

Then we were off to Curacao; a Dutch Caribbean Island. It is known for its beaches tucked into coves and it expansive coral reefs that are rich with marine life. The capital, Willemstad is lined with pastel-colored colonial architecture facing the harbor, floating Queen Emma Bridge, and a stretch of hotels along the beach. We spent a few days relaxing on the white sand beach and dining out on the freshest seafood and of course laying back and sipping those colorful, tropical drinks. We really didn't do much else. We were there just to relax.

Our last stop was Aruba, where we enjoyed more beautiful white sand beaches. What else is a holiday for? As I was walking along the beach one morning, June called out, "Oh, here comes my little Hershey Bar."

I looked terrific and worthy of being mistaken for a Hershey Bar, because we had been baking in the sun for three weeks. Don't tell me that Black people don't tan. Lucia Breault, an Italian friend, once asked if I tanned. "You put meat in an oven and it cooks, doesn't it?" I photographed June on the beach wearing some of my beachwear designs.

After we returned home from our month-long honeymoon, we invited Kay Thomas, from *The Daily News* to dinner at our apartment. I shared some of our photos with her. She featured two pages of June on our honeymoon in the Sunday magazine section.

Several weeks later, June's mother called to say that she has planned a reception for us in St. Louis. That was an obligation, I thought I could gracefully survive. My mother was also invited to attend. Mother had made previous plans for a holiday in Florida but took advantage of a twenty-four-hour stopover.

I took one look at the cheap wedding gifts on the table, at the reception, then whispered in June's ear,

"Why don't you return all those gifts to the store and perhaps we can get a toaster?" She hated me for that. I returned home shortly after the reception, while June stayed on with her family for a few more days.

Shortly after June returned home, *Look* magazine featured us as the newly married couple and one of the young designers of the 70s. Naturally, June wore one of my designs and I wore a Ralph Lauren white suit with a Panama hat. The photo also included my famous "Hug Me, Kiss Me, Fuck Me" scarf. The "F" word was substituted with "Hug" in the final editorial.

June was a sensational cook, she introduced me to Julia Child's Mastering the Art of French Cooking book. She also introduced me to homemade mayonnaise. I always thought it only came in a jar, instead of being a combination of oil and eggs. I observed her preparing escargot, which I also thought was bought in the shell. My experience in the kitchen was limited, so I was relegated to making salad and it was the best damn salad on the East Coast. She was not only a great cook but also a great lover.

Jon's Summer Salad

- 12 leaves of Romaine lettuce
- ½ cut red onion
- 20 slices of can or fresh pineapple
- 15 pitted dates chopped into circular pieces

Dressing

- ½ large fresh squeezed lemon
- ½ cup of grape seed oil or olive oil 1/4 teaspoon salt
- ½ teaspoon pepper
- 12 tablespoon of red Balsamic vinegar
- 4 tablespoon chutney
- ½ teaspoon of dried mustard powder

Stir until ingredients until they blend well together. Add to salad and mix well. Serves 4 persons.

CHAPTER TEN

Marital Changes

The first year of our marriage was blissful, then suddenly everything began to crumble. Suddenly she had five different personalities that jumped out of the closet and I didn't recognize any of them. My infidelity was getting the best of me and I was having enormous guilt. I wanted to be married and yet wanted to continue my extra-marital affairs. I had an insatiable appetite for sex with both sexes. I sat down with June one night and told her of my affairs. I couldn't stand the guilt any longer. We talked and talked and cried our eyes out until there wasn't another drop. We began discovering more about ourselves, expressing our innermost feelings, and realized our marriage just wasn't working.

There were too many differences. She knew I had bi-sexual relationships before we were married. I just wanted a momentary fling on the side. It was all about my insecurities of feeling I was going to miss something. It appeared to me that once I was married, everybody wanted me and I took advantage of that.

Life wasn't all that bad just because June and I weren't getting along. I was one of the honored designers at the Crystal Ball at the Philadelphia Museum of Art along with Halston, Stephen Burrows, Stan Herman, and John Kloss.

I invited Norma Jean Darden as my guest model. Norma and I checked into our hotel, then walked around the neighborhood and discovered a wonderful Soul Food restaurant on the South Side.

We ordered everything that wasn't nailed down. At the end of our fantastic dinner, we couldn't get up from the table because we were totally stuffed.

Somehow, we managed to return to the hotel to dress for the formal evening at the museum. Everyone was requested to wear white. All of the food courses were white, so we passed. We were still recovering from our Soul Food dinner.

First Lady Pat Nixon was the guest of honor and the security people locked us in a private reception room for the introduction. Carol Channing was the Mistress of Ceremony. Norma modeled a simple white empire gown with a very low-scooped bra top neckline, the dress slithered down her body with a fluted bottom.

Norma and I had a delightful evening. We had made a previous commitment in New York at the end of the evening, so we excused ourselves and then quickly dashed out of the Museum, which was located in the middle of a very large park. I thought we could easily hail a taxi; however, as we exited, there were no taxis in sight. Suddenly, a drunken driver appeared and offered us a lift to our hotel. We gladly accepted because it was the only thing moving. Riding with him was very tense because he swerved back and forth across the highway. Fortunately, we arrived at the hotel in one piece.

We dashed into the hotel and grabbed our bags, and quickly checked out, then hailed a taxi to the train station. After rushing about, we boarded the train, which appeared as the last milk wagon to New York. I think the train stopped at every street light along the way. After we settled down on the train, Norma was still dressed in her formal white gown and her eye makeup had streaked down her cheeks. I laughed for twenty minutes. We arrived in New York several hours later, with our bags in hand, just in time for the next party. You know we couldn't miss a party.

Months before all the havoc, June and I were the toast of the town, going to and doing everything together. Since my marriage was not working out, I asked Chadbourne Springs from the Community Church to suggest a marriage counselor, which he did. During our second, visit the counselor asked, "What are you thinking?" I stood up and responded, "What this visit is costing and I'm not going to pay."

June also wanted to travel around the world and be away from home most of the year. I couldn't see how our relationship could work over a long-distance phone call. I'm a 'Hands-On' kind of guy. That was not how I imagined our marriage to be.

We talked about separating. A short while after that, and to my surprise, June sent a divorce summons to my office. I was shocked—that pissed me off. She demanded alimony, my apartment, and its contents, and me out of it. I was not a happy camper. I felt that this was a personal matter that could have been settled amicably at home. I was speechless and devastated. When I returned home that evening. Everything went downhill from that moment. She had already started the divorce proceedings in court. I hated having a stranger decide the direction of my life, especially someone who had not lived with the facts.

Those were horrific times. I couldn't stay in the apartment in the evenings, so I went out every night, dancing and drinking at discos with friends. There was so much pain. I really loved June, but had too much pride and couldn't let my guard down.

I began taking piano lessons in the middle of all the chaos and was getting a grasp of the keys. I returned home one day, and sat down at my Baby Grand piano then placed my fingers on the keys, I began pressing the keys down, but there was no sound. Finally, I stood up to check the strings, to my surprise, I could not believe what I saw. She had cut all the strings in my piano. Whenever she got angry, she would destroy or throw things. On my way to work the next day, I took my very expensive Chinoiserie porcelain lamp with me for fear that it would wind up in little pieces as so many other things had met their fate. Thank God I did, because it was my first important purchase in the mid-sixties.

Years later my mother used a wrench to remove the hardware of that very expensive Chinoiserie lamp. I reminded her how important the lamp was. Then she said, "I'm your best friend, do you think the lamp is more important than our friendship." I shall never forget her comment, it brought me to tears. Of course, Mother was more important. Then I explained how special the lamp was, because it had survived my chaotic divorce.

June wasn't the only one that was destructive. One night, I was sitting in the living room, while she was on the phone in the bedroom. I heard her accuse me of something that I had not done. I walked into the bedroom and asked, "What did she say?" She blurted out that she was on the phone. I reached for a scissor and cut the phone wire. "Now, you are not on the phone, and don't ever accuse me of something that I didn't do." The other thing that I truly hate, is when someone tells me they know what I'm thinking.

Times were stormy on the home front and I think both of us suffered from a broken heart. Most people think only women get hurt, but I'm here to tell you, I was an emotional wreck. I lost weight and was depressed for a very long time after our marriage ended. I don't normally get depressed, EVER! Those were dark days in my life.

That relationship meant something very special to me. Perhaps I didn't realize it until it was too late. My other regret is that we didn't remain friends. But I shall never forget my love for her.

As they say, "It is better to have loved and lost than never to have loved at all."

June was the love of my life. It's too bad our marriage didn't last.

I loved June with or without those outside affairs. There will always be a place in my heart for her. When I open to love, I never, ever forget. I often wonder what life could have been and all the possibilities if we had stayed together. Sometimes I find myself staring at children wondering what our children would look like. Judy Garland's *In Person at Carnegie* album helped me through my depression. Her music was an emotional lift that cheered me up and gave me direction and hope. Once June moved out of the apartment, I called the piano man to replace the strings. Once that project was finished, I resumed my piano lessons, but quickly got very bored, so I hired a pianist to come to my apartment to rehearse with my backup singers for my Cabaret act.

June summoned me back to court numerous times. I wore an old raincoat on the last day so that I wouldn't look prosperous. I had hired four lawyers during the proceedings. One of the lawyers said, "Why don't you settle."

I quickly responded, "Settle your ass, you're fired."

June saw the divorce wasn't going her way, so she departed for Europe.

CHAPTER ELEVEN

Facing Hurdles
and Bouncing Back

I had a little success, as did other new talents in the Sixties. I felt so positive each day because I was making progress with my designs and connecting with the right people who exposed me to a new world of fashion. I was ripe as rain and ready for new challenges.

I'd known my friend, Clarence Ross, for four years. He was interested in investing in my company. Elaine Monroe, dress buyer from the Sutton Place Boutique at Bloomingdales gave him an excellent reference. He insisted on three factors: sales, design, and production. Unfortunately, he couldn't find a production person, so he passed. I know he honestly investigated because I met with him on several occasions. He also feared that I would take off on another vacation, not understanding that the trips were an inspiration for my fashion. Finding more money for expansion was the key, but the money simply was not there. Money was the biggest frustration while operating my company, there simply was never enough.

I had just presented my Fall Fashion collection to buyers from Bloomingdale and other stores. The very next day, the Internal Revenue surprise me a visit to collect back taxes. I hid in the armoire in the middle of a collection of gowns. Perhaps, I thought my problem would go away. I just couldn't face the problem of not having enough capital to pay the operational expenses of the studio and the I.R.S. Although I had confirmed orders of twenty-thousand dresses from stores across the country. I couldn't produce the orders, because my bank pulled the plug and wouldn't lend me any more money, because of the IRS situation. I was so frustrated because after I paid the back taxes, it left me high and dry. I didn't have enough capital to stay in business. To be undercapitalized is a bitch.

I called *WWD* to inform them that I was closing my business. Lois Weinbaum, the editor told me she was going to feature one of my designs on the cover the next day. Then *WWD* pulled the editorial. Suddenly all the stores that had placed orders, canceled their orders and that left me high and dry. I was truly out of business. Minnie Turner had worked with me from the very beginning. She was very disappointed because we were really beginning to gain ground when everything fell apart. Just before closing the door for good, I had an exhibition of Barbara Pearlman beautiful sketches. I finally closed my Smart Little Studio in January 1972.

Over the years I had gotten lots of national publicity in magazines, newspapers, and television, so I thought that exposure would have helped me find a backer...wrong. I had managed Jon Haggins Inc. for six years without any outside assistance and thought it would be easy getting financial backing from some adventurous investors or an angel from the sky......wrong.

I discovered the opposite; everyone beats their chops, but nobody was truly interested in putting their money where their mouth was. Helen Gurley Brown, editor in chief of *Cosmopolitan* magazine sent a letter of introduction for an interview to Ed Parnes of Mollie Parnes and Ben Shaw, two Seventh Avenue Angels. Ben graciously met with me, reviewed my credentials then asked:

"How would you like to be an assistant for Donald Brooks?"

"I wouldn't," I responded.

I couldn't believe his chutzpah. I also met with several other potential backers, but nobody was willing to put their serious money where their mouth was. I also thought my success with my Bymini Collection would have made a difference. It didn't.

It was a trying time. I received many offers from manufacturers to design for them, but they didn't respect my talent and didn't want to pay for my service. Therefore, my opinion was most manufacturers have a very strange notion that designers don't know anything about business, they only know how to sketch.

I hit the downside of fashion, a bumpy road that a lot of new designers meet—insufficient capital. I couldn't wait until I found someone to back me. I had to find employment, so I freelanced. It was a very difficult time for me because I had been independently on my own since I was twenty-two years old.

Like the song says: "Pick yourself up, dust yourself off and start all over again."

I'm like a bowling pin that gets knocked down and gets up again and I never stop, I'm always reaching for the brass ring.

Suddenly, I was thrust into working for a manufacturer. My first designer job after closing my company was at Portfolio Dress Company. That's where I met Jordan Samuelsohn. I brought Minnie Turner, my assistant, with me. We were a team. On the first day on the job, I felt like a caged bird. It was the worst feeling. It was more of a mental thing, that I wasn't used to. I designed classic ladies' dresses for that company during the day and taught a fashion design class at FIT in the evenings.

It was sheer hell working all day and then teaching in the evening. The Portfolio people called an emergency meeting at 5 pm. I couldn't stay, because I had to race off to FIT to teach a class at 6 pm. I didn't explain why I couldn't stay. They told me, "If you leave now, don't come back." Don't you dare threaten me. I left and didn't return.

I took a little time to reflect on my next move. I needed to spread my wings and soar like an eagle. I had designed several collections for other companies during the late 1960s, such as scarves for Glentex, loungewear for Dutchess, and Stella Fagin. I also aspired to produce a designer perfume. That never happened, unfortunately.

Louise Cohen introduced me to her friends from St. Louis, her hometown. They owned Barad Sleepwear Company and were looking for a lounge/sleepwear designer. Well, I fit the bill due to the fact that I had designed sleep and loungewear for Dutchess. I immediately signed a one-year contract and began designing beautiful, practical sleepwear with daring necklines and soft draping.

A mid-day meeting was scheduled in St. Louis with Barad's production team. So I called Norma Jean early that morning and told her I was going to St. Louis. Then asked her and her boyfriend, Henry, to meet me at 7 pm at Sayville's Long Island dock. I arrived for the production meeting. They introduced me to the staff and the production team. I left after the meeting. The airline had a stopover in Chicago. Somehow, I made the connecting flight to Mc Arthur Airport by the hair on my chinny, chin, chin. I arrived at McArthur Airport in Islip, Long Island, at 7 PM, to meet Norma and Henry at the Sayville Long Island Dock. They were arriving by bus from Manhattan, as I stepped out of the taxi. We took a ferry across the bay to the Pines on Fire Island. Synchronizing our appointment couldn't happen twice in a lifetime.

We spent a restful weekend at Stephen Lewis' summer home. I recall being pushed into the deep end of the pool when I didn't know how to swim. I was so angry, that I forgot that I didn't know how to swim. I managed to save myself and got out of the pool safely.

Norma Jean Darden models my sleepwear gown at my apartment, 1973

I designed a salad or another easy dish each summer so that no one had to slave over the stove. One summer it was Romaine lettuce with dates, pineapples, and red onions, and the next year spinach salad with bacon and other goodies. The most delicious summer dish was a Vichyssoise. Not only were those dishes delicious, but also the easiest dish to prepare. Those were wonderful summers in the Pines.

June had started the divorce proceedings and I continued. I was preparing to depart for an out-of-town in-store appearance to promote my sleepwear collection. My final lawyer demanded an additional retainer, so I sent him a pair of my very expensive candelabras and told him to hold them until I return. I paid the lawyer the moment I returned and retrieved my candelabras. June had ventured off to Europe to pursue her career as a model, while I stayed in New York and finalized the divorce in 1973.

I made several personal appearances for my sleepwear collection in major stores around the country. Several months later, I was back home in Manhattan. My phone rang, it was one of the Barad brothers. He called and yelled at me.

I said, "Nobody yells at me," and then I hung up.

They didn't like my attitude. So, they decided not to renew my contract after it expired.

Several months later, FIT honored me for having been one of the successful graduates along with five other designers. Ironically, I had been out of business for a while. I called several friends to retrieve some of my designs. Stephen Lewis wrote a little ditty for me. I was backstage when I heard my name announced. Then I suddenly heard thunderous applause. The entire audience gave me a standing ovation, as I entered the stage. I was very moved by the honor. That was my moment. I had a captive audience of one thousand important Garmentos at my feet. The lights were dimmed in the auditorium; the only available light was from the podium. Thank God, I remembered my speech. I stood at the podium for a moment taking it all in and then said: "There are two things we designers have in common, one: we are graduates of FIT and the other: they're working and I'm not." The thunderous laughter stopped the show. It's been said, "It pays to advertise."

I received an offer the next day from Puritan fashions to design a line of day dresses. I knew that wasn't where I wanted to be, but I needed the money. When I arrived at the appointed time, Carl Rosen, the CEO, introduced me to Lee Mellis, president of Nancy Valentine, and officially offered me the position. I accepted it as it was the only card in town at that time. After the interview, Lee gave me a tour of the offices and the design room.

I asked, "Where's my office?"

"We can put some walls here and make an office for you."

On that note, I quickly ducked into another office and said, "This will make a terrific office."

"That's the production man's office," he responded.

"Why don't you build him an office instead."

I had my office repainted and added a wall of mirrors and new furniture, new plants, and a new red phone.

The Puritan Group manufactured cheap dresses for chains and large department stores. Fashion editors Nancy Benson from *Cosmopolitan* and Susan Taylor from *Essence* featured some of my designs in their magazines.

Friday was always a special day because I'd arrive at work with my bathing suit under my clothes. My neighbors Ben and Charlie would pick me up at noon and off we'd go to the beach. I didn't return to work until Monday morning. The minute all the furniture and fixtures were in place, Carl came around and fired me.

Shortly after that incident, Bob Groberg from *Vogue* magazine introduced me to Mort Schrader. Mort had a draggy dress division that needed some life, so I was hired as the designer. I refused to decorate again because that was my downfall at the last company. I gave the salesmen a list of previous customers, but they refused to use it. They only wanted to do business their way, the old-fashioned way.

After several months of designing for that company, they called a meeting at Five PM, as I was preparing to leave. Here we go again, I told them I couldn't stay, because I had made previous plans and couldn't reach the party to cancel.

They told me, "If you leave, don't return for work the next day."

So, I left and that was the end of that position.

I called John Pomerantz, President of Leslie Fay Corp, and asked for a design position. He hired me on the spot for the Leslie J. division. I designed a loose-fitting dress with an insert at the neck. *Essence* magazine wanted to feature the dress in an editorial, but they needed it three inches longer. It took three days to convince them what an editorial would mean for the company. When the magazine hit the stands, the company had to keep its doors open until 8 pm, just to accommodate the buyers. They had never had that kind of reaction from an editorial.

Working there was sooooo boring, because how many fabrics could I possibly look at before I shot myself. I always arrived at my desk around 10:30 or 11 AM to start the day. Boy! I hated that job so much, that I made lunch appointments at the best restaurants every day of the week, just to get away from it all.

Bob Legary, president of the division, arranged model fittings at noon. I couldn't make it, because it interfered with my lunch appointments. On one occasion the model, who was from another country muttered something to me, with a thick accent, then asked if I understood.

"I was born in this country and I speak English and you don't," I responded.

I didn't like her attitude.

I recall quietly dining with Cathy Dives, an editor from *Harper's Bazaar*, and my friend Myrna at Barbetta's restaurant, suddenly the CEO of my company approached our table. I whispered in Myrna's ear, "Please cover your dress," because I had given her one of the samples.

Here is an example of the kind of company I was working for: the production man called me into a meeting to discuss reducing the cost of a dress.

"Maybe we can shorten the sleeve and remove the pocket," he suggested.

"Why don't you erase the print while you're at it," I responded.

A conversation like that would have never occurred, while I was operating my company.

I will never forget the day I was fired. I felt a dark cloud over the design room. Bob called me into his office and said, "You are much too talented for this job. You should be on Seventh Avenue." Well, I knew that.

"You can take as much time as you like to clear your desk."

I told him to cut the crap and give me my check, cause I'm outta here. I returned to my desk and called all my friends and told them the free lunch is OVAH!

Jordan Samuelson called several months later and asked if I would be interested in designing for Parkland of Dallas under my name, I jumped at the chance to design a day into evening dress collection called "Impressions by Jon Haggins." He rented a showroom from Halston at 550 Seventh Avenue. I introduced Jordan to Louise Cohen as our sales manager. We got off on a rocky start because Parkland refused to invest enough money to make the company work efficiently.

First:There was no design room in New York.

Second: Minnie produced the samples in her apartment in New Jersey.

Third: Louise and I stuffed envelopes with press material and licked stamps in my apartment.

I designed soft drapey jersey dresses for Impressions. The disadvantage of working with that company was: that they insisted that I use fabrics that they had previously purchased. I would have been more inspired if I had chosen the fabrics.

Altman's Department Store displayed six six-foot portraits of me with my designs in their Fifth Avenue windows. I also made a personal appearance in the store. Altman's also ran several ads in the newspapers. Franklin Simon Department Store also followed suit.

Elsa Klensch was a reporter at *Women's Wear Daily* in 1972. She ran into my new showroom and needed a tip for the 'Eye' column. Norma Jean Darden had just popped in and purchased one of my designs, Elsa featured that dress.

The strangest thing happened in the middle of my contract with Parkland Manufacturers. They sent my monthly check, and it bounced. I called to ask why they said they canceled our contract. They gave no special reason. I still can't understand why they simply didn't warn me. That was a time when a lot of strange and disappointing things happened. I was on my own to figure out the next step.

CHAPTER TWELVE

Show Biz

Norma dropped by Jeff Hunter Theatrical Agency where Ted Wilkins, an agent, mentioned my name. He knew of me, because of my fashion career. Norma called and told me he wanted to meet me. I called him for an appointment. When I arrived at his office, he asked if I had taken dance and singing lessons.

"No, where do I go? "

Ted suggested Ora Witte for voice building. She was an old lady with a lot of experience. Ora advanced my voice to a point where I hit notes that I never dreamed of. She also taught me the difference between head and chest voice. Unfortunately, I can't read music, but I have a good ear.

I was very concerned about making it in showbiz. Ora reminded me, "If you can make it in the garment business, you can make it anywhere. All you need is perseverance, determination, and drive." I will never forget those words. After taking lessons with Ora for a year, she suggested George Walston. George coached and helped me establish a repertoire of songs. I worked with him for several months, then asked, "How much time do you think it will take to build a repertoire so that I can perform in front of an audience?"

"It's up to you."

Singing and dancing had always been a secret ambition. Ted also suggested Luigi's Studio for dance lessons. My first Jazz dance lesson was torture, I had stretched every muscle in my body, even muscles I didn't know I had. I couldn't get out of bed the next day. Every bone and muscle in my body ached for a week after the first class. I began thinking that I didn't have any rhythm because Jazz movements are different from social dancing.

I also studied acting at Herbert Bergorf School on Bank Street. Everyone had to perform a monologue in front of the class. I chose 'In White America.' I wanted so much to relate to the writing, but somehow I didn't feel it. So, I decided to fly down to Sanford to visit Grandad for the weekend. Grandad began sharing some of his horrific experiences of growing up in the segregated South. His folks were simple sharecroppers that had inherited 40 acres from their father in Monticello, Florida. He shared stories that he'd heard from his parents of how White folks humiliated, tormented, and murdered Blacks. Hearing his trial and tribulations, established an empathy for my monologue. It made the experience real for me. I think learning from him assisted me in visualizing the words on the page. I was able to find my center and discover who I am.

After I returned to New York, I was able to digest the monologue and delivered it with conviction, strength, and tears. There was nothing more real for me than the truth, especially hearing it from someone who had experienced it. I was blessed to have an elder tell his story and to respect his feelings because he was there and knew from his own experience.

Several weeks later, Norma Jean Darden and I were at Reno Sweeney's, a popular cabaret in the 70s. She introduced me to Lou Friedman, the owner, and told him that I was a singer. He invited me to sing at the showcase the following Monday night. I worked diligently with Bob Esty, a pianist, and pulled together a couple of songs.

Then, I called Lois Weinbaum-Perchetz, at *WWD*, and told her that I was going to appear at the club. She ran an item in the 'Eye' column announcing my first appearance. The club was filled when I arrived. No one believed that I was going to perform, so they had to see for themselves. Even I couldn't believe I was going to sing in front of an audience. I was a nervous wreck, so I pasted the lyrics on the wall leading to the stage, so as not to forget the first line of the song. I figured if I sang the first line correctly, the performance would sail smoothly.

Singing was not like designing, because, after I design the collection, I had to wait for a reaction from the editors and buyers. The reaction from singing was immediate, instant gratification. Singing in front of an audience was incredible

Energetic Cabaret days

therapy. It's like going to a shrink because I was bearing my soul. When I first began performing in front of an audience, I thought I should sing for them. But after a few years, I realized that I was not projecting who I was, then I relaxed and began singing for myself, and liked it.

While freelancing as a designer for a variety of companies, I consoled myself by singing in a variety of cabarets around town, which soothed my soul. Show biz was a whole new, equally frenetic world.

The Cabaret life allowed me to get in touch with my feelings. The owner of Reno Sweeney once turned off my microphone, while I was performing. I just pushed the microphone aside and continue to sing louder and more brilliantly. The audience loved it and told me I didn't need a microphone.

I loved the attention I was receiving. Then decided I wanted to be a full-time cabaret singer. I developed patter between songs, for example:

"I'm from Sanford, a small town in central Florida. It's the last stop on the auto train." I don't think anyone in the audience knew what the hell I was talking about.

"I didn't always talk like this and I didn't always dress like this."

1978

1949

I held up a poster-size photo of granddad and me. The photo was taken when I was six years old. Grandad was in the middle of repairing the interior of an old bus. I was dressed in dirty clothes because I came in from playing in the yard. I jumped in front of the camera, with one hand on my right hip and then looked straight into the camera, upstaging granddad. The entire audience stretched out on the floor laughing because I had become so polished, a slicked-up big city guy with a very sophisticated act.

Several years later, Ted Hardin photographed me for a Cabaret poster. I posed with one hand on my right hip and later, compared it with an old photo of me and Grandad, I was amazed that the pose was identical to the old photograph with Grandad. I guess the pose was in my subconscious. Amazing how things change and then again they don't.

Peggy Grant, my agent often sent me to open calls. I hated open calls because the casting agents treated everyone like cattle. I was a wreck when going for an audition because that's when my shyness came out. I'd relax my nerves by throwing my arms loosely in every direction and wiggling my body. It appeared as if I was having a fit. Upon arriving at the audition, I would distract everyone by throwing the door open and then make a mad dash into the casting office. I hated auditioning. There was one time I didn't care, and low and behold, that's when they called me back for a commercial, unfortunately, I was in Florida and wasn't available.

Peggy also called me to do under five roles, which meant I was paid twice as much as an extra. I worked on 'Love is a Splendor Thing,' a daytime series that aired on CBS. The director teamed me up with Myra Lee because we were the only people of color. Well...we showed them what rhythm was all about. One of the scenes required background dancers in a restaurant. The director asked us to cool our dancing down, not so much dancing in the camera. We agreed until the camera started rolling, then we zoomed right into the camera. I hinted to Myra that she should stick with me, cause we're going places. I will never forget how splendid she looked in a green pleated designer evening gown.

Myra and I became fast friends after the show. I discovered that she loved the beach as much as I. I invited her to join me for a weekend at James and Kedakai Lipton's beach home in Amagansett, Long Island. Kedakai used to model in my fashion shows. James was the host of the Actor's Studio TV show. James and Kedakai were the most entertaining couple I've ever met. They know all the Broadway performers. Our weekend was spent socializing from house to house.

Myra and I needed a little break, so we walked over to Calvin Klein's house to talk with him and Jane, his first wife. Later when we returned to the Liptons', they insisted on giving us a lift to wherever we wanted to go, but we only wanted to walk. I turned around, as we were walking, and saw their car coming up the road, so we quickly hid behind a bunch of bushes until they pass. They were waiting at the market when we arrive.

"Where were you, we didn't see you?"

"I wonder why?"

Back home in Manhattan, I appeared frequently on the Joe Franklin Show, I even sang on the show. Joe loved to hear his phone ring. Whenever I'd call, he'd say, "Call me Wednesday, great news."

On Wednesday, he'd say, "Call me Thursday."

I'd call until he confirmed a date for an appearance on his show. Everyone received equal treatment. His office was filled with piles of memorabilia. I can't imagine how he ever located anything. I was also a frequent guest on Midday Live with Bill Boggs TV Show and Jack O'Brien-WOR Radio show.

The '70s were difficult for me. Somehow, my engagements as an extra on several Soap Operas only gained me nineteen weeks for my employment record. I needed twenty weeks, so I asked Mr. Ross if I could work for his company for one day because I needed one more day to receive unemployment benefits. He hired me for a day as a receptionist to answer the phone. At least, I thought I was answering the phone; however, I was totally confused and wasn't proficient at the job. I mixed up everyone's call. I was not good as a receptionist.

A young man was standing in line at the unemployment office, turned around and spotted me, then commented, "I'm surprised to see you on the unemployment line."

Joan's Comedy

I continue performing around town. I asked Joan Shepard a reporter at *The Daily News* to be the opening act for my Cabaret Show. She told me she would think about it. I always found her to be amusing, clever, and outspoken. Joan agreed a week later, and we opened on February 14,

Cabaret poster

1977, on Valentine's Day, in the Valentine Room at Once Upon a Stove. Joan was billed as 'The Funniest Mouth in Town'. The club was packed. I think every reporter from *The Daily News* showed up because they couldn't believe she was performing.

Joan opened her comedy act with: "I came to New York on the train, most Colored people came here on the bus. Of course, I came from the better Colored section of South Philadelphia, with matched Samsonite luggage. I didn't know nuthin' 'bout no Louie Weeton. I got here and got a good job with an advertising agency. Then got the right apartment with much canopy and much doorman. The apartment was so small that it made my clit twitch when I wrote the check.

Well, after working at that company for a while, I decided to quit. When I told my boss, he said, over the phone, you know they can't tell. I wasn't born yesterday. I knew what he meant. Well, I was depressed for a while......'bout two years. But you know what you do when you get depressed...you call a Jewish girlfriend. They have the fur coat and the Mercedes. They know what to do.

"Selma, what is a girl to do? What should I do?"

And Selma told me, "Girlfriend, you need a therapist. "

I couldn't afford no therapist. So, I went to that old walk-in therapy clinic, Bloomingdales, on the sixth floor where the rooms are. And a young man walked up to me and invited me out for tea. Now, let me clear the room, I don't cruise, nobody here has ever seen me in the meat rack on Fire Island. You might have thought it was me, but that was some other light-skinned Colored girl in the bushes. The boys on Fire Island taught me something. When you look at a guy, and if he has skinny little fingers...... forget about it. But if he has long, thick fingers and a good separation.... girl ya gotcha yourself something." Then Joan said, "Now, put your dick on the table, girls; let's tell the truth."

Everybody fell into a coma or shock. I was downstairs in the dressing room and couldn't believe my ears. But, hey, it worked and people are still quoting her. Joan should have been billed as, "The Dirtiest Mouth in Town."

I continued to build my repertoire of songs and expanded my performance with a five-piece band and two backup singers. Rod Hausen, my musical conductor, arranged for us to rehearse at Catch

A Rising Star Comedy Club, which was better than a rehearsal hall and it saved me lots of money. We also performed in a variety of other clubs in Manhattan such as The Grand Finale, Tramps, The Colony Club, Casablanca, Copacabana, Red Parrot, Studio Fifty-Four, Xenon, Freddy's, The Bushes, The Ballroom, The Waldorf Astoria and Dangerfield's. We performed at Dangerfield's on consecutive Sundays for a month.

Jon Haggins at Dangerfields'

1118 First Ave. (61st St.)
May 1st, 2nd & 3rd
9:30 & 11:30 P.M.
Elliot Finkel Trio
Reservations: 593-1650
$5 Music & $7 Minimum

"Jon Haggins is a wonderful, touching
and incomparably imaginative singer.
Watch him in 1978."
— Joe Franklin, WOR TV

Dangerfields, 1977

We were also booked at Pipe Dreams in East Hampton with a house band. The band wanted us to rehearse and rehearse.

I said, "I've had it, we already know the tunes."

Then I pushed the button on the tape recorder and told them to learn it.

The band sabotaged us the first night by playing the tunes in a much slower tempo. No matter what I did to pick up the pace, they would not follow. We hung in until the end of the set. Then I ran in the men's room and screamed, "Those Mother Fuckers."

A young lady approached me as I came out of the bathroom and said, "Great show." And I screamed again, "Those dirty SOB's sabotaged me." I was so angry and had no idea who the hell I was talking to.

"Slow down, Jon, I'm Elaine Monroe."

Then I laughed and was delighted to see her, she was my former buyer at Bloomingdales.

I spent a lot of time in the Hamptons during the summer months and folks got to know me. They would pick me up in their fancy cars and ask, "Where are you singing this weekend?" Then offered to take me where ever I wanted to go. Singing brought me out of my shell and allowed me to cover up my shyness.

During the day, I had a lot of free time to relax on the beach, getting blacker and blacker. Olivia Shaw, my backup girl, and I were walking away from Two Mile Hollow Beach in East Hampton when a guy spotted her very high heel mules and suddenly stopped his car. I looked up when he asked about her shoes. He was a design buddy who was fascinated by her shoes.

"I'd kill for those shoes."

On another occasion, my group was booked at The Salty Dog in Sag Harbor, Long Island. Twelve friends decided to join us. The agent couldn't accommodate all of us in her home, so she tried to book us in a local motel. The owner of the first motel refused to book us because I was Black. The agent repeated the story to me.

I said, "We have another problem. There are two homosexuals in the group."

"Oh no! " she responded.

The next motel owner said," As long as their money is green, they're welcome."

We decided to take an early train to Sag Harbor to take advantage of a day in the sun. We had reserved all the rooms in the motel. After checking in, we were walking to our rooms when the phone rang at the front desk. The manager called out, "Haggins, telephone." We were so paranoid, because we had been rejected at the first motel. I thought she said, "Faggot telephone." Our mouths dropped, we couldn't believe what we thought we had heard. Then we realized she'd said, "Haggins, telephone." A friend was calling to invite us over to relax and enjoy his pool.

Shortly after we arrived at his beautiful estate, Olivia ran and jumped in the pool. I was quietly relaxing on a chaise next to the pool.

Suddenly Olivia screamed, "Give me a hand."

Naturally, I put my hands together and applauded. She was so angry, that she got out of the pool without any help from the peanut gallery. We spent the rest of the afternoon noshing on delicious fresh fruit, peeling grapes, and just being lazy. The host of the party called all of his friends and told them, they had to come to the club to catch our show that evening. Everyone showed up at the club and we truly had the best time. We gathered after the show and venture out for a dinner at a lovely restaurant. The owner of the restaurant recognized me and asked me to sing a song. And I did happily. It was a great evening in Sag Harbor.

I spent a lot of weekends in the Hamptons during the seventies and when I returned home, my color was deep, dark chocolate. I called Ted Hardin and suggested he photograph me sitting on the floor wearing a white short-sleeve shirt and white pants, grinning from ear to ear while eating a slice of watermelon.

"The NAACP is going to come after me when they see this picture," Ted remarked.

That was a photograph that only my mother would love.

The strangest weekend was at Maggie Skipper's house in Bridgehampton. I didn't like the beach in front of her house, so I hitched a ride to Two Mile Hollow Beach in East Hampton, where I spent a relaxing afternoon. Once I returned from the beach, I decided to take a nap. Suddenly, Maggie ran into my bedroom, screaming and disrupting my nap. I was so shaken. I thought there was a major disaster. I ran into her room and discovered she had left the French doors open. The bugs were naturally attracted to the ceiling light. She wanted me to kill the bugs on her ceiling. I told her fugetaboutit, I was going back to sleep. Then she told me, if her boyfriend were here, he'd kill them. So, I suggested she call him.

She made me crazy as a bed bug, I returned to my bedroom to finish my nap. Later that evening, I dressed in all white and walked five miles in the dark to the main road to hitch a ride to a club. I returned the next afternoon and packed my bags to return home. After she drove me back to Manhattan, I thanked her and then begged her not to invite me again.

Once I returned to Manhattan, I continued my acting classes at Herbert Bergdorf Studios and began taking a TV commercial class at Weiss Baron. Those classes helped me get in touch with myself to perform better, although I never capitalized on my acting or commercial lessons. Cabaret singing was fun for a few years until I realized I wasn't making enough money to support myself.

There was always another way to skin a cat, so to speak. There were times during my non-working period in the seventies when I

At the piano in my home, 1973

couldn't afford dance lessons, so I'd rush out to buy the local theatrical newspaper to check out the dance auditions. I checked as many as I could, just to get free dance lessons. One of the auditions required a turn. I was coordinated for everything but the turn; the choreographer looked at me, and I said, "I don't do turns."

For the "One Mo Time" audition, everyone was required to tap. I arrived with my tap shoes in hand. One of the dancers in the dressing room showed us a combination as everyone shuffled along. I observed.

"Do you tap?" he asked.

"No."

"Then why are you here?"

"To learn," then, he laughed.

Well low and behold, they placed me in the front row for the actual audition. The choreographer showed us a tap combination with a turn. Everybody turned to the right and I turned left. I was called back for the singing and a reading audition. I didn't get the part, but I sure as hell had the right attitude and I had a lot of fun.

There were good times and horrible times while singing in cabarets. There were times when the club was filled to capacity and

Cabaret days

other times when the audience was small, but I always remembered one thing: people are paying their hard-earned cash and they deserved the same show. After all, there are no discounts in cabaret.

Norma was one of the actors in 'The Cotton Club Movie' as were Gregory and Maurice Hines. I was invited to the Rap party (that's when the movie finished filming). What a fantastic night of celebration, there was lots of food, drinks, gayety, and laughs. Towards the end of the party, I asked one of the guests, if he had a ride back to Manhattan and he said, 'yes'. I asked Norma if she needed a lift. So, we hopped in his limo, and off we went. Once they crossed the Queens Borough Bridge, they dropped Norma off and then dropped me at my building. Norma called me after I arrived home to ask:

"Do you know who dropped you off?" I had no idea.

"It was Bob Evans, the producer of the movie."

That didn't matter to me, because I had the best time ever.

CHAPTER THIRTEEN

Party Time

Carrie Donavan had been appointed, Editor in Chief of *Harper's Bazaar*. She was honored with a party in a large photographers' studio. I was one of the guests. That's where I met Sarah Pentz from Channel Five. After talking with Sarah for a while, I invited her to my apartment for my Annual Christmas Trim the Tree dinner party.

Christmas has always been a special time to spend with friends and share good feelings and memories. It was a perfect way to bring people together. I invited ninety people to my Party. I pre-dressed the tree with lights and requested each guest to bring an ornament. It didn't matter where the ornaments came from, as long as they had the Christmas spirit and imagination. Norma Jean's boyfriend Henry once asked, "Easter is coming, does that mean we have to bring an egg?"

I called my cousin Ethel because I knew she would have all the answers for planning an incredible dinner party for ninety people. I asked if I should buy a fifty-pound turkey.

"They don't come fifty pounds,"

"Why not?"

"Then she suggested I buy a twenty-five-pounder."

I dashed to the supermarket and purchased a twenty-seven-pound turkey. That was my first attempt at cooking a turkey, so I opened a cookbook. Ah! Twenty minutes per pound! I held up my right hand and counted on my fingers and concluded that it would take nine hours. Well, after nine hours, the turkey was petrified.

Sarah Pentz arrived accompanied by a cameraman to film the special occasion. The food was carefully placed on the buffet table as the party began. One of the dinner guests asked,

"Where is the stuffing?"

"Inside," I answered.

"Where inside?"

"In the plastic bag," I responded.

Some of the guests were Calvin Klein, Alexis Smith, Egon Von Furstenberg, Fred Williamson, Robert Di Niro, Clovis Ruffin, Angelo Donghia, Etta Froio, Grace Jones, Susan Taylor, Catherine Dives, and many others too hot to name. I served a real soul food dinner, which included sweet potato pie, potato salad, black-eyed peas, turkey (actually not the turkey), ham, and lots of southern potato salad. I never serve bread, because I don't eat it. The party lasted well into the night and everyone had a grand old Soul Food time. After all, I was the darling of the fashion swells.

I feel very fortunate to have known so many people from a variety of professions, such as the literary world, doctors, real estate developers, interior designers, fashion designers, artists, editors, writers, buyers, photographers, show biz people, restaurant and night club owners, advertising, public relations, producers, record companies, actors, dancers, caterers, waiters, singers, models, television and radio personalities, architects and probably others that I have forgotten.

One thing I hate at New York City parties, is someone approaching me and asking, "What do you do?"

I have three responses:

"I go to lunch."

"I talk."

"What did you have in mind?"

Why don't they start by asking my name?

One of the neighbors in the building produced a local newspaper.

The paper featured my party, however, I had not invited them. I have a feeling that the person, must have spied from across the way into my floor-to-ceiling windows.

I often invited friends to my apartment for cocktails and smart little dinner parties. Here are six favorite dishes that I often served:

1. Stuffed fish with shrimps, green peppers, onions, garlic, and raisins. Then, I stitched the belly to appear as if the fish was still swimming in the sea.
2. Chicken Liver, dipped in a flour batter with a little salt and pepper. Then dropped a little cooking oil. The onions were dropped in after a few minutes. Cover the frying pan and allow the livers to steam.
3. Romaine lettuce salad with red onions, cubed pineapples, and pitted dates and a homemade vinaigrette with a combination of oil and balsamic vinegar, chutney, and fresh lemon juice, mustard seed, salt, and pepper.
4. In a "Reynold's Bake in bag"; place the chicken in the bag and add salt and pepper to taste, new white potatoes, garlic, onions, sweet potatoes, and carrots. Close the bag and stick it in the oven for one hour and a half. Everything baked together gives the best flavor from all the ingredients.
5. Meatloaf with lots of catsup, onions, garlic, green and red peppers, eggs, bread crumbs, and salt and pepper.
6. Turkey in the bag; bake the same way as the chicken with salt and pepper. It will turn out very moist and succulent.
7. Shrimp in a butter sauce. Sauté red, green, and yellow peppers with white onions, garlic, salt and pepper, fresh lemon juice, and of course lots of butter. Plate it over a bed of Fettuccine Pasta.

Whenever I spot a guest standing in one spot at my party, I simply pull out one of my old tricks to mobilize them. I walk behind them and open the window. The cold air forced them to move.

After having ninety people for dinner in my small apartment, I realized that I need more space, so I asked the rental office if they had a larger apartment. Fortunately, there was a corner three-bedroom apartment with floor-to-ceiling windows on the seventeenth floor. I signed the lease and moved in January 1973.

Once I moved in and settled down, I invited my long-time friend Pat Davis to join me in Rio for Carnival. Then bought two air tickets, but didn't have a hotel reservation. While having lunch at Orsini's Restaurant, with Bea Feitler from *Harper's Bazaar* the next day I told her I was on my way to Rio tomorrow. Bea was originally from Rio. She asked where was I staying. I told her I have no idea. She suggested I call Roberto Rodrigo, and he would find an apartment for me. I raced home after lunch and called him. He asked me to call him from the airport when we arrive.

It was a very hot day in February when we arrived. I did follow up with a call. He asked us to take a taxi to his home, and he would find an apartment for us. We arrived at his home, and beyond the gate was a lush garden of tropical trees and fragrant colorful florals. Old fashion shutters open onto the garden, allowing fresh air to filter in. The music from the Lady Sings the Blues movie echoed throughout the garden. Sweat was pouring from our bodies when we arrived. Rodrigo suggested we freshen up with a shower to cool off.

He called around and found a three-bedroom, floor-through apartment at 120 Rua das Acacias. We loved the space and stayed ten blissful days. The apartment was also conveniently located, between Copacabana and Ipanema and only a block from Ipanema beach. As we were casually walking towards Ipanema beach one day, I stopped at a newsstand to pick up a newspaper. To my surprise, the cover had a large photo of New York City covered with five feet of snow. I said, "Lucky us."

We loved spending our days on the beach. At the close of each day, we met friends at Casalinho for a refreshing Caipirinha and an appetizer. Natalie Wood popped in the restaurant one afternoon. She was wearing a babushka covering her head. What a grand lady she was.

Carnival was held on Avenida Presidente Vargas. One large colorful float followed another with dancing girls and boys in colorful costumes.

It was amazing and festive and I loved it. That was also a time when the carnival was intimate. Long before the new Sambadrome, which was designed by Oscar Niemeyer in 1984. The Sambadrome became the international grandstand for Carnival, where many samba schools competed for the best music and costumes. The parades attract thousands of Brazilians as well as foreign tourists each year.

When I returned to New York, my skin color was a dark, radiated purple aubergine. I recall my mailman barely recognized me. I threw a housewarming party shortly after I returned and invited lots of friends and acquaintances. Champagne continued to flow and the food keep coming. Guests included numerous friends from the fashion, Hollywood, decorators, and the media industry such as Clovis Ruffin, Angelo Donghia, Alexis Smith, and Robert de Niro. Alexis Smith danced in front of my vintage jukebox. The Juke Box featured some of my favorite music, all you had to do was push a button to select the music. Several guests presented me with housewarming gifts such as several silver candle holders. *WWD* featured the party in the 'Eye' column the next day.

I was shopping in a Deli across the street from my apartment building and I observed a lady buying ice. I suggested she call Diamond Ice because they always deliver when I need lots of ice.

"Oh, you live in 17L and have great parties, why don't you invite me?"

"I don't know you."

She also added that I was an architect, and I was having my apartment renovated all of February. Not true because I was in Rio for Carnival. Boy, was she the nosey one?

I frequently hosted smart little dinner parties. As I was relaxing at home one day and not hosting a party, a friend called and asked," What do you have to drink?"

"Whatever you bring," I responded.

One of my most memorable occasions aside from my dinner parties was being invited to dinner at a friend's apartment. He had flown his chef in from Los Angeles to prepare a sumptuous dinner complimented with the best wines. After dinner, guests were chauffeured by Limousine to Yankee Stadium for the Muhammad Ali and Ken Norton fight. A parade of spectators kept streaming in, wearing the most beautiful fashions of the day. The fight was over in a minute and a half. I think Ken Norton won that fight, however, the title was given to Ali, because there wasn't a knockout.

I turned around after the fight, and low and behold, stood Norma Jean. I asked if she had a lift back to Manhattan, then offered her a ride in my limousine. Upon returning to Manhattan, we stopped at Regine's for a quick spin around the dance floor to end the evening.

One summer day, I returned from the beach only two hours before my smart little dinner party. The local butcher was only a block away from my apartment, lucky me. That was a time when we could find a genuine butcher. I often had the butcher cut the chicken, because, I recall, when I was in my science class in High School, the teacher asked me to cut open a frog and I couldn't do it. I never paid attention to what it cost to cut a chicken. So, one day, I happen to look at my receipt and was disturbed that he charged more to cut the chicken. But I had no choice, so I paid it. I also raced to the grocery and picked a few items and then raced back upstairs to prepare everything.

A tip for preparing potato salad: The fastest way to make a potato salad is to rinse the unpeeled white potatoes and drop them in boiling water. Allow them to boil and soften. Then dump them in the sink and pour cold water on them, to cool them off. Now you can push the shell of the potato off by hand.

Norma's boyfriend Sam arrived early, while I was in the middle of preparing dinner, I asked him to peel the carrots.

"That's women's work."

"Then you don't eat."

Fortunately, everything was prepared before my first guest arrived at 8 pm. What a day that was.

On another occasion, I invited twenty friends from the Hamptons, Rio, and Manhattan for an eight o'clock dinner. Everyone arrived on time dressed in all-white outfits, with very deep tans. It was just a beautiful coincidence. We were joyfully sharing cocktails until approximately 8:23 pm when the air conditioner went kaput and I thought, "Oh my God! I have to call the maintenance department." I looked out of my floor-to-ceiling windows that faced the Westside of Manhattan and watched the entire city slowly fade into darkness. It was as if a black curtain was drawn over the city. I knew then that we were having another blackout. That was the Blackout of July 13–14, 1977. The only available light was from the full moon. So, I quickly lit twenty candles in silver candleholders. Then placed the food on a table, ala buffet, and called out, "Dinner is served." I only served white wine at my parties to prevent them from staining my furniture.

Nothing was going to interrupt my evening. One of my guests played the piano, while everyone gathered around and sang. What a wonderful time we had, nobody paid attention to what was happening on the street. At 3 am, I gave everyone a candle and said, "I've gotta go to sleep. It's been fun, but ya gotta go."

The blackout only inconvenienced me in a minor way. There are so many things that I took for granted, such as:

I opened my apartment door and the hall lights were not working.

When I turned on the tap, no running water.

I just assumed everything automatically worked. The next morning, I ran down seventeen flights to the street and walked over to Waterside where I stretched out in the plaza. When I returned home later that afternoon, everything was functioning again. Thank God!

I often had financial crises. Joan Shepard suggested I throw a Thirties-Style rent party. I thought it was a good idea. Everyone came and paid six dollars then received an 'I Gave Already' T-shirt and dinner, which was served by top models Carmen Bradshaw, Naomi Sims, Norma Jean Darden, and my maid Mabel. That's what I called doing without.

Cy Coleman accompanied me on the piano, while I sang one of his little ditties, 'Would You Believe.' Somehow, I was in the middle of the song, when I forgot the lyrics and asked him to help me out. I never stopped for a moment, then finished the song with great pride. Everyone had the best time, but I didn't make any money. Some of the guests were Larry Fisher, the real estate mogul, Clarence Ross, James and Kedakai Lipton, Tammy Grimes, and many other unforgettable faces. A few days after the party, I told Joan Shepard that I was a simple man.

"There's nothing simple about you, Jon."

I also recall having a drink at B. Smith's Restaurant, when a young man approached me and said he had a terrific time at dinner in my apartment. Then he added, "Let me buy you a drink." When I finished that drink, another young man walked over and said he had a great time in my apartment and offered to buy me a drink. I didn't remember either of them as guests, perhaps they were a guest of a guest. I appreciated the gesture and the fact that they reciprocated.

CHAPTER FOURTEEN

Letting Go

I was in my early thirties when I called Mother and asked for my father's address in Tampa. She asked, "Do you really want to visit him?" I said, "Yes, I want to visit him on my own terms, as an adult." The airline offered a five-dollar stopover, so I took advantage of the offer. Tampa was my first stop. I didn't know how I'd react when I saw him. Would I rejoice or cry? Would I feel a special connection? I was terribly anxious and felt uneasy. Meeting my father was like meeting a stranger because that's what he was to me. I didn't remember what he looked like?

He met me at the Tampa Airport. However, the strangest thing happened. I knew him instantly as he casually walked toward me. He was wearing a pale blue loose-fitting short sleeve cotton shirt and casual tan pants. He was six-foot-tall, fit, and a handsome dude. I did not feel anything emotion for him. I was a nervous wreck and I'm sure he was too. The last time I saw him, I was thirteen, when he visited me at Grandad's home. Now, I was thirty-two years old. I was anxious and emotional. I didn't know what to expect from myself or him. We cordially greeted and hugged each other. Then I picked up my bags and we walked to his car.

It was a hot day in Tampa. The sun scorched the sidewalk. Dad drove me to his home, where he introduced me to his wife and kids. They were young adults. The first thing they said was, "Here's our brother." I turned and looked at them as if they had lost their minds. I didn't know them and my instinct said, "You don't want to know them?" It wasn't something they did or said, I was just in shock and didn't know how to react.

We casually sat on a bench in the backyard, under a large oak tree that shaded us from the scorching hot sun. Dad asked if I wanted lunch.

"No thanks, I had lunch on the plane."

We slowly sipped ice-cold lemonade and talked about, nothing in particular. There was never any emotion or meaningful conversation.

What I wanted most, was some private time with him, which never happened. I met him on his turf, which was awkward for both of us because neither of us knew how to react. Perhaps, he was equally as nervous, because I could smell alcohol on his breath. I wished we could have spent just one hour alone, just the two of us because I had so much to say to him. I will never forget one thing he said: "I always wanted my son to visit me."

I had originally scheduled to spend two hours with him, but I was so choked up. I wanted to get the hell out of there. It wasn't something he said or did. It was just an emotional experience that I just couldn't handle, especially after so many years of not having him in my life. The hour slipped away as he did from my life. I told him I had to return to the airport to catch my flight. He asked for my phone number and address as I stepped out of the car. I didn't answer. I rushed to the men's room and washed every part of my body that was exposed to him. I wanted to wash away the memory of our meeting. It wasn't anything that he did, it was just me. Then, I rushed to the bar and ordered a drink, actually a double to calm me down.

I called Grandad before boarding the plane. He always recognized my voice right away,

"Hello, Wesley."

He always called me by my middle name. It was always so good to hear his voice. I couldn't wait to see him. Once I landed in Orlando, I took a taxi to Grandad's house. The driver asked if we were going in the right direction, and I said, "Yes." We drove a little further and he asked again.

"Does this look familiar?"

"Yep, looks like the last shopping mall."

Finally, we arrived on French Avenue in Sanford. I vaguely remembered the Avenue from my childhood. I knew we were somewhat in a familiar area. When we arrived on the street where Grandad lived, I was looking out the window and didn't see his house.

"Oh, my gosh! What happened to Grandad's house?"

I was looking at the opposite side of the street and didn't recognize the block until we reached the house on the corner. The driver turned around the dropped me off in front of Grandad's house, then he got out of the taxi and grabbed my bags.

"Where are you going with my bags?" I asked.

He was bringing them to the porch. I forgot that was what drivers do in southern cities.

I told Grandad about my meeting with Dad. To visit Dad on my terms was important to me. It helped me realize he was only responsible for 'planting the seed.' Grandad asked if there was anywhere I wanted to go or anything I wanted to do. I said, "No. I just came to spend a little time with you, Grandad."

CHAPTER FIFTEEN

Biking

My most favorite pass time was biking around Manhattan. From the moment I stepped on the peddles, I felt powerful and in control. With each brisk stroke, I gained more speed as the wind gushed against my face. Biking built strength in my legs, pumped my heart, and allowed oxygen to flow into my lungs. I felt I could conquer anything and ride to the end of the earth. Somehow, biking made me feel like a kid again. Exploring the city on a bike has been a wonderful escape because I didn't have to use public transportation. Bill Cunningham and I were the original New York City bikers, we biked everywhere because it was the most convenient way to get around town.

Manhattan is an eclectic borough where people have migrated from around the world to make up a beautiful mosaic. I enjoyed biking around many unbelievable pockets of the city, discovering many changes every day. Manhattan is developing at such a rapid pace. I have said, "If I go away for a weekend. When I return, the neighborhood will have changed."

There are a lot of neighborhood pockets in Manhattan. Chinatown for instance is filled with many winding labyrinth cobblestone streets. I found a variety of Chinese restaurants where delicious Peking Ducks hang in the windows. Have you ever tried dim sum? It's divine, waiters push a cart around with an assortment of dishes from which to select. All you have to do is select a dish, and they place it on your table and stamp your check. At the end of the meal, the cashier adds up everything to finalize the bill.

Canal Street is filled with many open street vendors, selling off-price products. Chinatown is also where I bought knockoff designer watches. I've had several people ask, "Is it real or fake." Who cares as long it works for a year or two. They also sell lady's handbags and scarves. Chinatown is a destination where you can discover fresh exotic fruit, such as Rambutan. There are several fish markets where the fish is always so fresh, that you wanna slap it in the face. I watched fish jump up and down in a bucket. Interesting to see Asian ladies place their fingers in the gills to test their freshness.

Just below Chinatown is the South Street Sea Port, which has a combination of turn-of-century townhouses and a large shopping market where everyone comes to shop. My favorite section is Pier 17, which has the best view of Brooklyn Heights and the Brooklyn and Manhattan Bridge.

The Brooklyn Bridge is my favorite bridge because there is a pedestrian, wooden-plank walkway, and a bike path that stretches into Brooklyn. It's the most romantic experience, even if you're alone. I have compared the height of the bridge to about ten floors of a building. There is a metal plaque at the mid-bridge point that offers a little history of the bridge. Coasting from the height of the bridge to a decline is a rush as I entered Brooklyn. Dumbo is relatively a new community. It's located between the Brooklyn and Manhattan Bridge. There are a variety of shops and restaurants for your choosing. And don't let me forget a spectacular view of Manhattan. Manhattan twinkles at night. What could be more spectacular than that?

I crossed the bridge again and biked up to Tribeca and SoHo, which is definitely a tourist destination. The cobblestone streets are a reminder of the past. There is a large assortment of high-end stores and restaurants that offer some of the best cuisines. I meandered through several vintage stores. Some of the establishments have been in existence since the beginning of time. Bleecker Street has an Italian feeling with a variety of restaurants, pastry, cheese, and pizza shops. I ventured through the winding cobblestone streets of yesteryear and discovered little coves and treasures within Manhattan. There is a new waterfront along the westside highway, it accommodates skaters, pedestrians, and bicyclists like me. Entering the West Village and Chelsea area was harmonious and serene. There are many new residential developments in the area. There are so many new shops and restaurants, that I can't believe it's the same neighborhood.

Just north of Chelsea is the Garment District, where garment manufacturers produce the latest styles, that you see in stores across the country. It's a bustling and vigorous neighborhood with a lot of energy. The garment industry is the No. 1 industry in New York next to communications.

And just two blocks north of the Garment Center is the Theatre District and Hell's Kitchen, which is now called Clinton. Well, forget that, cause I still call it, Hell's Kitchen. Hell's Kitchen offers a variety of International restaurants. Are you tired yet?

You can't bicycle through Manhattan without visiting the Upper westside where Lincoln Center sits and there are also a variety of restaurants and high-end shops. Central Park is an excellent spot for cycling. The roads are smooth and there is a lot of competition from other cyclists. I never challenged the racers, because they always leave me in the dust. However, when I see a weekend rider, I love passing them with a smile. The last stop of the day was Harlem. I love Harlem, because of its history. The Apollo Theatre on 125th street is a landmark, Miss Mamie's Spoonbread Soul Food Restaurant at 366 West 110th Street. Spoonbread serves the best soul food in New York City. Let me not forget Striver's Row, Convent Avenue, Sugar Hill, The Abyssinian Church, St. John Divine, Riverside Church, Riverside Park, and many other attractions.

Well after all that riding, I was worn out. I needed an Epsom salt bath to soothe my weary muscles.

CHAPTER SIXTEEN

Making Possibilities

There was a time in the mid-seventies that I was so depressed, because my phone didn't ring for days. Out of disbelief, I called the operator to find out if my phone was still working; fortunately, it was. I slept to avoid depression, in hope that the day would end quickly. And if and when the phone rang, I'd waken and pretend I was alert and happy. The other activity that saved the day was going to the beach or taking a long walk with my neighbor, Pat Suzuki. I explored every possible idea to become employed, but all my efforts were fruitless. I couldn't get arrested in the garment business, even if I stood on my head. No one would hire me.

With all my years of experience in the fashion industry, manufacturers wanted me to prove I could do the job.

"Hey, you don't ask a secretary to type for nothing, and you don't ask a porter to sweep for nothing, so why do you expect me to work for nothing?"

When a manufacturer approached me to share my ideas, the only thing I have are ideas, and they have to pay me for my ideas. As Joan Shepard said, "Put your dick on the table, boys, let's tell the truth."

I learned several useful phrases in the garment business; that are necessary for survival:

"I'll think about it."

"No thanks, it's not for me."

"Call me when you get some money."

"Don't ask me unless you're prepared to pay."

Phyllis Halterman from Dancer Fitzgerald Sampler showed me a ray of light the day she called and asked me to consult on a Hanes Men's Underwear Project. I perked up and was delighted that she thought of me. First thing, I asked was how much are you paying? I asked for twice as much and got it. I was a happy camper, because the project was something I understood.

I told my friend Latease that they pay me for my opinion.

"Is that why you're not working?" she quickly responded.

Jeanne Boone, a producer of 'To Tell The Truth' TV Show, invited me to appear as one of the impostors. 'To Tell The Truth' always had two impostors and one real person. We met at the Mark Goodson executive offices in the Seagram Building at 375 Park Avenue. Frank Andrews was an occult that read palms. I didn't know anything about his profession, so I went to the library for a little research. Meeting Frank was a mystical experience.

I arrived at the NBC Studio at 30 Rockefeller Plaza, promptly the day of the taping. During the rehearsal, the announcer asked,

"Number one, what is your name please?"

"My name is Jon Haggins."

The announcer said if that happens during the actual show, the segment would be disqualified.

During the actual show, I didn't make eye contact with Peggy Cass, one of the panelists, for fear that she might recognize me, because if you remember, she came to my studio and purchased twelve of my 'Hug Me Kiss Me Fuck Me' scarves several years ago. Fortunately, she didn't recognize me, but I felt very uncomfortable lying. I blew my cover when one of the panelists asked,

"What University is the occult studied?"

"Durham," I responded.

The correct answer was Duke University.

Everyone gathered at the end of the show. I told Peggy that I thought she'd recognize me.

"Why aren't you here as yourself?"

I told her that Jeanne invited me to be an imposter.

On another occasion, I held a little dinner party and invited Jeanne Boone and her sister Elayne Steinbeck, the wife of John Steinbeck who wrote 'The Grapes of Wrath, East of Eden' and many other award winning novels. It was a quiet party with lots of booze and food.

I also opened a T-shirt business in 1975, with my friend Kiko Morgan, where I designed T-shirts with amusing words and phrases printed on the front such as:

"I Want to Make it with You and You and You,"

"Stud,"

"Next,"

"Me Me Me,"

"Hey! Big Spender,"

"Rich Bitch,"

"Oui Oui,"

"Merde,"

"Hug Me Kiss Me Love Me"

"Send a Boy to Rio."

Pat Davis wearing one of my T-shirt designs, 1975

Nancy Benson featured my 'Hug Me' T-shirt in *Cosmopolitan* magazine. *Women's Wear Daily* also featured them as the sexy new T-shirts. A variety of small shops in New York City sold them and they became collectors' items.

My T-shirt company was short lived, but a lot of fun, because I could say anything without restrictions. I walked into Cartier Jewelers one day boldly wearing the 'Merde' T-shirt. They raised their eyebrows, but never said a word.

On another occasion, I was walking down the street with my nine year old nephew, he was wearing a 'Stud' t-shirt. Two young men were walking towards us were wearing my T- shirts that read, 'I Wanna Make it with You and You and You' and 'Oui Oui.' I had a big smile on my face as they passed.

While sharing a delicious lunch with Nancy Benson, one of my favorite people, she asked if she could use my apartment for a photo location. My three-bedroom corner apartment was on the 17th floor, with lots of natural day light beaming in through the floor to ceiling windows. The apartment was perfect for photography, because it had southern and western exposures with an aerial view of Manhattan.

"Absolutely, you may use my apartment."

That request sort of sparked a thought: if I charged a rental fee, perhaps I could afford to keep myself in the style that I had become accustomed.

I called Polly Mellon at *Vogue* the next day to tell her that I was making my apartment available for photo sittings. She called her friend Korken Patcharian, a photographer. He rushed over to see the apartment and loved it. He used it for a background for a Revlon Ad with Lauren Hutton.

Others publications and department stores used my apartment for shoots, such as *Harper's Bazaar, Town & Country, Essence, Glamour, Ebony* and Abraham & Straus department stores and other product companies. Celebrity models, Beverly Johnson, Renauld White and Susan Blakely were frequently photographed in my apartment. Diamonds and baubles from Harry Winston also floated through the apartment with a bonded bodyguard, of course. The guard watched over those precious gems during a *Harper's Bazaar* photo shoot.

Jon's three-bedroom apartment

PHOTOS BY DICK LEWIS

Renting the apartment was lucrative for a while. It was the fastest and easiest way to earn money with the least amount of energy. It afforded me time to lunch, shop, visit museums or do whatever I wanted. The big fringe benefit of the shootings was, they always had the best food for the crew, the models and me. At the end of the shoot, they'd break the set and leave the food and the flowers. I often shared the food with neighbors. Occasionally, my apartment reminded me of a funeral parlor, because of the abundance of beautiful flowers that were left.

One of the magazines left fifteen pounds of grapes, and I didn't know what to do with them, so I called a friend, who offered a recipe for wine. After buying all the ingredients, I think it would have been cheaper to buy a bottle of wine. They forgot to tell me, not to cap the bottles. Within a couple of weeks, I had created bombs that exploded all over my kitchen. Fortunately, I was not at home when the bottles exploded. There was this juicy, gooey, sticky stuff all over the kitchen and it took days to clean up. I quickly threw the balance of the bottles down the incinerator for fear of another attack.

A nudie magazine also shot in my apartment. I asked one of the nude models to answer the door when the messenger arrived with a package. When she opened the door. "Wow! Wow!" He scratched his head and walked away as she closed the door.

The New York Daily News featured my apartment as "A Familiar Setting." *Essence* also featured it as a glamorous setting. It was also a perfect apartment for parties and boy, did I have parties. I survived on location rentals for two years, until I became tired of strangers traipsing through my apartment and wearing out the furniture.

Without an income, I had to make some serious decisions regarding some material items that I took for granted. Surviving was at the top of my list. At first, I thought I couldn't live without daily delivery of the newspaper, fresh cut flowers delivered twice a week and dear Mabel, the lady who cleaned my apartment three times a week.

I regretted having all those silver candlestick holders that everyone gave me for a house warming. They were looking tarnished and I would have to polish them. I didn't like it, but life had to go on.

I woke up one morning and realized I didn't have any money...
...I was broke. I sold my precious furniture, my baby grand piano, jukebox, Louis XVI desk, oriental rugs and all those silver candleholders in order to pay the rent. I was totally depressed. I was left with four couches , an etagere, dining table and chairs and two walls of mirrors in the living room.

One day a guest commented, "You don't have any furniture."

"Who do you know that have four couches in their living room?" It's the minimal look.

I sat on the arm of one of the couches for a very long time, just staring in the mirror. I stared directly in my eyes, just to get in touch with my inner feelings. To look directly into my eyes was the most difficult thing to do. It brought me back to reality.

I was in an awful state of mind, but I became a better person from that horrible experience. I knew deep down inside that there was a light at the end of the tunnel.

I had to do something quickly. My friend Latease introduced me to her friend, who owned a Temp Agency. I was embarrassed, because I had previously had a high profile and now I had no money. I figured, if I went to an agency where they didn't know me, it would be less humiliating. I felt so desperate and alone.

The moment I arrived at Georgie Girl Temp office, Latease's friend asked, "How are you, Jon?" I almost sank through the floor and died three deaths. I didn't want anyone to see me in that predicament.

Then she asked, "How many words do you type?"

I was such a nervous wreck, I said, "Forty minutes per word."

I quickly corrected myself and told her, "Forty words per minute." She insisted that I take a typing test. The irony of working for a Temp Agency was my earnings would only covered my food and entertainment. I had a very large three-bedroom apartment on the east side of Manhattan to support. Working temp was almost a joke, but I didn't laugh when I received the checks. The day I signed on, I asked them not to send me too far north, south or west or insist I wear a jacket, because that required dry cleaning and that cost money. I wanted to limit the area, because I didn't want to spend carfare or a lot of time getting there.

My first assignment was with Equitable Life Insurance Company, where I worked in three different departments. One day, I was asked to make four copies of everything that I typed. I thought it was going to be easy, until I tried to squeeze the paper in a Selectric typewriter. I pushed and pulled, but to no avail, I just couldn't get it to work. Eventually, I looked up and discovered the manager had been observing me from his desk. So, I walked over to one the other secretaries and asked, "Could you show me how to get the paper in the typewriter?" She laughed and helped. "While you're at it, could you show me how to change the margins, because every typewriter is so different?" I managed to get through that day.

I often skipped out of the office, pretending to go to the men's room. Then I crossed the avenue to visit an A&R producer at a record company. I wasn't gone long enough to be missed. When I returned no one was the wiser.

One of my jobs, was to answer problem calls for the company. I had absolutely no patience when answering the phone. I didn't want to hear long drawn out stories, of their complaints, because I had things to do. "Edit! Get to the point!" was my response.

The third assignment could have been very embarrassing for me, because I recognized several names on my boss's Rolodex and hoped none of them would call. I feared they might recognize my voice. I didn't want anyone to know I was that desperate. The personnel manager wanted to hire me, but I turned him down, because I knew that was not what I wanted to do for the rest of my life. And, besides, working as a temp couldn't pay my rent. I called my friend Kiko in Chicago and told her I was temping.

"Why don't you get a job that pays you instead of you paying them?" she responded.

I could always count on Kiko to be witty.

My next assignment was with *Newsweek* magazine where I worked as a receptionist for all the big wigs, such as Katherine Graham, the publisher, and Ed Kosner, the editor. I never said anything to anyone, but saw everything. I only answered their phones after the tenth ring; therefore, I had a lot of time on my hands.

I used my time wisely, for instance I wrote, '*Touchin' My Body*', a song that I used in my cabaret act with two backup singers. We performed all over town and thought we were cute with a little choreography.

One day, Georgie Girl Temp Agency called at nine o'clock in the morning and asked me to assist on a project at the French Bank on Wall Street. They pleaded with me, because they didn't have anyone else. Lord knows, I didn't want to go. When I arrived an hour later, Miss Manager with a very thick French accent reprimanded me:

"You are late!"

"So, dock me," I responded.

She rubbed me the wrong way; because it wasn't my fault the agency didn't give me enough notice. I was assigned to type lots of money exchange forms that I didn't understand. But I stuck with it, I was busy, didn't even take a lunch break. I hate numbers on a typewriter, because they are so far away from everything. At four o'clock, I walked over to Miss French Manager and asked her to sign me out for four-thirty. With her thick French accent,

"It is not fur-turty,"

"Lady, I didn't even come up for air today."

"Are you comin' to..ma..ho?," she asked.

"No, honey, I quit."

Georgie Girl was furious with me, when they found out what I did. They didn't offer me another assignment for a while.

I knew my days were numbered at Georgie Girl. My last assignment was at the Urban League. When I walked into the office I said to myself, "Oh, my God! So many Colored people." I was only joking to myself, since that was the first place where there was a cluster of one type of people.

I was amongst a very large secretarial pool of twenty. I had to make this a fun experience, because it was going to be my last stop on the temporary train. I had a goal. I negotiated with my supervisor to leave an hour earlier, if I didn't take lunch. He agreed, which gave me time to start designing and sewing my smart little fashion collection at home.

One day, my supervisor asked me to take a letter. All the secretaries laughed, because they thought I couldn't do it. I recall watching Ann Sothern's TV Show, Suzy the Secretary, from my early television years. She always crossed her legs and licked the point of her pencil.

"Where's your pad?" he asked.

"Oh yes, my pad."

I asked one of the secretaries to hand me a pad and they laughed again. They didn't know that I had been transcribing lyrics from records for years, which was good practice for taking shorthand. I had my own code and managed to record every word he dictated.

As I began to type on a Selectric typewriter, nothing appeared on the page. I asked one of the secretaries what is the problem? She told me I was missing an element. I thought she was referring to me as a little loose in the head.

"What's an element?" I asked.

I was relieved to discover that she referring to the little ball that hits the ribbon and makes the impression on the paper. After fixing that problem I began typing again and nothing appeared.

"What's going on now?"

"It's your ribbon, you have to change the ribbon."

"Child, I don't know nuthin' 'bout changin' no ribbons. I only know how to type forty words per minute."

One of the young secretaries changed the ribbon and made my life easier. Then she asked if I had just taken a typing class.

"Yes, I took a typing class in the eighth grade on an old manual typewriter. That's where we had to really bang the keys to make an impression." The modern secretaries just lay their finger over the keys and it's like magic, everything happened. I worked at it the old-fashioned way.

After I finished the letter, all the secretaries threw their hands up and applauded. You can't judge a book by its cover. I had the last laugh. Once that was settled, I was asked to correlate a bunch of papers. I spread the papers all over the floor and they laughed at me again. Spreading them on the floor was logical for me.

I began to miss the fashion industry. I knew from the day I began temping at Urban League, that my goal was to start my own small design company again. Do you remember when I started, I negotiated with my supervisor to leave an hour earlier? That hour made the difference. I quit on September 20, 1979, to follow my dream.

I wanted to have a useful life, filled with the joy of doing what I enjoyed the most, and that was designing from my heart. It was a trying time and I had rolled with the punches. In the arts, versatility is often the name of the game.

Gordon Parks once said, "I do many things, just not all at the same time."

After six years of ups and downs as a performer in cabarets around town, and my short stint as a Temp, I felt my creative juices flowing. I was inspired to design again.

CHAPTER SEVENTEEN

Return to

Designing Again

Nancy Benson, the fashion editor of *Cosmopolitan*, said, I am only creative when working for myself. She also told me that I had to start designing again. Nancy was very supportive of my talent for many years. She believed in me when no one else did, and I thank her for that. In the fashion business, "You're only as good as your next idea." Through thick and thin, Nancy always came to see my collections and if I didn't have a collection, we'd have lunch, because, "We just L...O...V...E to lunch." That was one of our favorite expressions.

Katherine Stephens and my mother also encouraged me to return to designing. So, within two weeks, I had designed a half-dozen dresses. I called my friend, Marcos Oxsendhandler, the illustrator at *The Daily News* to invite him to lunch. We had been friends since our early days at FIT. Fortunately, Liz Rittersporn, a fashion reporter, picked up the phone and asked what was I doing. I quickly told her, I have started designing again.

She was delighted and then set up an appointment to see my collection. After reviewing my fashion, she sent Marcos to my apartment to sketch two of the gowns for the fashion pages. Liz's article appeared in *The Daily News* the next day, "Jon Haggins' Original Material." That was a day after I quit the secretary job. I can't imagine how those secretaries reacted when they saw the article. I was that mystery man that dashed through their space.

I invited ten friends to a mini-fashion show in my apartment on September 21, 1979, and served white wine and cookies. Oh, how the ladies love white wine and cookies. Some of my loyal fans were Katherine Stephens, Barbara Barrows, Nancy Benson, and Dolly Reade Borgia. They purchased several items on the spot, and that created an instant infusion of much-needed cash. Katherine Stephens told me she thought the occasion was so chic.

Nancy Benson from *Cosmopolitan* magazine featured one of my designs. That was the beginning of my return to fashion. And the start of something BIG! My fashions have been featured on eighty-five pages and seven *Cosmopolitan* magazine covers during my career as a designer.

Lynn Cohen owner of Off-Broadway Boutique disappointed me on my first visit. She told me she wanted something new and that I didn't have it. I returned home and wept. I didn't know what to do; I had considered returning to the cabaret world.

I called Beverly Madden of Turtle Green Boutique the next day. I'd known her since her early days at De Pinna Department Store. She loved and bought several styles, which restored my confidence. After Beverly purchased several styles, I mustered up enough courage to call Lynn for another appointment. I was determined to sell her; she bought several styles that time and the rest is history. I think her mood during my first visit affected her buying spirit. It only proves that you have to try and try again until you win. Lynn displayed my fashions in the windows, and she sold every dress that she bought. Barbara Leary, the buyer at Bonwit Teller, also bought several styles, as well as other specialty stores.

Fashion is such a volatile business, and everything changes from moment to moment and day to day. Ora Witte, my vocal coach, was right when she said," All you need is drive and perseverance."

Here is a tip for reaching dress buyers: call them early in the morning to set up appointments. That's before they ventured into the market. Buyers can usually be reached between 8:45 am and 9:30 am, and then again between 4:30 pm 'til 5 pm. Large stores have the same schedule. If the first call doesn't do the trick, call them until they confirmed an appointment. I biked to their offices with a sack of dresses on my back because I was determined to sell.

Another one of my former buyers, Barbara Weiss, from Snooty Hooty Boutique, set up an appointment at Joanne Roaman's JSR Buying Office. Joanne's office assists many small boutiques with fashion direction. She was also responsible for finding manufacturers with the right merchandise for their boutique.

My fashions were soft and drapey and very economical. For example, if a dress cost $600.00 and you have it for ten years; it only costs $60.00 per year or pennies per day. My fashions are for a woman to enjoy, as I said before, my dresses are like lovers — you never lend them out.

As I was beginning to re-start my fashion business. Everything began to happen simultaneously. Joanne Roman from JSR Buying Office was instrumental in introducing me to her friends at Dan Lee, a manufacturer of Mother of the Bride Evening dresses. She thought it might be a perfect fit. I met with them and asked if they would allowed me to show my small designer collection from their empty showroom. They agreed, and we confirmed our arrangements. My friend, Andrea Skinner stopped by one day, and looked around, then said, "You will never last here, because MOB's (mother of the bride dresses) is not your style."

I called Grandad in Sanford Florida, as I was returning to the fashion business. He told me he wasn't feeling well, so I called Mother and asked her to bring him to New York. I also reminded her of how generous he was to take care of me for six and a half years when she was unable to. Mother listened and thought about it for a moment.

Then rearranged her schedule, so she could drive to Sanford. She drove because Grandad was afraid to fly.

Everything began to happen simultaneously. The very same week I began working as a designer for Dan Lee, I had also scheduled my last Cabaret Act at West Bank Café. The opening night was very emotional. I began with a little patter regarding my childhood in Sanford. I reflected on my Grandad not feeling well and coming to New York. Then I began to sing, "Wish I was A Child," suddenly a flow of uncontrollable tears streamed down my face during the first verse. The band members were puzzled as I turned toward them during the musical break. I quickly pulled myself together and finished the song stronger than ever.

That was the first time I revealed personal emotions in front of an audience. I talked with several friends after the set. One of them asked if I was having a nervous breakdown.

"Oh, no, that was just a little 'Judy Garland'."

But what happened was real and I felt deeply emotional. I was overcome with love for my Grandad.

Mother returned to New York with Grandad and checked him in a hospital. She wanted to make sure he was taken care of and would have a speedy recovery. I visited him almost every day. After Grandad was discharged, he stayed with Mother for a short while. Mother was overbearing and they didn't get along, so he called me to pick him up. He wanted to stay with me for a while. I was more than happy to share my apartment with him. I lived on the 17th floor. The apartment had floor-to-ceiling windows. Grandad was afraid to go near the windows. I gave him the keys to the apartment if he wanted to go out for fresh air. However, he chose not to. I think he was intimidated by the big city. He frequently called me at work during the day to check in. When I returned home in the evenings, we talked for hours. Those were the happiest few days of my life. We spent a little precious time together and I was delighted to have him stay with me. I'm sure he also enjoyed our time together, but he yearned to return home. I told him, "There will be no reason for me to return to Sanford after you pass. What matters now, is that I love you."

"I love you too, Wesley."

He stayed with me for a week, then bought a train ticket to return home.

Several years later my phone rang in the middle of the night, actually, it was 3:00 am. My bedroom was dark. I had finally fallen into a peaceful sleep. Then reached for the phone without turning on a light. It seemed as if I had been asleep for hours. My eyes were still closed as I stumbled in the dark to stop that annoying ringing noise.

"Hello, hello. What is it? What's going on? What could be so important at this hour?" I listened for a minute with one ear pressed against the receiver. It was my mother. She called to inform me of Grandad's death. I had only spoken to Grandad a few days earlier. I promised that I would visit him for Christmas.

I hung up the phone, walked into the living room, sat on the arm of a sofa, and stared out the window at the full moon that brightly lit the sky. I began reflecting on our years together. I gazed at the concrete skyline of Manhattan and began to cry. I cried for hours. I recalled this fantastic and inspirational man. My heart was broken and missed him already. No bandage could ever cover the pain and emptiness of missing Grandad.

Uncle Robert called and said, "You of all people should be there."

"No, I made my pact with Grandad and I'm not going."

My first six and half-and-a-half years with Granddad, a "single parent," were the years that largely inspired and formed me. Those years also inspired me for the "Yes I Can' approach to life. He was my guardian angel. With his passing, Sanford, Florida, would never be the same. My family didn't know I made a pact with Grandad. He understood that I was not going to return. Funerals are for the living, and I didn't have to prove my love, or anything to anyone, because he knew how very special he was to me. He knew I loved him very much. After carefully thinking about our conversation when he was in New York, I kept my promise and did not return to Sanford for his funeral. I wanted to remember him as I last saw him. It was his passing that I never wanted to witness. Granddad passed away September 1, 1982, two weeks before his 84th birthday. With his passing, Sanford, Florida, would never be the same. They had lived together for me, and were wrapped and tied together in a bundle and laid away to rest.

My design position at Dan Lee only lasted four months. The owner came into my office and said, "I hate to be the bearer of bad news, but you're fired." When business isn't good in the garment business, the designer is the first to go; it's never the production man or the salespeople. Designers get a lot of abuse from the manufacturer and that's why I preferred to be independent, therefore I could control my destiny. I took this with a grain of salt and quickly packed my bags.

Susan Stack, a friend, stopped by and offered to help wheel my rack of samples to my apartment. We stopped on the corner of thirty-fifth Street and Seventh Avenue for her to make a phone call. Suddenly, two young men approached me, pretending to recognize me from Studio Fifty-Four. That was a distraction for them to grab my garment bag of samples. I tussled with one of the guys for a moment, until he produced what appeared to be a knife. I released the sample bag, then he ran off into the crowd. I was speechless. My mouth just hung open. I couldn't believe what was happening in broad daylight. Susan and I stood there on the crowded corner for a few minutes just to catch our breath. I spotted a policeman and told him what happened.

"What were they wearing?" the officer asked.

"How would I know, I'm not their designer!"

The strangest coincidence of the day was; that I had just returned from the bank and had lots of cash on me, thank God the robbers didn't rob me of the cash. The sample bag contained a bunch of abstract dresses that appeared to be rags. The dresses conformed to the woman's body, once she had them on. One would have to have a road map to understand those garments.

After they robbed me I felt nothing. I walked home and dropped off the rack, then dashed to a party. I blocked out the incident on the avenue until I returned home later that evening, then I went into shock.

The very next day, I met a friend for lunch on Seventh Avenue.

But when I arrived at the very spot where I was robbed, I freaked and became very paranoid. It took quite a while after that incident to adjust to passing that spot.

Several months after I was fired from Dan Lee, I was honored with a Harvey's Bristol Crème Black Designer's Award, along with twelve other designers. The show was held in the auditorium at The Fashion Institute of Technology. I invited several friends, they wore my soft drapey dresses that glided over their bodies. Myra Lee wore a wine-colored silk pleated silk chiffon off-the-shoulder dress. I asked her to pull it up before sitting because silk does not retain pleats. She didn't listen. Myra stood up after the show, and the dress retained the shape of her fanny.

There were 1,000 guests in the audience. I was very excited about receiving the award. Each designer showed twelve fashions. One of my models' walked out onto the stage and quickly turned to show off the dress when suddenly her dress blew up over her head. She stole the show. The entire audience stood with a roar and applauds, "Bravo." My fashions were a Wow Experience!

Mother and I at the FIT Awards show, 2005

Ray and Pat Cortell, long-time friends who owned a very large wholesale travel agency, was also in the audience. Ray called the next night and asked if he could financially back me and make me the next Gloria Vanderbilt through public relations and advertising.

"Do you want to start tomorrow? Is the Pope Catholic?" I asked.

Ray was so impressed by the crowd's reaction to the show, He asked me to put together a business proposal for a fashion business. We quickly got all the legal stuff out of the way and we opened the company in July 1980. The next thing on our itinerary was to present a holiday fashion show in August, which gave us only four weeks to produce the clothes.

Ray asked. "Is it possible to get everything produced in time?"

"Of course," I responded as an eternal optimist.

My sister Carolyn had separated from her husband and had three children to support. I asked her to work with me in the new Jon Haggins Division. She didn't have any professional fashion training, but I had faith in her. I just knew she was capable of anything she wanted to achieve. Isabel Serrano, a sample maker, took her under her wings and worked with her until she got the hang of constructing a garment. We started Carolyn off with very simple cotton striped outfits and she gradually worked her way up to more complicated items with zippers.

The first major article of clothing that Carolyn constructed was a forest green silk chiffon gown with six layers. Each layer measured four hundred inches in circumference. The layers had to be finished with a thin baby hem. After she completed it, I asked her to cut it off and start over, because I didn't like the way it was finished. She re-hemmed the gown with a tiny baby hem to my satisfaction. I don't think she'll ever forgive me, because she had to stay late into the night. After a short time, Carolyn became my number one sample maker and my assistant.

Everyone's energy was frantic. It was great to be working with all my friends. We were a great team. Joan Shepard worked as my PR lady. She ran around the studio yelling, "I love it, I love it."

The strangest thing: Ray's father always arrived early each day and would read everyone's mail before it was delivered to the addressee.

Helen Gurley sent a letter that he read before I arrived at the office. I thought that was invasive.

The show was titled, "Jungle Fever." The models strutted to a soundtrack of birds, hyenas, waterfalls, elephant calls, the roar of lions, and other sounds of the jungle. The first model appeared in a very skimpy little animal print, nothing bathing suit, that fit the mood of the show. She carried a basket of bananas that she offered to the audience. Each guest received a bottle of ruby red nail polish that was labeled 'Jungle Fever'. It was the first time I had ever designed hand-knitted garments. My favorite gown was that forest green chiffon bat-wing top with an enormous circular skirted gown that Carolyn made. That gown closed the show. WWD called the show "Congo Conceit." Elsa Klensch from CNN TV and Marion Etoile Watson from Channel Five featured the show.

Marion asked, what kind of woman do I design for? "A woman with a heavy pocketbook." The show was held in a small space, but it was a very happy time for me.

Ray Cortell re-introduced me to the fashion industry with weekly ads in WWD. I hated the ads. The advertising company didn't have any fashion experience; their business had always been travel-related. Fashion is a very specialized business and has to be treated as such. Ray didn't understand why I felt as I did; after all, the owner of the ad agency was his best friend. I refuse to attend the ad meeting because I didn't see the point.

Ray organized a trip for Pat and me to go to Munich, to introduce my designs at Moda Voka. Moda Voka is the German Fashion Week. Pat arrived earlier than I, so she met me at the airport. I was extremely hungry upon arriving, so we dashed off to a Bavarian Restaurant. I did not know one word of German, and no one spoke a word of English. I had to become resourceful, so I picked up a menu and walked from table to table until I saw something I like. Everyone was very helpful, they helped me identify the items on the menu. I kept my finger on each item until our waitress arrived. There's no fool like a hungry fool. I ordered by grunting and pointing to each dish.

The very next day, the Public Relations lady of the Bayerischer Hoff Hotel invited us for tea and a fashion show. The Bayerischer is a traditional five-star hotel, located on Maximillian Statsa. She asked, where had we been. Pat blurted out, "The California Club." The PR lady looked surprisingly shocked. Several days later we passed 'The California Club' and discovered it was a sleazy hooker palace. Oh, my God! What a first impression. We had visited the Cadillac Club, which was a Black Officers Club.

We thanked the PR lady at the end of our visit then departed the hotel, then crossed the street to the American Express office to get some cash from Pat's Gold American Express Card. Pat handed her card to the agent. He took out a little black book and looked up her number, then looked up at her and grabbed a scissor. He cut her card into itsy bitsy pieces. Ray had stopped the card because he was upset with Pat. Pat totally freaked out; I remained calm, overtly.

"Let's go back to our hotel and call Ray. I'm sure he'll rectify everything," I assured her. And he did. He arranged with the hotel to advance us some money and to forward the bill to him. We spent the rest of the week in peace and money.

We jumped on streetcars all over town without paying, because no one came to collect. We didn't know that public transportation works on the honor system. Oktoberfest festivities were in full swing. People come from around the world to drink large steins of beer, socialize and devour lots of bratwursts. We also ventured out on the double-looped cyclone. As we were returning to the starting point on the ride, "Thank God! This is over, " Pat yelled out.

I whipped out another ticket and said, "One more time!"

Pat told me that she was having the best time of her life. She got a chance to relax away from her marital problems. Her marriage was on the rocks and she needed a distraction. While we were talking with a group of young people in a local bar, Pat met a young man that charmed her. She was free for the first time to do whatever she wanted.

I ventured out one night to a small local bar. While sitting at the bar, someone called out my name from across the room. He recognized me from the back of my head. He was someone, I knew from New York. The most amazing thing about that experience was, that I never expected to see anyone I know, especially in a small bar in Munich.

Several days later, I decided to visit two friends in Koln, Germany.

The hotel concierge suggested I take the train up the Rhine River, for a scenic view of castles, on top of the hills. Unfortunately, I had only slept for an hour, before the train was scheduled to depart. I dashed out of the hotel and hailed a taxi to the train station. The train was departing as the taxi driver and I ran as fast as we could with my bags. I yelled, "Stop! Stop!" It was to no avail because German trains always depart on time. I called my friends Dietrich and Igor in Koln to inform them that I would be on the next train.

I wasted no time boarding the next train. I sat in a compartment facing forward and immediately fell asleep. When I woke up, the train was going backward. I thought I was losing my mind. Thank God, an English professor was sitting next to me and clarified the train situation, for instance: why the trains pull into a station one way and continue their journey in the opposite direction. He also explains the history of the castles and cruise boats on the Rhine.

My friends were waiting at the station when I arrived. They greeted me and drove me to their apartment, which was located in the heart of town, near the historic Dom Church. They also invited Waltrad, who I had previously met in New York. She was born on the same day and year as I, so I called her sister.

Dietrich had confirmed dinner reservations for us in Bonn. Time quickly passed as Dietrich told us we only had fifteen minutes to get to our dinner reservation. He drove one hundred and thirty miles per hour on the Autobahn. My heart remained in my throat for two days. All heads turned as we entered the five-star restaurant. The owner rushed over to Dietrich to inquire as to who I was. We returned to Koln after dinner and hung out at a local bar, before retiring for the evening.

The next morning was an adventure for me. I wanted to have a local experience. I insisted on going to the bakery alone to purchase some bread. I asked the shopkeeper for funf pumpernickels (five pumpernickels) and then paid with Deutsche Marks. I had no idea what the bread cost. She gave me some change and I left the shop. My twenty-four-hour stay ended too quickly. I wish I could have spent more time with my friends. However, I had other obligations in New York. I truly enjoyed my short visit. My friends said, "You have to come back and stay at our home in Sardinia." It took me twenty years before I decided to return. Unfortunately, they had just sold their home in Sardinia.

Upon my return to my New York office, Marion Etoile Watson and Joan Shepard were discussing how their family came to America. They were in a very serious discussion regarding the slave boats, the plantations, and the total experience.

"Jon, how did you get here?" Marion asked.

"Lufthansa."

Because I had just returned from Germany.

I knew my remark would lighten up the mood. We laughed for twenty minutes.

Eartha Kitt visited my studio in 1980 and bought a gown with a slit on the left side. That was her trademark. Pat Cortell approached her and asked about her confrontation with Lady Bird Johnson. Eartha didn't want to re-live the unfortunate incident where Lady Bird Johnson invited Miss Kitt to her 'Women Doers' Luncheon on January 28, 1968, for a discussion of what women could do to help eradicate crime on the streets.

After Pat asked her that question, Eartha quickly walked out of the studio and headed toward the elevator. She didn't want to discuss the incident, because it was too painful to address. Pat ran after her and apologized. Eartha accepted her apology and returned for her fitting. The next time I saw Eartha, she was performing her latest disco song titled, "Where is My Man," at studio 54. She looked radiant.

My spring fashion show was held at the Plaza Hotel in the Terrace Room. It was part of Eleanor Lambert's Design Group presentation. I introduced my easy, crushable, packable cotton jersey separates and I talked about how they were to be worn.

My 'Heat Wave' summer fashion show was held in FIT's Katy Murphy auditorium. I featured lots of pink: 'Think Pink' was the theme. I gifted the audience with a bottle of Pink nail polish. A recording of Marilyn Monroe singing 'Heat Wave' and the sound of an airplane taking off created an aura of a holiday in the sun. The show opened with thirteen models sashaying on the stage wearing lots of packable, cotton-knit, striped travel clothes with matching travel bags.

My favorite designs were made of silk chiffon and silk organza. They were perfect choices for the summer show. A Brazilian Bahiana woman inspired the white organza gown. The gown was designed with cascading ruffles that plunged to the waist, and a billowy, bouffant skirt. The model held a large umbrella, high above her head. The umbrella was covered with a layer of white silk chiffon. The model pulsated her hips and danced to the audience's delight. I closed the show with a cerise color organza gown with a décolleté neckline to the waist. It also had cascading circular ruffles that embellished her face. Let me not forget, it was backless with a very large bouffant skirt. Nancy Benson, featured those two gowns in *Cosmopolitan* magazine.

Elsa Klensch from CNN TV asked for a sound bite regarding the collection. I looked straight into the camera and said, "My clothes are sexy like me. Don't you think?" She said, "Cut."

Ray spoke with Lufthansa Airline, regarding a cross-promotion of a ten-cities tour across America. Lufthansa could promote their airline and have a drawing for a free ticket around the world. Jon Haggins Inc. would sell the fashionable, travel packable that a woman could take anywhere for a weekend. The kit included everything except personals. AMC Buying office was gung-ho for the idea. They wanted to place the kit in all of their stores, but in the end, they decided not to go forward with the promotion.

Jon Haggins Designs – Diva gowns, 1981

Bahia gown

Bahiana woman, 2016

189

Ray rented a showroom at 530 Seventh Avenue in January 1981. It's my favorite designer building. My 'Sophisticated Lady' Spring fashion show was held in Parson's School of Design auditorium. Bill Cunningham popped backstage and took a few pictures before the show. It was a very exciting day for me because I hired a trio to play live jazz for the show. For the finale, I walked onto the stage and sang 'Sophisticated Lady' as the models paraded out. Well, that drove Ray and his family insane. The whole family was furious with me and said, "We're not going to support your singing career." Ray didn't understand the originality of the show. He pulled the plug and closed my business in April 1981. He used the excuse that the fashion business was just too expensive for his pocketbook.

Another thing I learned about working with friends — is you don't. I was sabotaged by what I thought were friends. I felt let down by the very people I trusted. They turned on me at the end. I even went out of my way to make larger samples to fit the model, so that she could earn a salary to support herself and her kid.

Ray continued to use my name after we parted. He told me he invented 'Jon Haggins'. I retained a lawyer to rectify that situation and proved him wrong. I was born with my name and I incorporated Jon Haggins Inc. in 1966, long before I knew him. I wanted nothing to do with the Cortells' after that. I wanted peace of mind, no more craziness that surrounded the Cortell Group.

After Ray pulled the plug and closed my company. I was depressed for a short while until my friend Katherine Stephens called to say, "I happen to have a little extra money that you can use to start your business." That perked me up and certainly boosted my ego, it got me going again.

My mother said, "Don't get tied up with another crazy maniac manufacturer. They'll wear you out. You should wait and surely you'll get what you want."

CHAPTER EIGHTEEN

On My Own Again

Nancy Benson phoned to inform me that she was featuring one of my designs in the September 1981 issue of *Cosmopolitan* magazine. That was my jump-start; it gave me something to sell. I quickly made a copy of the gown that I had previously designed during my relationship with Ray. I packed the gown in my backpack and rode my bike to several buying offices and small stores. I offered the stores an editorial credit in *Cosmopolitan* magazine if they bought the dress. I was amazed that I sold $40,000 of that dress in two days. I was a happy camper.

I had received a lot of press attention during the ten months with Ray, so I had to keep the momentum going. I opened my second design studio at 260 West 35th Street on the 13th floor on July 6, 1981. The 13th floor was most appealing because there was a large 49 by 12-foot terrace on the front space. That's where I spent weekends planting hibiscus and ficus trees and colorful petunias. I asked the landlord to paint my front door a bright fire-engine red. He showed up with a murky color that I hated. Dee Macklin, my salesman said, "That's not even bright brown."

I used my imagination to design every inch of the 5,000 square feet. It was a smash if I must say so. I included lots of double doors that were adorned with gold-plated latches. I was inspired by the Loretta Young show from yesteryear, where she entered a room through double doors. A large mirror on the back wall reflected the outdoor terrace. The floor-through space was lined with windows on three sides, which allowed cross ventilation. The studio included a private office, a salesman's office, a reception area, a showroom, two closets, a kitchen, and a very large design room that I converted into a space for presenting my fashion shows. That was my first experience designing a space. I guess if you have an eye for design, you can design anything. All it takes is a little imagination.

I returned to the fashion scene with a new design studio and more energy than ever. Carolyn, Isabel Serrano, and Dee Macklin worked with me until there was a cash flow. I could not have gotten a more generous pack of people when I started on my own again. Carolyn was very supportive and very talented as my assistant. She understood the construction of my designs.

The studio was a great space for shows, parties, meetings, and working. Some of my happiest times were spent in that loft. Having independence and my own company allowed me lots of freedom and the best working environment. I didn't have to answer to anyone, and I had complete control of my ideas. Once the samples were made and sold, we worked with a terrific contractor to produce the collection.

My mother was always there with her love and support each time I started my own business. The most important thing she said was, "Don't do something and hate it. Do everything with PASSION.

As guests arrived at my studio, they were immediately attracted to the brightly colored hibiscus, petunia, and ficus trees that lined the outside terrace. My studio transported everyone away from the traditional showroom on Seventh Avenue. We often served lunch and held parties on the terrace. Two TV shows featured my fashions on the terrace.

George Parker from Dupont, once told me that he arrives in his office at 7 am. I asked, "Why?" He explained that it allowed him time to have a leisurely coffee and read the paper, so by 9 am, he was ready to rock and roll. That set my brain to ticking, if I practice what he preached, perhaps I too could have a jump on the day. I followed his advice and arrived at my office at 8 am, checked the mail, read the trade paper, and watered the flowers on my terrace. So, when my staff arrived, I was more than ready to start my day. Owning my studio was very inspirational because there was always something to do, such as creating new fashions, sales, promotion, bookkeeping, and public relations. Never bored, always thinking about how I could make things better and more fruitful. A dollar saved is a dollar earned.

I approached several designers in the loft building and suggested that if we unite, we could promote our building as the Designer Building. I told them we'd become a stronger force if we pool our money for a full-page ad in *WWD*. The cost for a full page was $4,000, however, it would only cost $125.00 per designer if we united. Uniting was the most difficult concept to convey to all those creative people.

They were skeptical and thought someone was trying to take advantage of them. It took weeks to convince the first ten designers to participate. Once the response was positive, then everyone wanted in for the next season. The plan allowed buyers, stylists, and editors to make one sweep through the building.

Ted Hardin photographed my beautiful fashions, and I converted his photos into large promotional posters. Then hired Jim Rogers to plaster them on empty walls up and down every major avenue in Manhattan. It was the most effective way to advertise

My designs, 1982 and 1983

and far cheaper than advertising in a magazine or newspaper. It was the same concept that I used during my cabaret days. The photographs featured me frolicking with several beautiful models wearing my fashions.

Summer '82 Evening Fashions Tuesday January 26th
260 West 35th Street NYC 10001 13th floor 12 noon
R.S.V.P. enclose card (212)564-2897

I used the watermelon photograph that Ted took several years before for a Summer Fashion Poster campaign and an invitation to my summer fashion collection. One buyer told me she carried the postcard invitation in her purse for weeks, and said, if I had that much humor, she had to see my collection.

Left to right: Olivia Chapman and Suzi Gilder model my fashions, 1982;
Olivia Chapman wore this copper gown to the Met Opening;
Plung dress – Suzi Gilder, 1983; Suzi modeling white cowl gown

Some of the slogans were:
If it's Sexy, if it's Glamorous, it's a Jon Haggins.
I'd flip for a Jon Haggins.
Jon Haggins fashions are Magic.
This is the man who dresses the stars, Jon Haggins.
To be without a Jon Haggins is to be without.
This is Jon Haggins, his fashions have Pizzazz.

I received instant recognition that brought back some of the old luster that I had been known for. Editors and buyers readily welcomed me back. Even my original designs continued to attract attention.

Ted and I thought if nine million people live in New York and at least one million walked the streets, and if only one hundred thousand remember the posters, then we've made our point. The posters got the attention of stylists, stores, and the general public. One day, I was

exiting the Coliseum on Columbus Circle and a homeless man yelled, "My main man, Jon Haggins." My friends laughed because they didn't understand what it meant. It meant everyone was paying attention.

Someone once asked, "What's the point of your poster?"

"What's the point of asking, since you noticed?"

Someone once told me that Calvin Klein thought it was tacky to plaster the walls with posters. A few years later I saw his posters plastered all over walls around the city and several other manufacturers followed suit.

Ted had been a great friend and photographer. He knew how to bring the best out of his subject. He also taught me everything I know about photography. Marcos Oxsendhandler from *The Daily News* once asked. " Is Ted your lover?"

"Absolutely not, I just adore him as a friend."

"Why do you ask?"

"Because you guys always work together."

Sarah Hardin, Ted's wife, and I threw a party for Ted at Area Disco. Ted's exhibit featured photographs of famous people from when he worked for *The Washington Post*. He was privy to photograph many international celebrities such as the Kennedy family, Sammy Davis Jr., Marilyn Monroe, and many others. Those photos were treasures.

My company began to expand quickly, so I hired an accountant and a lawyer, every company must have both. As our production was increasing, I hired additional staff to meet our deadlines. One of the most important things in business is following through with commitments. Timing is everything. If you can't meet your commitments, you are out of business.

My front staff included a sales person, who made appointments with buyers. I also hired two outside salesmen, who did a remarkable job selling my fashions and calling in the orders. My company was expanding at such a rapid pace that I had to employ several more people to execute the styles, for instance, five sample makers and an assistant designer.

Left to right:

Pink dresses, 1983

Jon and girls modeling

Fashions in 1982

*Norma and I at the
Met Museum Opening, 1983*

Norma Jean Darden worked with me as a public relations person for a year. We created Cerise, as our public relations contact. We needed a name that would last, no matter who the public relations person was. Whenever someone called and asked for Cerise, we immediately knew it was an RSVP for the fashion show. Cerise needed a last name, so we chose Stephens. Cerise also received fan mail from around the country. One day a young lady called to say Cerise was her schoolmate.

Everything was popping in the studio and I was working with a group of very creative people. The energy was running high and everyone was very enthusiastic and excited to be a part of the Jon Haggins Inc Studio.

Venturing into the market to find new fabrics was always a discovery. I was always excited to experiment with new fabrics. I loved draping the fabric on the mannequin or on a live model to create a new design. Working with my staff to create those designs was an amazing evolution where everything came to fruition. I was a touchy, feely designer. The fabrics inspired me to create the most extraordinary creations.

CHAPTER NINETEEN

ShowTime

I presented a Fall and Summer collection each year. And insisted on presenting a different theme for each show. The music always set the mood. Creating theme music required at least a week of reviewing lots of records and tapes. It's amazing how much energy and thought goes into preparing a fashion show: first I had to come up with a concept, select fabrics, sketch the dresses, and have my staff execute the ideas. Invitations had to be written, printed, and mailed. After the collection was completed. I had a go-see or model call, where I selected and fitted the models for the show.

I hired twelve models, two makeup artists, two hair stylists, and six dressers to create the right look for each show. I also hired a music coordinator. The cast of 23 people plus my design and showroom team of 11 helped produce the shows. Let me not forget, I scouted for jewelry accessories, shoes, and stocking to compliment my collection. The garments were paired with the accessories and the accessories were bagged and hung over the dress hanger.

All the machines and the cutting table were removed. The stage was assembled and the lights were hung. The design room was transformed into a theatre the night before the show.

At 3 pm, the day of my show, we were ready to rock and roll and greet the audience of buyers and editors. The music started and ding dong, show time. The first model walked on stage and others followed, until the end of the show. I step on the stage with several models for the finale and receive lots of applause. A lot of energy goes into preparing each collection. Once the show was over, I was thoroughly exhausted. I often felt a little depressed, because we had put a lot of energy into producing the show. It's just a mental thing, but that mode only lasted a very short while, it's like giving birth to a baby, I suppose. That's one thing I have not done or want to experience. Another way to describe the feeling was to let the air out of the balloon.

Once the show was over and the crowd disappeared into the afternoon. Somehow, everything goes back to normal.

Left to right: Angle wing gown, 1984; Jon Haggins Design –
Essence Magazine, 1986; Jon Haggins pink chiffon gown in
Cosmopolitan Magazine, 1981; Suzi Gilder models my design, 1982

It was always a relief when all was done. Then, I looked forward to receiving editorials in newspapers, magazines, and television coverage.

I was never bored, because there was always something to do, such as designing, helping with public relations, sales, bookkeeping, calling and reminding stores that the invoices were due, watering the flowers on the terrace, and helping to make an appointment for buyers to view my collection. I can usually determine the best styles within a few showings. There was never a dull moment from the time I arrived in the morning until I left in the evening.

I bought a large free-standing Christmas tree to celebrate the first Christmas Trim the Tree Party in the studio. I adorned it with colorful lights. Guests were requested to bring an ornament. The ornaments could be bought or homemade. It didn't matter. I also prepared food,

which included Turkey with all the trimmings.

Several stylists sorted out my fashions for TV shows and commercials, such as the Weight Watchers Commercial. I designed numerous dresses for the commercial. Lynn Redgrave was the first celebrity spokesperson for Weight Watchers. The commercials featured low-calorie meals and desserts with the tagline, 'This is living'.

I was invited to the set where they were shooting the commercial. The costume stylist was puzzled and didn't know how to cover one of the dresses, so I suggested buying several yards of red fabric to drape it around Lynn's shoulder. That would allow Lynn to easily remove it to reveal her gorgeous figure and say, "This is living." It worked.

While on the set, I observed a food stylist painting the food to liven it up. I had no idea that was done to make the food more appetizing. Lynn put the food in her mouth while taping, then spit it out when the cameras were off.

Debbie Allen called and made an appointment. She bought several gowns. The fun part for my staff was seeing her in the dresses. I also designed several dresses for *The Debbie Allen TV Variety Special*. She ordered two short snazzy gold and bronze dresses with a shirred bustier for her and Phylicia Rashad, her sister. They danced in Times

Square with a bunch of sailors. Debbie also wore another one of my designs, a long satin bias cut backless slip dress that slithered down her body with a scooped neckline in the front. It was one of her previous purchases. She performed some dirty dancing with Michael Phillip Thomas from *Miami Vice*. Debbie also appeared on the June 1990 cover of *Essence* magazine wearing that little black slip dress adorned with a pair of animal print sneakers.

Debi Allen in my fashion

Debbie also returned to my studio and bought several dresses, when she starred on Broadway in *'Sweet Charity'*. She claims she has the largest Jon Haggins designer dress collection. She invited me to her farewell party. As I entered the restaurant, someone asked if I had seen her?

"What is she wearing?," I asked.

She was wearing a green silk taffeta strapless catfish dress that hit her in all the right spots. It was the most beautiful dress I ever designed. She introduced me to Eddie Murphy and Gregory Hines. That was so much fun hanging out with the stars.

Debbie said, "Jon Haggins designs fit me like they were all made to order, and only for me. His use of fabric and color combined with his understanding of how to accentuate true femininity created the most unique, classic fashions, that are still the most beautiful you'll ever see on any Red Carpet."

I designed several gowns for the models on *'Star Search TV'*, Ed McMahon was the host. I also designed costumes for an off-Broadway show, *'Cry and Say No'*. The most fun was designing outfits for Marion Etoile Watson, when she hosted *'Good Day New York'*. Her first outfit was a peach-colored, crepe fishtail jacket with a black linen skirt. A messenger arrived at the end of each day to pick up an outfit for the next morning. It was hell working without any lead-time, but working with TV is an around-the-clock job to make it happen.

After working diligently for weeks, I flew to Chicago for a weekend. I was so preoccupied with the show, that I woke up in the middle of the night, thinking, "What's she wearing today? Does she have enough clothes to wear?" Unfortunately, the station ran out of money for her wardrobe, so my service was no longer needed.

There was always lots of excitement when celebrities such as Diana Ross, Helen Gurley Brown, Phylicia Rashad, Rue McClanahan, Linda Thorson, Kaity Tong, Rolanda Watts, Sheryle Lee Ralph, Grace Hightower rushed in and bought my latest designs. The day Diahann Carrol visited my studio, the entire block lit up with excitement. She was so glamorous. Everyone on the block was confused and thought Elizabeth Taylor had stopped by my studio. Obviously, both stars were glamorous, but I still don't understand how they confused those two ladies.

Helen Gurley Brown, editor in chief of *Cosmopolitan*, bought several of my designs and wore them on the *Tonight Show* with Johnny Carson. One of my designs was a little complicated, so she called and asked for a diagram of instructions. Those were a few of my early eighties dresses that I still love and they will never go out of style.

August 1983 was a hectic time because I was presenting my holiday fashion show. New York City had a 'Brownout' in the garment district. Fortunately, my block was not affected. Someone told me that a manufacturer brought his collection down to the sidewalk and set up shop for the buyers. That was very inventive. 'If they can't get to you, you come to them.'

I showed a collection of soft drapey silk daytime dresses in monotone prints and lace dresses combined with silk chiffon. I was also booked for a week-long singing engagement at Freddie's Cabaret. After the finale dress exited the stage, I dashed over to Freddie's Cabaret Club for a tech rehearsal. I lost my voice during rehearsal because I had worked through the night converting the design room into a theatre for the

Show finale, Jon and Christine Clements

fashion show. I ran out of the club after the voice check, hopped in a taxi, and headed home. Once at home, I immediately took an Epsom Salt bath and a two-hour power nap. I repeated the salt bath and did several pushups later, then I felt renewed. So, I dressed and walked out of my building, and hailed a taxi. The driver asked, "Aren't you Jon Haggins? I've seen your posters all around town."

The first show was fantastic. I was flying off the walls. I made each experience live for that moment and changed the patter for each audience. The waiters laughed, so I knew I was funny. After all, they get an opportunity to see everyone's act and it takes a lot to make them laugh.

Two young ladies sitting at a front table were talking as I began my patter. I simply stopped the show and looked directly at them, smiled, and said, "I'll wait." They buttoned their mouths and never uttered another word. After a week of singing the same old songs, I thought to myself, "Thank God! That's over. I don't have to sing those songs for a while."

The most interesting new experience for me was working with Soap Operas. Carr Garnett commissioned me to design special dresses for *As The World Turns*. Then he returned and requested four red taffeta Christmas bridesmaids' dresses. Working with Carr was a total pleasure because he knew exactly what he wanted.

Lee Austin, the costume designer for *One Life to Live*, also asked me to design twenty beautiful dresses for Deliah's fashion show, a character on the soap. She was having an opening of her first fashion collection in a very ritzy hotel. The actresses were fitted in my studio. My mother kept asking about her favorite character "Mimi."

On the day of the taping, the director wanted the actresses to instantly become runway models. He wanted them to glide across the stage. Unfortunately, he didn't understand the workings of a fashion show, so I stepped forward and directed. I just couldn't help myself. I said, "Let's get this thing rocking and rolling." I got everyone coordinated and stepping high. Peabo Bryson sang the new theme song over and over until everyone got it right. Can you imagine the royalties he received each time the show airs? Once everything was moving, I bid everyone farewell, because I was heading out to Fire Island for the weekend. The weekend was restful, exactly what I needed. It was simple, I read, dined, danced and relaxed, and took in a little sun on the beach.

A friend introduced me to Shelley Frankel, a jazz and body conditioning instructor at Clark Dance Center. Shelley had performed in many Broadway shows and understood the workings of the body. There were many stressful days in the fashion business and I needed a form of relaxation. She taught me discipline because whenever I felt I couldn't make it through the class, she'd steal my shoes. Then I'd have to stay until the end.

I recall one evening we were doing a warm-up exercise, suddenly I dropped to the floor because my back gave way. I returned the next day and took a tap and her jazz class, I felt renewed, with no more aches and pain. It was all about stretching and relaxing my muscles that made the difference.

'Tango Argentina' opened on Broadway. I was so inspired by the mood of the Tango dance and the fast feet. The Tango became the theme for my next fashion show. Arthur Murray Dance Studio advertised a free half-hour lesson. Norma and I signed up for a tango lesson to learn the basic steps. We knew we would use the dance for the opening of my fashion show. Our instructor asked, "Why do you only want to learn the tango?"

"Cause it's so dramatic."

While Norma and I were rehearsing the death drop in my studio the next day, she dipped to the floor and caused stress on my back. I was in serious pain. I rushed to a back specialist, who examined me and wrote a prescription, then told me to go home and rest.

"Can I ride my bike, should I bathe in Epsom Salt?" I asked.

"Absolutely not!" he explained.

So, I left his office with the prescription in hand and rode my bike to the drug store, and bought a large box of Epsom Salt. I arrived home and put a cup of salt in a bath of warm water. I was back to my old self the next day.

On the day of the Tango fashion show, the music was cued. Norma and I stepped on the stage with our arms elegantly wrapped gracefully around each other. She wore a light grey satin cowl back bias cut dress with a diagonal, circular flounce. I wore a black tuxedo with a black bow tie. The stage collapsed shortly after we steps on it. Norma lost her balance and landed in the lap of a fashion journalist, who was seated in the front row. Norma quickly gain her composure and stepped back on the stage and said, "I just wanted to get familiar with the audience." Then, the first model paraded out in a fluid blue jersey tango dress with a ruffle flounce. Followed by twelve models who moved to the tropical beat of the Tango music. They were wearing dresses and gowns of a variety of colorful fabrics. The dresses were long and lean, made of chiffon, tulle, sequins, satin, silk, lace, soft drapey jersey with ruffles and fly-away toile sleeves, and asymmetrically shaped dresses. The sequin gowns reminded me of a mermaid's skin. it was a show of energy, color, and excitement. The models moved to the rhythm of the rumba, the tango, and the samba. What an exciting time for me and the models. It was a very uplifting show and everyone felt Latin, at least for the day. The show was a tropical paradise. The tropics have always been an inspiration for my fashions. My Tango Show was one of my favorites. *Essence TV* also featured the show. My Tango Fashions started a trend that hit Fashion Avenue two years later.

Rosanna Scotto booked me as a guest on the Regis Philbin ABC-TV show. My models paraded down the stairs in Tango dresses. That was another opportunity for the models to practice the Tango. Bob Mackie called to congratulate me after the show. Norma asked, why don't you design clothes for the winter.

"Winter is a fur coat," I responded.

I arrived at my studio one morning and discovered it had been burglarized. One of the windows was wide open, a clothes rack was empty and a closet door was open. I always closed the closet doors at the end of the day, so I knew something was wrong. My entire Spring collection was stolen, one week before the show. They also took some audio equipment that I didn't want anyway. I was mad as hell, for about twenty minutes. Then I called a local hardware store to ask if they had bear traps. They told me bear traps were illegal. So, I did the next best thing, I bought ten pounds of cement mix and nails and collected several empty bottles, which I broke into tiny pointed pieces and placed them in cement along the edge of the terrace. Diane Von Furstenberg was also robbed the same night. Ironically, I had had a party on the terrace several months earlier and left the windows open all night. When I returned the next day, everything was still intact. But the minute I closed the window, they broke in.

I knew the show had to go on, because, there was going to be an audience. We worked diligently and duplicated all of the samples, and the show did go on.

The show was originally called, 'Southern Nights in New Orleans.' I dressed two kids in Mardi Gras costumes. Ethel Beatty, who portrayed an Ingénue in Bubblin' Brown Sugar on Broadway reprised her solo 'I've Got It Bad'. That was the original Southern jazzy touch that opened the show.

Norma Jean entered the stage holding up *Women's Wear Daily.* She said, "Originally, this show was called, Southern Nights in New Orleans, but after the robbery, we're calling it "*Sleepless Nights in New York.*" Then she added, "Nobody has to worry about a thing because now I bring you the King of Polyester, Jon Haggins."

I wrote a check for Olivia Chapman, after the show, she was one of the models. However, I miss-addressed it as Olivia Shaw. She called after arriving home and asked,

"Who is Olivia Shaw?"

"Oh, my God! That was one of my backup singers from my cabaret days," Gosh, I thought I was losing it, so many young ladies and so little time.

After the second robbery, I came up with the bright idea of spreading black axle grease along the window ledges and never had another problem.

I was invited to the Metropolitan Museum of Art Annual Costume Event. My date was Olivia Chapman. I arrived at her apartment wearing a black tuxedo. She wore one of my favorite copper color strapless

gowns with a lettuce ruffle top. We looked fabulous if I must say so. As we exited her apartment building, a driver was sitting in a Rolls Royce in front. He asked us to get in and he would drive us where ever we wanted to go. So, he opened the door and off we went to the Metropolitan Museum. He was so generous and didn't charge for the ride. It was like a Cinderella ride to a beautiful event, and what a night it was. That was also the night John Lennon was shot in front of the Dakota Apartment building, where he lived, it was not a way to end the evening.

Olivia Chapman wore this copper gown to the Met Opening

June, my ex-wife had disappeared and I had not heard from her for many years. She returned to New York in the summer of 1984 and asked Norma, "Who is the hottest designer?"

Norma told her, "Jon Haggins."

I was quietly working in my studio one afternoon when the doorbell rang. I opened the door and discovered, she had hired a man to deliver a divorce summons. She was still up to the same old tricks that she performed many years before. I called her lawyer immediately and suggested she check with the City Courthouse because our divorce was finalized in 1973. As you remember, June had started the divorce in 1971, and I followed through. I guess she figured she could come back and collect after all those years. I also suggested that if June had called me, I would have personally given her the news. Norma later told me that June said she had no idea she was divorced. She also told

Norma, that it took her three years to get over me.

Several years later a young attractive lady was walking toward me on the sidewalk near my apartment building and I said, "You look familiar."

"Oh, Jon," she responded.

"Oh yes, I know who you are."

It was June, my ex-wife. I knew she looked familiar, but meeting her on the street was out of context.

I had considered marriage again, but after a short engagement, the affair petered out. Somehow, that one and only marriage had left me scared. There is a fine line between loving and divorce. A divorce is a difference of opinion.

My other loves have been men. Unfortunately, none of the relationships lasted more than a few years. When I look back over my life and think of my parent's and my grandparents' relationship, there were many separations and divorces. I think there is a pattern here, and I question it. My relationship with June ended for two main reasons: One, I was unfaithful.

Two, because we didn't have the same vision.

There have only been a handful of great loves in my life and I put June on the top of the list. She broke my heart.

Well anyway, back to the studio. One day, one of my workers was stitching a garment very slowly and I asked if she was picking her nose between stitches.

"This is not a factory," she responded.

"It's not a molasses shop either, my dear,"

On another occasion, I observed a sewer stretching and I asked if she was taking a break. Time is money and I was always a stickler for it. I believe if you put in a full day's work, you deserve a full day's pay. I also said if you arrive ten minutes late, please make it up at the end of the day, because every ten minutes add up and we lose productive time.

One of my favorite designs and the most popular dress was created while I was feeling fancy-free. I gathered a roll of tulle and some pink taffeta, then created the most wonderful, fantasy dress. It was a simple strapless sheath with a double tulle over-skirt. A perfect prom dress for every young girl.

Pink cover Cosmopolitan, 1983

I called Sean Byrnes, a stylist for photographer Francesco Scavullo and said, "Have I got a cover dress for you."

"Then we have to see it."

Sean loved it and Francesco photographed it for the August 1983 cover of *Cosmopolitan* magazine. That little pink taffeta, strapless prom dress with a bouffant tulle over-skirt, became a hit the minute the magazine landed on the newsstands. My phone didn't stop ringing for months. Everyone wanted that dress.

I placed signs all over the studio reminding everyone to "Think Pink." As the dresses were being boxed and shipped,

"Those dresses are still smoking," Carolyn commented.

I sold approximately twenty thousand of that dress because it was featured on *Cosmopolitan's* cover. The cover is the first thing that catches your attention as you pass a newsstand. That little pink dress hit Madame Consumer in her pocketbook. Janet from the Manhattan Transfers bought one to wear for her performance at Radio City for *'The Night of One Hundred Stars'.*

I was invited to a *Cosmopolitan* magazine Christmas party. Francesco Scavullo, said he'd like to photograph me, I turned him down by saying, "I have Ted Hardin as my photographer." That was one of my big regrets.

After Mother retired, she often visited my work studio to see my latest fashions and to spend a little time with Carolyn and I. I also invited Mother to assist with sample/sale merchandise. Some of my clients were stars from Broadway shows. Having mother at the studio brought her a little joy and it helped to fill her day. One of her other favorite things to do was to get together with friends and arrange bus trips to the Burlington Factory in Pennsylvania to shop. She also passed her time at home crocheting beautiful, colorful bed coverings and throws. Her retirement gave her a chance to reflect on her life. She often talked about her grandchildren and how she looked forward to seeing them.

She spent a lot of time tending to her lush garden, where she grew red roses and rhododendrons, and of course lush green grass. She claimed to have the best garden on the block, She was always working around her house to improve it because she knew the real estate value would go up year after year. She did everything with pride. Her neighbors were congenital, she felt their comradery. Neighbors on her block stopped in periodically. That sort of reminded her of her early years in Florida, where neighbors looked out for one another.

One afternoon the doorbell rang at my work studio. I opened the door and asked the lady standing there if she had an appointment.

"I'm your mother," she responded.

I didn't recognize her because I was preoccupied with what I was doing and I wasn't expecting her. She had just come from the hair salon and had a new hairstyle. She looked terrific. Her visit was a pleasant surprise. We spent the rest of the afternoon catching up and sharing thoughts over lunch.

I loved visiting my mother during the weekends, not only to spend time with her but also because I ate well! She prepared what I considered a "mountains" of the best southern food ever— fried chicken, collard greens cooked with pork fat, Southern potato salad prepared with eggs, mayonnaise, sweet pickles, celery, salt, and pepper, etc.

Southern Potato Salad

Ingredients

- 5 medium white potatoes, peeled and cubed
- 6 hard-boiled large eggs, chopped
- ½ cup thinly sliced white onions
- ¼ cup chopped sweet pickles
- ½ cup of Miracle Whip
- 2 stalks of celery
- Salt and pepper to taste
- ¼ cup of mustard

Directions

Place potatoes in a large pot, with the skin on, and then add water to cover the potato. Bring to a boil, Reduce heat: cook, uncovered until tender, 10-15 minutes. You must also boil the eggs. After cooking the potatoes and eggs, then doused the potatoes and eggs in icy cold water. It makes it easier for the skins to "pop" off the potato. Slice the potatoes into cubes size pieces. Then add eggs, onions, pickles, mustard, celery, and mayonnaise. Season with salt and pepper to your taste and mix well. Don't forget to chill the potato salad in the refrigerator before serving. Now you have the best potato salad on this side of the Dixie Line.

Mother always prepared enough food to "feed an army," there was always more than enough to take home in a doggy bag.

Mother was known for her delicious crème cheese pound cakes. The cake was light, fluffy, and oh so delicious! She piled mounds of crème cheese, butter, and sugar into her cakes. Her aromatic cakes permeated her block. The neighbors rang her doorbell to request a hot slice. Her cakes always disappeared the moment they were removed from the oven. Her cakes were THAT good!

One bright, sunny Saturday morning, Mother drove me to my friends, Pam and Larry McGonigle's home in Norwalk, Connecticut. Mother gave everyone instructions on how to make her famous cream cheese pound cake. Larry and Pam's son, Ryan, stood by and assisted by preparing the baking pan with self-rising flour. Everyone pitched in. Three cakes were baked and devoured while they were still hot. The consensus was: Willie Mae's pound cakes were the best this side of the Long Island Sound.

Willie Mae Haggins' Recipe for Cream Cheese Pound Cake

- One eight-ounce package of cream cheese
- 2 cups Self-rising flour
- 2 cups of sugar
- 2 sticks of sweet butter
- 2 tablespoons of vanilla extract
- 6 large eggs

Blend well:
- Cream cheese
- Sugar
- Sweet Butter
- Vanilla Extract

Add:
- 2 cups of sifted self-rising flour
- Break 6 large eggs into a bowl
- Add flour and eggs at the same time
- When you remove butter from the wrapping, save the wrapper to oil baking pan
- Sprinkle a little flour in the pan
- Use a two-part cake pan so you can remove the cake easier
- Preheat the oven for ten minutes until the temperature reaches 350° before putting the cake in
- Bake for one hour (if the stove turns off and on, you might need an extra ten minutes) Do not open the oven until one hour and five minutes
- Take out and sit on top of stove until cool
- Use a knife to remove the cake

Mother really enjoyed the day out of the city and the experience of sharing her cake recipe. Her cake recipe has been shared in Chicago, Florida, and Connecticut.

CHAPTER TWENTY

Awards

The eighties bestowed several awards for my achievements in the fashion industry, for example, a three-time winner of the Harvey Bristol Cream — Salute to Black Fashion Designers Award. I was one of the twelve designers to receive the Harvey Bristol Cream Award at Avery Fisher Hall at Lincoln Center in 1983. It was a big night because I was amongst peers. My friend, Phyllis Hyman. the tall, elegant and talented lady accompanied me to the occasion. Phyllis was a powerhouse of a singer and she could whistle. I think she was one of the best in the world. My mother, sister, and Uncle Bill attended the award ceremony.

Phyllis Hyman and I, 1988

Jon honored at FIT with models Toukie Smith and Suzi Gilder

From the 1960s onward Jon Haggins' designs were seen on the covers and inside popular magazines and dozens of other publications and his clothes were also carried at major department stores. In the Jon Haggins Fashion Archive, you will find sketches, correspondence from the publications that featured his outfits, and other items that document his career as a fashion heavy hitter.

Later in life, the multitalented Haggins also performed as a vocalist in New York City's trendiest night clubs, writes about travel extensively and hosts a series called *Globe Trotter TV*. Haggins authored an autobiography, *Yes I Can: A memoir*, *The African-American Travel Guide To Hot, Exotic, and Fun Filled Places* and a follow up book, *Chasing Wild ASS*

Jon Haggins (with model and actor Tookie Smith,
left, and two unidentified women on the right)
Fashion Collection
Schomburg Center for Research in Black Culture
Photographs and Print Division
Photographer: Carlo Alabanese

Debbie Allen was the host of the evening. She wore that pink strapless taffeta bodice, sheath dress that was on the *Cosmopolitan* magazine cover. I designed it with yards of tulle covering the skirt. When Olivia Chapman entered the stage wearing the same style dress in white, they did a double-take. Both young ladies dance together as if they were sisters and hadn't seen each other for a long time. I just sat in the corner of the stage and watched and took it all in as twelve models entered and sashayed across the stage wearing my designs. After the award ceremony, we celebrated with dinner at a restaurant across the street from Lincoln Center. It was an amazing night of fashion and glamour.

Phyllis Hyman and I often got together for dinner or we'd go to a party. Several people told me she took drugs, I never saw her indulge in drugs when we were together. I don't take drugs, therefore, she respected that. She was always up and in good humor when we were together. I recall the night we caught Melba Moore's cabaret show. Melba walked over to Phyllis with a microphone and asked her to sing. Phyllis didn't hesitate, she had not warmed up, she didn't need to. She sang 'It don't mean a thang' from her performance in Duke Ellington's Broadway show, 'Sophisticated Ladies'. Talks about stole the show, that's exactly what happened. Phyllis loved to hang out and we hung out on many occasions.

On one of Phyllis many engagements at the Blue Note, I walked in and presented her with a large black woolen stole that I designed. I thought perhaps it would keep her warm during the cold winter nights in New York City. She asked if anyone had a request? I said I wanted her to sing, ahhhhh, and then I couldn't remember the name of the song.

She said, "some fan you are."

I also recall visiting my friend Kiko Morgan in Chicago and saw a billboard on Lake Shore Drive announcing Phyllis's upcoming appearance at McCormick Place in two weeks. Well, I returned to Chicago to catch her show. I called her at the hotel and asked if I could get eight tickets for the opening night performance. She gave us tickets in the front row. I took seven guests backstage after the show and introduced them to Phyllis. Each time Phyllis returned to Chicago for a gig, my friend caught her performance and took her out after her show. They were true fans. Everybody loved Phyllis.

I spoke to Phyllis a few days before she was to headline at the Apollo. I told her I would attend, however, I was also invited to a dinner party the same night. I chose the dinner party instead. When I returned home that night, my answering service had fifty messages. Everyone was calling to tell me that Phyllis had committed suicide, that was June 30, 1995. Just before her 46th birthday. My heart sank. I was totally in shock and could not comprehend such an act. Although several years before I asked if she use protection when she had sex, and she said, "no." I reminded her how dangerous that was. She said she didn't care. I was a bit surprised. What a pity, because she was one in a million. She was unique and a gifted individual. Later, I learned that she had attempted suicide earlier that year. Strange as that was, you think you know someone, then discover that they only let you know what they want you to know. Phyllis always had a positive attitude and was in good humor whenever we were together. I truly miss Phyllis and her spirit.

I produced fashion show extravaganzas in several New York Discos. On the night at Studio 54, I was celebrating my most successful *Cosmopolitan* cover featuring the pink strapless dress, there were 3,000 people in the club. Salsa music was hot and ringing through the rafters. I can still hear the music ringing in my head. I felt very Latin that night. A friend who owned a florist shop lent us a bunch of tropical trees for the occasion.

Alison Williams, one of the dancers in 'Dream Girls' on Broadway, danced a brilliant salsa. The audience raved about her performance.

I opened the show singing *'Touchin' My Body'*. A little ditty that I wrote. Ethel Beatty and Shailah Edmonds sang backup. I began walking backward at the end of the song. I was ending the song on a very, very note, then suddenly, I fell off the stage backward into the abyss. The ladies took a quick surprise glance at me, then rushed to the front of the stage to finish the song. I have told

Ethel and me singing at Studio 54, 1983

that story many times and swear the girls pushed me. It's my story and I'm sticking to it. The club manager crawled over to me as I was lying on the floor.

"Why don't you take a bow?"

"Honey, I've had it, you take a bow."

Fortunately, nothing was broken.

Then twelve models entered the stage dressed in that famous pink dress that appeared on the cover of *Cosmopolitan*. One additional model entered the stage wearing a black version of the same dress. She appeared as the black sheep in the family. They looked like a flock of sheep dolled up in tulle.

Kiko Morgan, my long-time friend, flew in from Chicago to attend the party. It was a very exciting time in my life. She was a guest in my apartment. Several days later, I held a dinner party for Kiko. During the evening, I had a few too many alcoholic beverages, so I disappeared into the bedroom for a little nap. I dozed off to sleep immediately. The phone rang. The room was dark, my eyes were closed, I picked up what I thought was the phone and said, "Hello." The phone continued to ring, I turned it around and said, "Hello," again. It continued to ring. Then I opened my eyes and realized I was holding a shoe.

I also produced another singing fest at Studio 54. This time I featured the Red Cha Cha dress that was featured in *Cosmopolitan* magazine. This close-fitting shirred jersey bodice was embellished with rhinestones sprinkled all over the fluffy net flounce. The rhinestones gave the dress a little pizzazz.

Pi Douglass choreographed a little number for Christina Clements. Let's make this perfectly clear, that was not just a plain old modeling job, it was choreographed. The dance required the model to be uninhibited. Christina was not that girl, but Pi tried his best. While he was giving her instructions on the moves, she was standing in the corner taking notes. He screamed, "Don't just stand there taking notes, honey. I want you to start moving. When Jon says, gloves by whomever, I want you to stretch out your arms and give 'em a glove, and when he says, shoes by Stuart Weitzman..., give 'em a long, long lean leg and point to the shoes, when he says, earrings by Kenneth J. Lane..., put your fingers behind your ears and lift and so on."

Everyone expected to see a fashion show, but instead, they got me and Christina. She wore 'The Dress,' while I sang 'Brite Lites and Limousines', another little ditty that I wrote. She was very timid that night and had good reason because she had to perform on a moving catwalk twenty-five feet above the dance floor. Nothing bothered me, I have always been adventurous; I even turned Pi's choreography around. Christina was petrified as she stood there. She was holding on to the railing for dear life. She did her best to get through it. One thousand red balloons embossed with my 'Jon Haggins' logo descended from the ceiling onto the dance floor at the end of the song. Christina was delighted that this little caper was over and she was still alive.

When I arrived in Puerto Rico the next morning, my eyes were bloodshot from not getting any sleep. A friend called me over and told me he had heard about my show at Studio. The news really traveled fast.

I also celebrated my designs on seven *Cosmopolitan* covers at Xenon's. The famous and near famous showed up from TV, fashion, advertising and the recording industry. I also sang with a five-piece band and of course, my backup ladies, Tish Hammick and Deborah Sharp. Deborah's voice was similar to Chaka Kahn; she was one of the stars in Little Shop of Horrors. My ladies wore strapless bustiers with a diaper skirt that was slit to the top of the thigh. Pi Douglas choreographed a very energetic number for the girls with their arms going in every imaginable direction. Deborah was also a few months pregnant and had a difficult time keeping her top up, because of her childbearing bosoms. One of the guys in the audience told me they were betting on how long Deborah's top would stay up. Fortunately, there was no faux pas.

I began with a little patter: "It's taken me a long time to grow into this song." Then I began singing: *'What Are You Doing the Rest of Your Life* and ended with *Touchin' My Body'*. It was a glorious night with an audience of 1,500 friends.

Gwen Barrett, the producer for Midday Live on Channel Five, originally entered my life in the mid-70s, when I was a Cabaret singer.

She came back into my life in the 80s, when Cynthia Malmuth, my public relations person, re-introduced us. We became fast friends because our personalities meshed. The thing I liked most about Gwen is her straightforwardness; she does not pull punches. She tells it like it is and she also knows how to party.

I was a regular personality on Midday and understood the workings of the station, so when an escort was sent to the lobby to accompany me to the TV studio, I made my way up to the makeup room where Carmen Gerber, an Emmy award winner created magic on my face. He managed to take twenty years off with a simple application. Most makeup artists in the TV business don't have the foggiest idea of how to apply makeup for people of color. I shared a tape of one of the shows with a friend and they asked, "What year did you appear on that show?"

"Yesterday," I quickly responded.

I think they asked because Carmen miraculously applied the makeup to bring out my best features.

Whenever Gwen was in a spot and needed a guest, she knew she could always count on me to deliver. One day, Bill Boggs, the host, was spending too much time with one of his guests, so Gwen signaled him to cut. She said, "I didn't bring my friend Jon Haggins here to waste his time."

And let's not forget I was the voice for FOX-TV's public service announcement, "It's Ten PM. Do you know where your children are?" I was also a travel contributor on NPR Radio with 25 million listeners across the country.

My fortieth birthday was celebrated at the Red Parrot Disco. The invitation featured a photo of me at the tender age of six. I called it my twenty-first birthday because I didn't have a party when I was twenty-one. That was the first time I sang with a seventeen-piece orchestra. I also presented another fashion show. The models descended down the stairs to the stage. A TV monitor featured my dresses from my appearance on Midday Live earlier that day. A staff member presented me with a huge birthday cake with forty candles and the DJ played Stevie Wonders' version of Happy Birthday at the end of the show. Cynthia, later told me that I had been the same age since we met a year ago. A year had slipped away and I was a year older than I thought.

I never needed a reason to throw a party. I love getting people together. I hosted a party for eighty people in a restaurant to view a fashion segment on *PM Magazine*. Stuart Eichner and his brother Bruce, owner and developer of City Spire, a seventy-three-story apartment building in Mid-Manhattan, allowed us to film a segment there. City Spire reminded me of the Metropolis. Phyllis Hyman was one of the guests at the party.

Eleanor Hendley from City Lights on KYW-TV in Philadelphia also featured some of my fashions. She asked, "Where is fashion going and where has it has it been?" "Fashion is Now! I want to inspire young people who are interested in fashion to think positively and set goals. First, they must have lots of drive and ambition; that will make a difference in their lives. Don't let anyone tell you "No." The word "No" does not exist. Also, you should not take anything for granted. No one gives you anything: you have to earn it, the old-fashioned way, by working to make it happen.

I have created trends and set styles that are still reverberating today. For instance, the monkey suit has evolved into today's hot-selling Catsuit. As my designs have endured, so have I, but not without many wrinkles, ironings, and much wear.

Then Eleanor asked, "If you weren't a fashion designer, what would you be. Would you be a truck driver?" I quickly responded, "Good heavens no. Don't be silly, my dear. I don't even know how to drive. If I weren't a fashion designer, I'd be an interior decorator. I love shapes and space."

After all the serious stuff, we lightened up our conversation and talked about my favorite subject, shopping. I love to shop, especially when it's a bargain. But I believe the only real bargain is when they pay you to take it away.

My business was progressing quickly, but I found it very difficult to operate because it was undercapitalized and needed an infusion of capital. When stores were delinquent in paying their invoices, it interrupted my cash flow. Janet Stewart, another designer in the building, suggested I factor my bills, which meant the factor would purchase my receivables, once the merchandise was shipped to the stores, then give me 60 to 85% of the invoice in advance until the stores paid. However, it was very expensive to factor the receivables. I tried that route for a while, but even the factor put me through too many combinations.

The fashion industry had radically changed from the first time I entered the business in the 60s. A new generation had arrived with new thoughts on how to conduct business. Black talent was no longer a novelty, and AIDS began to bash Blacks and Whites. There is no racism with that virus. Nor is success proof against it. Patrick Kelly and Willi Smith all died of the disease.

When I first entered the business, a confirmation from a store was an order. They only returned or canceled merchandise if was damaged, or if the merchandise didn't arrive in a timely fashion. However, the new buyers requested manufacturers to accept returns on any merchandise that they don't sell. There is no way a small manufacturer can absorb the cost. After all, we have to purchase the fabric, pay the workers, rent, taxes, electricity, phone, salesmen, cleaning, etc.

Cosmopolitan magazine featured one of my dresses on a full page. Bloomingdales placed a large order for that style. The order was delivered on time without any problems. However, the buyer called a month later and asked, "Do you want to go forward?"

"What does that mean?" I asked.

"I want to return the dresses we didn't sell."

"Let me think about it," I responded.

After I hung up, I called the accounting department and asked if the check was ready. It was. So, I hopped on my bike, rode up to Bloomingdales and picked up the check, then deposited it.

A week later the buyer called and asked, "Have you thought about it?"

"Yeap!, I'm not taking them back."

Well, that was the end of doing business with Bloomingdales. Lord and Taylor was a similar story where the buyer wanted to return and exchange dresses for the style they were selling. No can do. A small firm can't afford to accept returns. A small manufacturer can't exist on those new terms. I couldn't take the pressure of doing business that way.

As many of the designers from my generation dispersed, disappeared, or went abroad, I found myself facing closure again, despite recognition. The world that had expanded in the Sixties was now shrinking every day. The Eighties weren't the Sixties and life had become more difficult for small fashion firms to survive. I quickly learned how fragile financing can be. After much exasperation and frustration of not being able to acquire a financial backer, I folded my new company in 1984.

After closing my studio, I found a position for Carolyn with another manufacturer. That's when she said, "I never want to work with you again." I asked myself, "What did I do to her that she felt that way?" I gave her a profession, so I did not understand her attitude. I knew a contractor that wanted her to work for him, but she turned him down. I have no idea what was going on in her head.

It was time to regroup. I worked briefly for a couple of manufacturers of cheap dresses. That was a very depressing time. On one occasion, I drifted into Macy's furniture department, laid across a bed, and dozed off to sleep, only to be awakened by barking dogs after the store had closed.

I began thinking about my next step in life, and my future. A Seventh Avenue manufacturer asked me to design a collection of dresses.

Then he asked, "What was I thinking?"

I quickly responded, "I get paid for my ideas."

Whereupon, he handed me a check for the amount I asked for. I rushed to his bank and cashed it. The manager of the bank presented me with a very large envelope with cash. I was a happy camper. Then I returned and offered my ideas. Once that project was finished, I was back to square one, with no prospects.

I received a phone call from Karen Thomas at *Essence* magazine. She introduced me to The Smithsonian Museum in Washington, D.C. Several weeks later, the museum invited me as a guest speaker. My message stretched far beyond fabrics, thimbles, and buttons. I use my creativity and rely on a positive attitude, which has helped me survive against all odds, maneuvering through many rocks in the hardest of places.

I also addressed fashion trends and what it takes to stay in the business. Networking is an important factor, in doing business. The more people you know, the better. You must make an impression and a connection with people, so they will remember you when an occasion arises. Nowadays, people call me for projects and I don't have to struggle to find them as I once did. So, I count my blessings.

To make a successful business, you need to start with a vision and a business plan and establish goals. Then check out your competition. It takes a lot of creative juices, persistence, determination, and strong follow-through to make a business successful. You must also have guts, good work ethics, stamina, and money.

You must also be prepared to work long hours.

You must be passionate about your business.

Your business becomes your lover.

Put your priorities in proper perspective.

Anything is possible when you put your heart and soul into it. Managing a business is not a party. If you think you have those ingredients, go for it.

My message stretches far beyond fabrics, thimbles, and buttons. I used my creativity and always had a positive attitude, which has helped me survive against all odds. I maneuvered through many rocks in the hardest places and still survived.

The new Smithsonian National Museum of African American History and Culture in Washington, D.C. also honored me for my contribution to the Fashion Industry.

The honors were mounting in the 80s: I receive the key to the city of Baltimore. Another highlight for me was a month-long retrospective exhibition of my fashion designs in the Johnson Museum at Cornell University in Ithaca, New York. Beate Zeigert, an associate professor took three months to mount the exhibit. The exhibition opened on April 4th, 1988. Bea was beaming with delight when she picked me up at the airport.

Essence, 1988

She said, "The crowd will expect you to make a speech this evening."
"What will I talk about?"
"Tell them you're having a good time."
"Suppose I'm not?"

Well, that was the beginning of my speech and everyone laughed. The Johnson Museum is a very modern structure that was designed by I.M. Pei. He is one of my favorite architects. I felt very much at home from the moment I stepped out of the car and into the building because Pei also designed the apartment building that I lived in for 20 years in Manhattan.

As I stepped out of the elevator on the second floor, a single mannequin stood at the end of a long corridor dressed in the gown that Lynn Redgrave wore to the Tony Awards. The gown was designed with large dramatic angel white shoulders attached to a very long lean slithery black velvet bodice.

The exhibition was divided into three rooms: graphics including some of my drawings and editorials, Clips from different TV appearances, and fifteen mannequins dressed in my designs. As I walked throughout the exhibition, I realized that my fashions were so contemporary they could be worn into the next century.

Essence, 1988

Cornell Exhibition

More honors followed such as: The Museum of the City of New York included my fashions in a retrospective in 2006-2007. The exhibition was called "Black Style Now." The museum had a red carpet that lead to the steps of the museum. The press stood on the other side of the rope. One of the reporters asked: "What does Black Style mean to you?"

"Blacks designers put the 'B' in fashion."

Several photographers joyously yelled, "There's Jon Haggins, he's a legend." I told them that I had no idea what that meant because I continue to enrich my life each day and I live in the moment, not in the past. One of the reporters was a young lady from the same TV station that airs my show. She was surprised to see me on the red carpet. Then asked why was I on the red carpet. I told her to see the exhibition. She had no idea that I was once a fashion designer.

One reporter asked, what do I think of some of today's fashion designers, like Puffy and Tommy Hilfiger. "They are stylists. Scott, Stephen, and I were touchy, feely designers who understood fabric and we made magic that allowed the fabric to come alive." Testifying to that fact two of my designs were on display in the museum, my bias-cut low cowl dress (circa 1983) and my bias-cut low back black velvet gown (circa 1984) that glided over the mannequin's body.

Debbie Allen, Olivia Chapman, and Lorraine Curry contributed several of my designer dresses for the exhibition. It was refreshing to view my fashions after so many years. The best part of seeing those dresses. Those dresses are still fashionable and can be worn today and into the future.

Gold cowl back

I had been on my own for twenty-six years. I also needed to think about something that would hold my interest and be fulfilling. Refusing this time to leave fashion designing, I became a consultant, doing specialty jobs, such as couture work for corporations, media tours, and producing entire shows for corporations.

Karen Thomas at *Essence* magazine recommended me to Elayne Stanback for a Cheseborough Ponds and Esteem hair product promotion campaign. I designed several colorful outfits to coordinate with their products. I was scheduled to travel to Raleigh, Greenville, and Fayetteville, North Carolina, where I would present a fashion show promoting their products.

Unfortunately, the travel agent booked me on a flight to Greenville, South Carolina, by mistake. I didn't notice until someone asked:

"What part of South Carolina are you going?"

"South? I'm going to North Carolina."

"This plane is going to South."

I shouted, "Stop this plane, I wanna get off!"

After collecting my bags in Greenville, South Carolina, the ticket agent said he'd have to charge me extra for the large garment bag. The bag was filled with garments for the fashion show. I stared him directly in his eyes and said, "I've traveled around the world with this bag and nobody's ever charged me extra." "O.K., I won't charge you this time. However, the next time you come through here, I'll have to charge you." I put my right hand on my hip, reared back, and said, "Do I look like I want to come to THIS town again?"

Arriving in some of those small towns took forever; I often felt as if I was in the middle of nowhere. I must have read every magazine and newspaper on the newsstand during the four-hour layover. Finally, the next plane arrived. It was too small to carry my luggage, so they delivered it on the next plane. I arrived at the hotel at approximately 3 pm. Our production team of models, makeup, dressers, and hair people occupied half of the hotel. I was a bit hungry after a long-delayed day. The restaurant in the hotel was closed until 5 pm. I couldn't wait, so I wandered across the highway to Stokey's Restaurant and ordered a steak with potatoes and vegetables. When the steak arrived, it had been badly overcooked. It was more like shoe leather, I could have bounced it off the wall several times and it still would not have made a difference. The so call fresh fruit was from a can. Not appetizing.

I managed to take advantage of a half-hour break before the garments arrived. I always travel with a bathing suit, because there's always a pool. It's a perfect spot to relax after my travel ordeal. I must have been a fish or an octopus in my other life because the octopus is the Renaissance man of the sea. They have many arms and can do more than one thing at a time.

Once the garments arrive, they were unpacked and freshened up, then fitted on the models. I might note that all of this had to be done before presenting the show. Despite all the confusion, the show was a smash. We presented the same show in Raleigh and Fayetteville. The people were the best thing about traveling to those cities, they were laid back and just nice folks.

I was also a national spokesperson for Proctor and Gamble's Ultra Detergents. I design several outfits for the press kit and promoted their Ultra Detergents on the radio and made personal appearances in malls in six cities around the country. I signed on because I could spend 5 nights in New Orleans. Imagine five nights in New Orleans: that's fifteen fabulous meals in fifteen different restaurants.

I also had a little free time to explore the town. I recall having two brunches and several Hurricanes. I was so twisted when I arrived at the dock and asked to buy a ticket up the Hudson.

"The Hudson?" the dock master asked.

Then, I remembered it was the Mississippi. That was a helluva cruise. I met several people and later dined together. I was so exhausted at the end of the evening. While standing in Preservation Hall, I fell asleep and only reacted when the drummer banged his drum.

I received a call, early the next morning from the young lady who was in charge of driving me to and from interviews and appearances. While driving along one of the long highways, she said, "I'm having an out-of-body experience.

"I hope it doesn't smell," I responded.

Several Procter & Gamble promotional trips across the country allowed me to visit my friend Kiko Morgan in Chicago. I loved visiting Kiko, because she was always in good spirit and full of life, and we could laugh together. Several of her friends often invited us to dinner, therefore she didn't have to cook. So, she always enjoyed my visits.

Well back in New York, I was sitting in my office, when Nancy White, former editor-in-chief of *Harper's Bazaar*, called to tell me that our friend Cathy Dives had died. She asked me to write a little something, that she would read at Cathy's Memorial. I reached into a cabinet and pulled out a sheet of apple green stationery, then wrote, "Spunky."

Spokesperson for Proctor & Gamble, 1991

Then I flew to Chicago for the day to promote Proctor Gamble's Ultra products. I didn't want to miss Cathy's memorial, so I return to New York after the promotion. Nancy read a variety of statements regarding Cathy, she held up the apple green page and I knew it was mine. She read what I wrote and everyone agreed that Cathy was 'Spunky'.

I flew to Los Angeles immediately after the memorial. This brings to mind that I once sent a condolence card to Norma Jean for one of her relatives. The card featured me in my apartment standing in front of my baby grand piano, with my hands flung in the air with a big grin on my face. Norma told me she fell off the toilet laughing when she received the card.

Seymour Schneiderman, who owned Symphony Fabrics, introduced me to a manufacturer. I designed cocktail dresses for that firm. The manufacturer was not happy, because I often invited a parade of fashion students from across the country to learn about the workings of the fashion business. He fired me after four months.

Once that position ended, Seymour allowed me to have free access to a desk space for a year, after I closed my studio. I shall never forget his generosity. He also produced fabrics that I experimented with. I designed a special collection of soft jersey and chiffon fabrics that I presented on *People are Talking* on Channel Nine TV.

I desperately looked for a design position, while I waited it out at Symphony Fabrics, but no one would hire me, because I was too knowledgeable and knew the inner workings of running a garment business. I was in a very precarious position because I had worked for myself and I knew my value. No one was willing to pay what I thought I was worth. There is an expression in the garment business, "Hire them cheap and keep them nervous."

My advice is: 'Be in control of your destiny.

Have a little adventure, branch out on your own, and go for the brass ring. Occasionally, when an idea doesn't work, re-worked it and started over. I never lost faith and never gave up on my dream. Working for myself meant I shared the good with the bad.

CHAPTER TWENTY-ONE

Discovering

a New Direction

I took a little time out, to reflect, and think about my future. Mr. Goma, a kimono designer from Japan called and asked me to produce a fashion show extravaganza in New York in 1989. It would celebrate the twentieth anniversary of Tokyo and New York, the sister cities. The show would also feature his exquisite hand-painted kimonos. Several American designers would use his hand-painted fabrics to create fabulous fashions.

I was delighted to participate because I would fly first class on JAL Airlines to Japan, to be introduced to Japanese culture, religion, and modern lifestyle. It was an amazing flight and the service on board was superb.

After I landed at Narita Airport in Tokyo, I asked a gentleman from JAL Airline, "Where can I post a few postcards? "

"Because you were so kind to fly on JAL, I'll take care of it for you."

"OK, here are twenty more."

While waiting at the conveyor belt for my luggage, a young man approached me and reached for my shoulder bag. I quickly responded by tugging with him.

"Where do you think you going with my bag?"

Then someone said, he was my driver. But no one had bothered to inform me in advance. I still had a little New York paranoia.

I was quietly and quickly whisked off to Nara in a cordovan-colored Jaguar. Dinner reservations were made at a lovely restaurant. The restaurant offered a variety of Japanese dishes, and they were, oh so delicious. After dinner, we checked into the most wonderful, vintage hotel where the Prime Minister and Japanese Royalty stayed. While checking in, the desk clerk looked me up and down and realized that I needed a larger bathtub, because I am very tall compared to most Japanese people. He accommodated me with all that was necessary. I was exhausted after a fourteen-hour non-stop flight and needed a little shut-eye. I also knew my host had planned a rigorous schedule, and I was due to rise very early the next morning.

The next morning, we were off to visit several temples, and pagodas after a typical, light Japanese breakfast. We also participated in a tea ceremony at the home of the highest Buddhist priest. One of the Japanese customs is to present a gift to your host and the host presents you with a gift in return. It is a way to show gratitude and appreciation. It is important to give and receive gifts with both hands; it's also a sign of respect. When receiving a gift, one ought to modestly refuse the present up to three times before finally accepting.

It is considered rude to give a present to one person in a group of many. You never open the gift in the presence of your host. Gifts are opened in private, because if the gift turns out to be a poor choice, "Loss of face" will result. The priest guided me on a tour of the oldest temple and explained some its history.

Kyoto was our second stop, where I visited Mr. Goma design studio and summer home. Both homes are perched high on a mountain that he owns. He installed a monorail between the two homes. I preferred to walk instead of taking the monorail. We were there in the dead of the winter. There was no central heating in either home. They used a floor heater and a center table, which was covered with a blanket. I slid my legs under the table to warm them, and I wore a thick sweater to warm the rest of my body.

One of the most intriguing evenings was spent in a typical old

Japanese Hot Springs. Everyone wore kimonos to dinner. My kimono was much too short—it reached the top of my thighs—but I wore it anyway. I also wore underwear to insure nothing was exposed. Everyone sat on the floor in a lotus position. The lotus position was not comfortable for me, because my legs aren't that flexible. One of the Geisha girls looked at my crotch and placed her hands over her mouth and giggled, because I couldn't get my knees to go in the right direction.

There were lots of futons, geisha girls and green tea. The Japanese stirred powdered green tea in hot water. They served it at every meal. I craved for a simple Coke Cola after a week of sipping green tea.

Everyone openly talked about sex and the Black man's myth and suggested what it would do to them.

They said, "If I put it in the front it would come out the back like a ventilator."

I even danced the tango with one of the Geisha girls and she loved it. They really know how to entertain. Everyone retired to the lounge after dinner for drinks and fun.

My final stop was in Osaka. A rendezvous in Osaka took us to several private clubs where a hostess was assigned to each guest. They made me feel like a King. The drinks were served, ever, so quietly, that every time I turned my head, another drink appeared. I thought, "Hmm...if I don't touch the drink, they will stop."

I asked my hostess if the men sitting directly in front of us were Japanese Mafia and she said, "Yeah," then laughed. I think she was pulling my leg. The club presented us with several designer gifts as we departed. Another helpful lesson I've learned from the Japanese custom is always presenting two business cards facing the other person. That allows them to share the second card with another important person.

I decided to explore Osaka on the last day. It was the first time, I was truly on my own. Everything was too expensive in the stores, so I bought nothing. As I was departing the department store, I forgot the name of my hotel. Fortunately, I had pinched a pack of matches from the hotel and found them in my pocket. I stopped at another hotel to ask the concierge to draw a directional line to my hotel on the map. That was necessary for me because I can't read Japanese. I'm a visual person.

I returned to the hotel, checked out, and summon a taxi to the

Osaka Airport. May I make note that the taxi drivers steps out of their taxi after each customer and wipe it down. One other thing, the back door automatically opens with a push of a button from the driver. I arrived safely at the airport.

After checking in at the ticket counter, I was on my way to customs, when I heard, "Mr. Haggins, where are you?" It was announced over the broadcast system. As I arrived at the door of the plane, the steward asked, "Where were you, we were waiting for you?"

"Shopping," I quickly responded.

The first-class accommodations were relaxing and peaceful.

Japan was an eye-opening experience. I was introduced to Japanese culture, religion, and modern lifestyle. The Japanese culture is so tranquil and refreshing. I was impressed with their creative energy throughout the cities we visited.

After landing in Honolulu, Hawaii, I was allowed to exit first. It was like parting water on a river, and I loved it. A young lady greeted me and offered me a lei as I entered the terminal. I said to myself, "Back to the real world." I carried two shoulder bags and a suit bag.

The customs inspector asked: "How long were you in Japan?"

"One week."

"Business or pleasure?"

"Pleasure."

"And you didn't buy anything?" he asked.

"Do I look like I can carry anything else?"

"Are you in the Army?"

"At my age, are you kidding?"

He became exhausted from my smart answers, then allowed me to pass.

Honolulu was sun and fun on the beautiful Waikiki beach. My friends Michael Langley met me for a drink at the old Moana Surfrider Hotel. It's the oldest hotel in Honolulu and it sits directly on the beach with the best views of the beach and the city. Several days later, Michael invited me to his home for Thanksgiving.

Michael picked me up after a day on the beach, then drove me through beautiful mountains and countryside on the North Shore. As we passed strange things growing out of the ground, I asked,

"What's that?"

"It's a Dole Pineapple farm."

I always thought pineapples grew on trees. As we were riding along the coastline, he pointed out the Big Kahuna, twenty-five-foot waves for serious surfers. Michael told me that more tourists drowned each year by the unsuspected waves when they step out on the rocks to have their photos taken. A wife says, "Charlie, now you go out there and stand on that rock and I'll take your picture." The next unsuspected thing happens, a Big Kahuna comes and takes Charlie away with the undercurrent. Then the wife goes home and collects the insurance money.

The Langley's estate was perched on top of the most beautiful mountain next to Elvis Presley's old estate on the North Shore, The Langley's home reminded me of a Frank Lloyd Wright design. Michael gave me a quick tour of his estate. It was so wonderful to see Jackie, his wife again and met their three kids.

The grounds were well manicured. Fresh starfruit hung from a tree. Michael told me, we had a rare opportunity to see the next island. It was like seeing the world from a postcard, like the song says, "Beyond the Blue Horizon, lies a beautiful sun." I knew I had to be dreaming.

Jackie had prepared the most festive and bountiful Thanksgiving dinner. What a terrific occasion to share with his family. I told Michael what happened upon arrival at the Honolulu airport. He said perhaps I didn't fit the inspector's description.

"Who goes to Japan for a week and doesn't buy anything?"

"So, I must be a drug dealer."

That never occurred to me, because I don't even smoke cigarettes.

The next morning, I was back on Waikiki beach, where I boarded an Outrigger boat without a life belt. There were several other tourists on the boat. We paddled out to sea, it was similar to the way the guys from "Hawaii Five-O" used to do it.

"Number two, please put your paddle in the water."

"Why," I asked.

As he turned the boat around to ride the swells to shore, a very large wave covered us and sank our boat. I continued to sit there looking back at the hotels and said, "I knew I should have sent my postcards."

My problem was way beyond the postcards: I didn't know how to swim, especially in ninety feet of water. The water was crystal clear, I could see the bottom, but who cares. I couldn't touch it, so I didn't want any part of it.

"Everyone out of the boat!" the captain yelled.

The woman in front of me yelled, "I'm only used to swimming in my pool at home."

The water was rising to my chest as I jumped out. I held my breath until I reached the end of the outrigger attached to the boat. The captain dumped the water and asked everyone to return to the boat. Then he told us that the boat would never completely sink because buoyancy was built in. I asked the captain if we could get an extra ride for the inconvenience and he did not comply.

The next day I returned to the same boat and a stranger walked over, looked at me, and asked, "Weren't you on the boat that sank yesterday?"

"Yes. How did you know?"

"I was looking out of my hotel window and couldn't believe my eyes."

"Does that happen all the time? Why are you back again?"

"I returned just for the fun of it, in addition to being a foolish tourist."

The absolute most fun was gathering a group of new friends from the beach at the end of each day. We'd meet for cocktails at eight and then off to dinner. I felt like a native Hawaiian because I had visited the island once before with Norma Jean Darden.

I was free to do whatever I chose. I was having the best time of my life. I booked myself at the hotel for another week and another week until I ran out of money. After the third week of sharing experiences with my new friends, they gathered on the beach to say:

"We know you're leaving today and we wanted to say that we have never met anyone like you. You brought so much energy and joy to everyone. It was a real pleasure meeting you."

That was the nicest compliment I have ever received.

I called Jackie from the airport to apologize for not seeing them again.

"We were so worried about you since you were here alone."

"Are you kidding? I shared dinner with ten people each night and had a great time."

Before returning home, I decided to visit Kiko in Chicago. When I arrived at O'Hare Airport, I was surprised to see snow up to my ears. Obviously, I was not dressed for the winter, I was still wearing tropical summer clothes from Hawaii. When I left New York several weeks ago, the temperature was seventy-degrees. So, the snow was a total surprise. I hailed a taxi to take me to Kiko's house. Once I arrived there, I asked her boyfriend Ken, if he had boots, a sweater, a hat, a coat, and gloves. I spent ten days with Kiko and wore out my welcome.

"When are you leaving?" she asked.

I packed my bags and returned home. Years later, Kiko denied she ever said that. However, I remember everything. She didn't hurt my feeling and I have returned many times to share special times with her.

Well, back to earth, I opened a small studio on West 38th Street to keep my hands in the game. I called Jim Leamy at Clairol and asked if I could design for his company. He told me, he was satisfied with the people he was working with.

"You don't want satisfied, you want the best; you want me!" I quickly responded.

He arranged an appointment for us to meet in his office on September 10, 1990. Eileen McGonigle joined us in the meeting. It was her first day on the job and also her birthday. When I discovered it was her birthday, I insisted that we celebrate by going to dinner. I returned at the end of the day with a birthday gift, it was a very large woolen scarf that I made. Then draped it around her shoulders and we were off to celebrate. We began going out every Wednesday and then every night of the week. My new direction took me to Clairol and Revlon where I designed special projects for the trade shows.

Eileen invited me to her home in Connecticut for at least a year, before I accepted. Once I accepted her invitation, I never stopped being a perennial guest. I loved visiting the home that she shared with her sister Carolyn. I also met several members of her family and lots of her friends. I wasn't working full time, so I was at liberty to spend four days a week at their home. We shared great adventures on Lucia and Joe Breault's seventy-five-foot yacht. One of the funniest things happened while sailing on the Long Island Sound. I took the helm as we were sailing beautifully, suddenly, Lucia asked me to look out for lobster traps, so I slowly turned the helm 360 degrees, as the boat slowly turned with me.

She laughed and said, "I can't believe I let you at the helm because you don't even drive."

On another occasion, Joe asked me to get a net from the hull. I only saw a bucket, so I grabbed it. The fish was flipping on the deck. I yelled, "Hey fish, jump in the bucket." The fish did a double-take and flipped back into the sea. Joe caught another fish and made ceviche. I refused to eat it because I saw it alive.

As we were returning to shore, Lucia released the dingy, so we could go shopping for fishing tackle. Lucia asked me to throw the bumper over as we were approaching the dock. I literally threw it, unfortunately, it wasn't attached to the boat. As the bumper floated down the river. I yelled, "Get that bumper." Another boater returned the bumper and saved my skin. After we bought the tackle, Lucia allowed me at the helm once more. As I made the next turn, we almost capsized. Fortunately, the day ended on a great note.

I loved visiting their friends' homes and relaxing. Her father always said that I was his son from another marriage.

Jon on Breault's yacht, 2015

The New York Times featured me as the perennial guest.
They asked, "What do you do as a guest?
Do you chop wood?"
"No."
"Do you mow the lawn?"
"No."
"Then what do you do?"
"I can be charming."

Most often, I'd take my bike on the train, however, I didn't that day. I recall arriving at the Westport, Connecticut train station. As I stepped off the train, I spotted a bus at the station. I asked the driver if he knew the direction to the Breault's home. While he was thinking about my request, a young lady stepped off the train and asked if I needed help.

"Yes, I was trying to get to my friend's home."

"My name is Doris, hop in and I'll take you."

I direct her to the Breaults' home. No one was there when we arrived. So, I asked Doris if she wanted to take a dip in the pool. She said no thanks because she lives in Wilton and was in a rush to get home. So I peeled off my top clothes and stretched out on a chaise and relaxed. Occasionally, I dipped in the pool to cool off. When Lucia and Joe Breault returned home, they looked out the window and said, "That looks like Jon." They came out and asked how did I get there since they didn't see my bike. I told them Doris dropped me off.

"Who is Doris?"

"I have no idea, except she lives in Wilton."

Eileen arrived later with her family and friends, then we shuttled over to Carolyn and Eileen's home. Everyone surprised me with a gigantic birthday bash. Papa Bud, their father, gave me the most memorable gift, a membership to AARP. I laughed for twenty minutes. I had just turned 50. It was the best gift. What a great surprise. Turning fifty was a milestone.

"How did it happen?" I asked myself.

It appeared to me, that only yesterday, I was forty and carefree. Not to say that I'm not fun and carefree today. But those years have passed ever so quickly.

"It's too soon. You're too early, come back in ten years," I called out.

Turning fifty suddenly sneaked up on me. I looked in the mirror and asked, "What happened?" A little gray, a little bald, I guess it comes with the territory.

Well, one day I was on a bus in Manhattan, minding my own business, when a three-year-old boy looked up and said,

"Don't look at me, bald head." I was shocked.

"Don't be rude, he's not your grandfather," his father said.

No, thank God I'm not! But after being reminded, I guess I am at the ripe old grandfather age. I feel fit, energetic, and still sexually appealing.

This is what growing older means to me: Maturing like a flower as it blossoms into the most colorful character. I can watch younger people spread their wings. I can also look in the mirror and like what I see. Now, I can take advantage of discounts on public transportation, hotel rooms, and car rentals, even though I don't drive. I can continue having many new experiences and adventures so that I don't have to repeat the same old stories. And I have lots of long-time, good friends.

I have had many wonderful experiences in Connecticut. I often took the 12:07 pm train from Grand Central to Westport. Carolyn and Eileen would meet me at the station with the car trunk filled with beach food and drinks. You know you always have to have your cocktails. Having all the food and drinks allowed us the luxury of staying on Compo Beach all day. I also recall, on one occasion, we ran out of Vodka, so, I did the very best thing, I asked the couple next to us, to prepare a drink for us. Carolyn was thoroughly embarrassed but graciously excepted the drink. Later, I asked to excuse myself, because I needed to go to the bathroom. A gentleman next to us said he would give me a lift. I thanked him and said, it wasn't necessary, but he insisted. Carolyn and I got in his car and he drove us to his home. While we were relaxing with a drink in hand, suddenly the wife stormed in and said, "I can't believe you guys are partying, while I'm slinging hamburgers on the beach."

I whispered in Carolyn's ear, "I think it's time to go."

Many days were spent relaxing on Compo Beach and watching the sailboats cruise up and down the Long Island Sound.

CHAPTER TWENTY-TWO

Tour / Travel Business

Manhattan Tours, was a customized tour company that organized all ground arrangements for groups visiting New York City. The tours allowed the students to have a behind-the-scenes tour of the fashion, beauty, and the interior design industries.

I was preparing six-thousand press kits to mail to Fashion schools around the country. Ethel, my cousin, arrived at my studio, in the middle of all the kaos. I asked her to help stuff the envelopes, with a postcard, a press release. Once that was done, everyone had to peel off the address label and stamps, then stick them on the envelopes. I thought it would cheaper to do bulk mail. However, it wasn't worth the savings, because we had to bundle the mailers according to the zip codes. After Ethel finished that tedious job for the day, she told me she would never visit my office again, if I wanted her to work, because the mailing was too much work.

I have lectured more than 15,000 fashion students from around the country. One of my favorite teachers was Barb Ebner from Wisconsin Technical College. She always brought a group of enthusiastic fashion students to experience Manhattan and the inner workings of the fashion business. One of her students asked if I took editors and buyers to lunch to get placement in their magazines or to get orders. I told them 'yes,' but it's not about getting tit for tat. It's about building a relationship. A number of my editors and buyers have become close friends over the years.

My first love was fashion; however, travel has always been my passion. Norma Jean called to tell me there was a trip to Abidjan, Cote de Ivoire. The sponsors were hosting a fashion show featuring African and Black American designers. Norma told me that I had to be included. So I contacted the sponsor and was hired as the MC for the fashion show.

Once I arrived in Cote de Ivoire, I saw men and women who owned their businesses and they walked with great pride. I decided to venture out the first day and explore the town. The souk was my first stop. That market offered everything from masks, wood carvings, clothing, bags etc.

One of the vendors called out, "My friend, my friend."

I responded, "I'm your best friend."

"No, you not my friend, 'cause you no buy nothing."

I returned the next day prepared for whatever the challenge was. The Souk is where everyone haggled for the best price. It was a new experience, but I learned quickly and blended in with the culture.

Norma Jean and I were out later that evening. The music was hot, I asked her to dance. She got up. As I spun her around, she had to step out of the bar to turn, because the bar was too darn small. The bar was the size of a large closet. We had a few laughs from that experience.

On another occasion, we were having a lovely quiet lunch in a little village, when suddenly a group of drummers appeared and began banging loudly on their drums. One of the guests commented, "The only sound I want to hear are the birds and the bees."

As we were returning to our hotel one evening, the Military Police stopped our car on the bridge and asked for identification.

"Je suis Americaine," I blurted out.

Then we were permitted to pass. I had no idea that the country was under Military control.

The Grand Bassam is located on a Palm-backed beach that stretched along the Atlantic coastline. The old French-colonial town center, once the nation's capital, was filled with decaying 19th and 20th-century mansions. I met with the mayor several days later and said, the Grand Bassam would be a fantastic resort area for tourists if they fixed it up.

He said, "We don't have the money."

"That's how you make money."

The fashion show was held in the Ballroom of our hotel, and I was the MC. Beautiful, American, and African fashions floated onto the stage. I disappeared for a minute, between the introduction of the fashions. Everyone was puzzled and asked, "What happened to you?"

"I went to the bathroom."

I knew the timing of the show. Everything went very smoothly. The President's wife was in the audience. Everyone loved the show and it was a perfect way to introduce American Black Fashion designers to an African audience.

To top off our visit to this incredible destination, we stopped at a local bistro and ordered fried chicken and French fries. Both dishes were the freshest. The Cote de Ivoire chickens are not pumped with all the steroids and hormones as in our chickens. I had never tasted chicken that had a genuine flavor. After I returned to New York, I couldn't eat chicken from the stores, because it simply didn't have the same taste.

One day, I was visiting my mother and began sharing my experiences in Cote de Ivoire. Suddenly tears began to stream down my face. Those were tears of joy because Cote de Ivoire was where I discovered my true enter.

Parsons School of Design hired me, as a fashion design instructor. My classes met on Thursdays. The chairman of the fashion department assigned me to a very unimaginative design class. The experience was totally exhausting. I felt as if the blood had been sucked out of my body. I returned to my office at the end of the day, and put my feet up on the desk to get my blood circulating again. After ten Thursdays, I sent a resignation note that BOLDLY stated, "I QUIT!"

Two weeks later, I was hired by Revlon to produce a fashion show in Ghana. The show would include Black American designers and designers from Ghana. I ran around Manhattan gathering clothes and accessories from a variety of designers. The inspiration for the show was a large photo of a Royal Village in Ghana. My concept was to open the show with the lights out. I would have a dark auditorium with an audio track of sounds of jungle animals. That was shot down because the wife of the president would be in the audience, so they couldn't allow it. So, instead, the show opened with a large band of drummers performing on stage as the models walked out. A dozen models, both male and female entered the stage. I had forgotten to bring a veil for the bridal gown. However, as clever as I am, I asked someone to buy several yards of sheer white fabric to drape on the bride's head. How could anyone resist the price? The bride walked out for the finale and she looked regal and exquisite. The show was a Wow! Experience.

An agent from Air Afrique, a Pan-African airline owned by eleven West African countries, approached me after the show and asked if I could get thirteen people together for a tour to Senegal for Black History Month. The price was $1,100.00, for the tour package. The tour package included a roundtrip airline ticket, hotel, tours, and meals. What could be better than that? How could anyone resist that price? I didn't have a clue about how to do it until I talked with my friend Hal Jackson at WBLS Radio. I told him of my dilemma. He immediately responded, "Hey, we can do a live show every Sunday and see what happens." I also sent press releases to the top one-hundred newspapers around the country. Well, my phone rang off the hook. I received 450 calls regarding the trip! One of the callers told me he was jogging and heard the broadcast, and had to book himself and his wife immediately. We managed to get 96 people on my first trip. I became

Travel. 1995

Haggins International Tours in 1995, and had the good fortune to invite my Mother to the Motherland — Dakar, Senegal. Sharing Senegal with my mother was going to be a very special experience.

Before departing for our trip, I asked if anyone had any dietary requirements, but no one responded. While I was comfortably seated in business class, a young healthy oversized man walked over to my seat and nervously shuddered, "I'm a vegetarian."

I looked up and quickly responded:

"Funny, you don't look like a vegetarian."

A nine-year-old boy seated next to me began laughing with me, and our laugh became infectious, tears began rolling down our cheeks. The boy continued to repeat my response and we continued to laugh.

Once we arrived in Dakar, we were transferred to the Teranga Hotel, a large imposing hotel that sits next to the sea. Mother had her own room. She always arrived at breakfast before I did.

I reserved two buses to accommodate ninety-six participants for our city tour. Everyone rushed to the bus after breakfast for our city tour. One day, this very tall, slow tourist, who was always late, finally showed up. I called out, as he stepped onto the bus, "Come on, Pokie."

His wife responded, "His name is not Pokie, his name is Herman."

"Well, to me he is Pokie." Then she turned to Donna Bethea, a new friend, and said, "You'd better control your huzzzz...ben."

"First, I can't control him and second, he is not my huzzzz...ben."

Dakar is a cosmopolitan city with skyscrapers and lots of bustling activities. No visit is complete without visiting the Soumedioune Market. Soumedioune, is located along the esplanade lining the Atlantic Ocean. Marché Soumbédioune, is an open-air market where local artisans and craftsmen sell their creations, for instance: a variety of African crafts, leather goods, woodcarvings, statues, gold jewelry, wooden masks, jewelry, clothes, leather goods, pottery, paintings, batiks featuring images of harvest or daily life in a village. It's a destination where I found local African cuisine.

It's customary to take a little time to negotiate for the best price, because It's part of their tradition and culture, and it's also an expected interaction. First, ask the vendor for his price, knowing you can reduce it by one third. Then do the old flinch game. Generally, the vendors will ask: "How much would you like to pay."

Think long and hard about it. Make a low ball offer of one-third or half the asking price and stick to it. Bartering and haggling in the markets is a cultural thing. The vendor will say, "That was my first price, give me your best price."

That calls for some serious negotiating. If the vendor doesn't agree, then walk away. Walk away several times, until he's convinced you don't want the item. That's when acting comes into

Mother in Dakar, Senegal

play. Then you pay what you want or...fuhgetaboutit. Walk away if the seller isn't willing to entertain your offer. The old walk-away trick distinguishes you from the inexperienced barterer. Remember, when you give a little and do it with a smile, everyone is happy. Just say it's o.k. we can still be friends. Remember, you don't need any of those wonderful, beautiful, irresistible items...but you want them. A sign of an inexperienced shopper in Africa does not understand the culture and the process of bargaining. It's customary to haggle with the shopkeepers in the market. Haggling is an art.

There were also several shops across the street from the market. That's where I found lots of antique carvings, in various sizes, and a display of hand-carved wood furniture.

Due to its proximity to the sea, fishermen returned to the beach in their colorful (Pirogues) boat, then locals gathered to negotiate the price for the catch of the day. It's a way of life in Dakar. I even haggled in a shop at the airport in Ecuador. It's my favorite thing to do, it's an obsession. We also stopped at the Camel Market, where I spotted a bunch of colorful woven baskets of all sizes. The craftsmanship was amazing. I bought several baskets to use for my laundry at home.

Mother was mesmerized by the Church of the Saviour's interior. Black saints were painted on the ceiling and along the walls, and white saints were captured in the stained glass windows. Our guide said. " The church is for everyone." We also stopped in front of the Presidential Palace for a photo op with a guard, who stood tall and proud as he protected the palace.

The IFAN Museum of African Arts features important collections from across Francophone Africa. The noteworthy collection presents an important glimpse into West African history and the visual cultures. The IFAN Museum is one of the oldest, and it was founded in 1936. It is the most prominent institution dedicated to the research and exhibition of West African art and artifacts museums in West Africa. The IFAN Museum of African Arts features a display of African Ritual masks, costumes, instruments, clothing, weapons, pottery, and history. It was notably supported by the first Senegalese president, Léopold Senghor, who served between 1960 and 1980. Seminal Artworks and Artifacts from Mali, the Ivory Coast, Guinea Bissau, Burkina Faso, and beyond inhabit the IFAN Museum of African Arts in the Senegalese capital.

After the city tour, we boarded a ferry to Goree Island. The ferry ride across the bay took thirty-minute. As we approached Goree Island, the pastel, dusty-rose-colored houses appeared mysteriously through a thin grey haze. After disembarking, we began a casual walk along the cornice to the Museum of History (the Fortress). As I entered one of several rooms depicting the slave trade, my mouth dropped, and I stopped in my tracks, disbelieving the sight of skeletons of our ancestors buried together in a large block of cement. Their mouths were open because they were crying out from the pain they had suffered. The skeletons graphically displayed elements of torture. I could hear their loud cries as I was reduced to tears. There were several other rooms displaying artifacts of shackles, chains, and whips from the slave era. Neither my mother nor I could comprehend what we were witnessing. We were in shock.

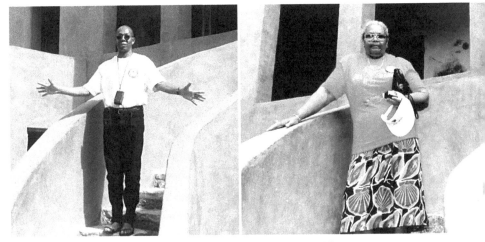

Me and Mother at the Door of No Return, 1995

The House of the Slaves, was the highlight of the Goree Island tour. Dr. Joseph Ndiaye lectured on the conditions and existence of the slave trade. He talked about how the Portuguese, Spaniards, Dutch, and the English perpetuated the trade within the four walls of that house. He was emphatic and outraged regarding the comparison of the Holocaust — which existed for only eleven years — to three hundred and seventy years of slavery. "Nobody ever talks about slavery. We need to be reminded, so this catastrophe never happens again. 'Roots' was only the tip of the iceberg," he firmly stated. He demonstrated how slaves were captured and then shackled with chains around their waists and wrists. He also showed how their ankles were attached to an iron ball and chain, totally preventing them from escaping. If a slave was defiant, he was forced into a 4X4 compartment with twenty-men cramped under the stairwell to lay in feces and urine. There was only a tiny opening in the wall to allow a bit of fresh air and daylight. Men were only allowed out once a day to stretch. The rebellious men were beaten and shackled, then thrown into the Atlantic Ocean to be eaten by sharks. The iron ball prevented them from escaping the inevitable.

Slave traders lived upstairs over the slave quarters. Many young ladies indulged in sexual favors to become pregnant. Once impregnated they were set free. Moments later, everyone gathered downstairs at the 'Door of No Return'. The 'Door' opens onto the Atlantic Ocean.

*Me and Mother at the Door of No Return terrace
on Goree Island, Senegal, 1995*

It's called the 'Door of No Return,' because once the captives passed through that door, they were shipped off to the Americas or the Caribbean, never to return to Africa. They would forever remain separated from their homes, families, lineage, culture, and customs. Everyone joined hands, formed a circle, and took a moment to reflect and remember in silence.

"We must never forget what happened here and never allow it to happen again," Dr. Ndiaye emphatically stated.

Everyone was asked to call out the name of the person who inspired him or her. That was a life-changing experience for everyone. I called out Richard Walker, my grandad.

The grueling trip across the Atlantic Ocean typically lasted between six and eight weeks. During the "Middle Passage," about 15% of captives died at sea, mostly from sea sickness, suicide, and at the hands of the crew. It is estimated about 10 – 28 million Africans were shipped across the Atlantic between the 15th and 19th centuries. The exact number remains a mystery.

Forced into a life of slavery in Brazil, the Caribbean, Europe, America, and specifically for my ancestors, South Carolina. The 'Door' served as a painful and symbolic reminder of the unyielding suffering of millions of slaves and the devastating, generational impact that was felt for decades to come. As emotional as it was to stand in the space where my ancestors were forced into slavery, it was also a moment of letting go, retelling—and celebrating—the life of our ancestors and loved ones. One young lady on the tour had an especially heartfelt reason for her trip to Senegal:

"I promised my husband that someday we'd go to Africa. I felt a sense of peace within myself after I sprinkled his ashes in the ocean. We did make that journey."

There wasn't a dry eye in the house after hearing her story.

We had a mission to 'Put a Book in a Child's Hand'. I asked everyone to bring Bic pens and paper for the school students. We walked to an elementary school on Goree Island and gifted the school with four boxes of books, pens, and paper. After we presented our gifts, the students showed their appreciation by singing a local song. They were so happy. One of the ladies from our group brought four pens.

"Where do you think you're going with four pens. This is Africa and the students need lots of pens for school."

After visiting the school and the 'Door of No Return', we stopped at a restaurant next to the beach, to reflect on our experiences on the island. Our table was shaded with a large parasol to protect us from the hot, burning, sun. I ordered a Flag Beer to compliment my Thiéboudienne, The national dish of Senegal.

Thiéboudienne is a hearty one-pot meal. It's a bold-flavored combination of potatoes, cassava, squash or pumpkin, and plantains. combination of fish, rice, and vegetables simmered in tomato sauce.

You can make it with any fish or vegetables you have on hand.

Thiéboudienne

Yield: serves 6-8

For the Fish and Stuffing

- ¼ cup finely chopped parsley
- 2 tsp. crushed red chili flakes
- 6 cloves garlic, minced
- 2 scallions, minced
- ¼ small yellow onion, minced
- Kosher salt and freshly ground black pepper, to taste
- 8 (4–oz.) filets grouper or red snapper

For the Thiéboudienne

- ½ cup canola or palm oil
- 2 medium yellow onions, roughly chopped
- 1 medium green bell pepper, stemmed, seeded, and roughly chopped
- 1 (12–oz.) can of tomato paste
- 6 cups fish or vegetable stock
- 6 small carrots, halved crosswise
- 1 large eggplant, cut into large chunks, or 4 small Thai eggplants
- 1 medium turnip, peeled and cut into 12 wedges
- ½ cassava root, peeled and cut into 1 1/2" chunks
- $^1/_3$ cup dried white hibiscus flowers (optional; see below for ordering)
- 2 tbsp. tamarind paste
- 2 tbsp. fish sauce
- 4 cups basmati rice
- Lime wedges, to serve

Instructions

1. Make the fish and stuffing: Mix the parsley, chili flakes, garlic, scallion, onion, and salt and pepper in a bowl. Using a paring knife, cut a 2-inch split lengthwise in each fish filet; stuff filets with the herb mixture, and set aside.
2. Make the Thiéboudienne: Heat oil in an 8–qt. Dutch oven over medium heat. Add onions and green pepper, and cook, stirring, until softened, about 10 minutes. Add tomato paste; cook, stirring occasionally until vegetables are very soft and paste is lightly browned, about 10 minutes. Add stock, and bring to a boil.
3. Reduce heat to medium-low, and add filets; cook until fish is just cooked through, about 18 minutes. Using a slotted spoon, remove filets and transfer to a plate, then cover to keep warm.
4. Add carrots, eggplants, turnips, and cassava, and cook, stirring occasionally, until tender, about 40 minutes. Using a slotted spoon, transfer vegetables to a bowl; keep warm. Add hibiscus flowers (if using), tamarind paste, and fish sauce, and cook, stirring occasionally, until hibiscus flowers soften, about 5 minutes.
5. Add rice, and stir to combine; reduce heat to low, and cook, covered, until rice is tender, about 45 minutes. Remove from heat, and fluff rice with a fork.
6. To serve, divide fish, vegetables, and rice among serving plates; serve with lime wedges (for squeezing over fish).

I loved sitting in the outdoor restaurant listening to the rushing sound of waves splashing against the shore while the children played nearby. I thought, how lucky those children are not to have been born 200 years ago, and how blessed they are to have gained a future. We walked to the dock, after lunch to wait for the next ferry to take us back to Dakar. Mother sat on the cornice and out of nowhere, a young lady approached her and called her "Momma," then began braiding mother's hair.

Goree Island was an exhilarating, educational, historical, emotional, and memorable experience that must be shared with family and friends.

After the ferry arrived, everyone boarded to return to Dakar. Everyone was still and quiet, while they reflected on their experience on Goree Island. Once we disembarked, we boarded a bus to travel south on a bumpy road with baobab trees in a distance. Locals gleefully smiled and waved as we passed several small villages. We were on our way to the village of Joal Fadiouth, the birthplace of President Senghor (the first president of Senegal).

Mother and I were parched and exceptionally thirsty, when we arrived on the shore of Joal Fadiouth, I raced to a nearby store and purchased several large bottles of Flag Beer to quench our thirst. The store had a thatch roof. Just ahead of us was a long weather-beaten, wood-planked bridge that led to a small island. We were cautioned to watch our step because over a period some of the planks had rotted or misplaced.

We entered a small village, after crossing the bridge. The streets, huts and shops were constructed from seashells and cement and the roofs were thatched. The huts were supported on stilts and raised five feet above the water. The only other means of transportation was a dugout canoe. The dugouts were painstakingly handcrafted from large logs. We were greeted with a grand welcome, and smiles with curiosity from the children. I don't know what it is about children, but they are truly special and adorable.

Children were curious and asked, "Where are you from?"

Mother sitting on the tomb of Jaol Fadiouth, 1995

After a brief walk through the village, we continued our walk to another long, wooden plank bridge that led to a graveyard with raised tombs. Mother was exhausted from schlepping; she quickly sat on one of the tombs. The guide informed her that it wasn't polite to sit on a tomb. She responded with a quick, wicked sense of humor:

"It won't hurt him, because I'm sitting on his feet."

Mother and group walk to Joal Fadouth, Senegal, 1995

Mother in Pink Lake in Senegal, 1995

After the tour, Mother joined a group of ladies in a Senegalese Restaurant for a large, circular plate of Thieboudienne. In keeping with Senegalese tradition, everyone used their right hand to pick up their food; because the left hand is used for sanitary purposes. To use the left hand is considered impolite.

We boarded the bus after lunch and continued our journey to the famous Pink Lake, where the water is really pink. The pink color appears as the sun reflects on the crystals that rise from the bottom of the salty lake. Young, slim, fit men mined the salt from the bottom of the lake, then tossed it in dugout boats. Once the salt dried on the muscular ebony skin, it left an impression of ringlets in zigzag configurations. It appeared as if they were wearing tie-dyed t-shirts. A couple of women walked deep into the salty water with colorful plastic pails to collect brown, grey or pink salt from the boats. Then they lifted the pails and balance them on their head, then walked and placed the salt carefully in cone shapes along the shore. The hot sun-dried and bleached the salt. Once the salt dried, it was bagged and shipped for commercial consumption. Mother pulled up her skirt and walked out into the lake just for the experience. Sharing the trip to Senegal with my mother was one experience, I shall never forget.

Baltic Sea Cruise

I shared another memorable travel experience with Mother. I told her I couldn't afford a Mother's Day gift but offered her a 12-night Celebrity Galaxy Cruise on the Baltic Sea.

"That's a very nice gift," she replied.

That was another opportunity to spend quality time together exploring the world. We flew on Lufthansa to Frankfurt in business class. That was a far cry from traveling in the back of a bus during Jim Crow in the 40s and 50s.

The Frankfurt, Germany Airport, appeared to be the largest I've ever experienced. Mother was 75 years old and had a little difficulty walking the long distance to our connecting flight to Stockholm. A young lady approached and directed us to a lounge, where we could rest and have a few snacks, before our connecting flight.

Thank God, it was a short flight to Stockholm. Stockholm is also known as the "Venice of the North," because it's surrounded by a body of water. We checked in at the Grand Hotel, a five-star property, which is favored by a selective clientele. The hotel faces a canal overlooking the Royal Palace. The first thing on our schedule was a tour of the Vasa Museum. The museum was inaugurated in 1990, it houses the oldest wooden ship. The ship appeared exactly as it sat in the harbor during the winters.

The Vasa Ship is the only remaining intact 17th-century ship. It was embellished with wooden carvings that told stories of the Swedish Royal family, and most importantly the King, Gustav II Adolf. It was the King, who ordered the ship to be built. The ship carried an unprecedented load of 64 bronze cannons. He watched in horror as the ship sank. It sank because of the weight of the cannons.

The Old Town, also known as Gamla Stan was our next stop. It's the largest and best-preserved medieval city center in Europe, and one of the foremost attractions in Stockholm. This is the location where Stockholm was founded in 1252. The Old Town has a labyrinth of narrow winding cobblestone streets that lead to a cluster of architectural wonders. The townhouses are painted in a variety of shades of rust and yellow ocher, which give Gamla Stan its unique character. The alleyways and meeting squares reflect German Architecture dating back to the 13th century, but most buildings are from the 17th and 18th centuries. Gamla Stan is also popular with Aficionados of handicrafts, curios, and souvenirs. Stortorget is located in the middle of Gamla Stan, it's the oldest square in Stockholm. Stortorget is the central point from which runs Köpmangatan, the oldest street in Stockholm. Gamla Stan is like a living pedestrian-friendly museum filled with sights, attractions, restaurants, cafes, bars, and places to shop.

The Riddarholmen Church was built as a Franciscan monastery for the Grey brother monks in the thirteenth century. It is also the royal burial site. There are several beautiful churches and museums in Gamla Stan, including Sweden's national cathedral Stockholm Cathedral and the Nobel Museum.

The Royal Palace of Stockholm is also located in Gamla Stan, since the middle of the 13th century, when the Tre Kronor Castle was built. Architect Nicodemus Tessin built the palace in baroque style and it is designed as a Roman Palace. It's the largest attraction in the district. It's one of Europe's largest and most dynamic palaces with over 600 rooms, divided between seven floors with a state apartment facing the city and smaller living rooms facing the inner courtyard. The Royal Guards have guarded the palace and the Royal Family since 1523.

City Hall is where the Nobel Peace Prize event is held each year. It's a grand old building, that was constructed with eight-million beveled bricks from the region. We were invited to a lovely dinner in the City Hall. Our dinner setting reminded me of the Last Supper because our group of twenty-eight sat at a very long table. The entrée included fresh, pink salmon from the Baltic Sea. It was moist and flaky and by far the best salmon I've ever tasted. At the close of our dinner, a band of waiters marched down the aisle carrying Baked Alaska cakes, lit with sparkling candles to top off our evening.

The Celebrity Galaxy Cruise Ship docked in Stockholm. We boarded the ship the next afternoon for our 12-night cruise on the Baltic Sea. Mother was impressed with the international staff, which represented

Mother and I on a Baltic Sea Cruise, 2001

50 nations. She relished having twenty-four-hour butler service at her disposal. I think, actually, I know she fell in love with the crew, because they were very attentive and called her "Mamma."

We arrived in St. Petersburg, early the next morning. I stood on our balcony, overlooking the dockyard as the ship was docking in the port. I called Mother to check out the dock, where a band serenaded the ship with 'When the Saints Go Marching In.'

After disembarking the ship, we toured the Hermitage Museum, it's one of St. Petersburg's most famous building, not only does it physically dominates Palace Square, but also the south embankment of the Neva River. It was the Winter Palace and a place of solitude for the late Catherine the Great. There are 1,057 rooms and 117 staircases. Of course, we had to visit Pushkin, the Summer Palace, which is located, just outside the city limits. Also known as the 'Palace on the Hill,' it sits on a hill overlooking an English-style landscaped park where a beautiful river flows through it. The palace was almost destroyed during World War II but has risen like a phoenix from the ashes due to an extensive restoration program.

The Church of Resurrection, also known as the 'Spilled Blood Church,' took 25 years to build. It was completed in 1907 with miles of mosaics. Seven attempts were made on Alexander VII's life. He was finally shot and killed on the spot where the church stands today. That was the derivative of the name.

Street vendors readily sold fake Faberge Eggs, a variety of Russian dolls, and trinkets. An American friend told me, I could buy a fur hat for $10.00, if I negotiated properly. I followed her advice and worked the nerves of the vendor until he compromised. Mother bought a similar hat on board for a much higher price.

I told her, "You should have followed my lead."

She also bought Russian boxes and dolls for our family.

Our cruise also stopped in Finland, Poland, Germany, Amsterdam, and Denmark. When we arrived in Copenhagen, Mother wanted to rest on the ship for the day, so I ventured off with several new friends. Copenhagen is a walkable city with lots to explore. It is also a biking city. Copenhagen was very special to me, because my friend, Nils Toft married Latease, my best friend. They have two sons, Michel and Julian.

I was able to retrieve Nils phone number from a phone book. Can you believe they even have a phone book? Everyone is listed in the phone book by their profession. I called his home and a strange man answered. I didn't recall Nils having a roommate. I asked, "To whom am I speaking?" he responded, "Michel." I had not seen Michel since he was about five years old, and to my surprise, there was a manly voice at the other end of the line. I asked for his father's work number, then called Nils to arrange to meet him and his sons at the end of the day. We met and shared a delightful dinner at a restaurant next to a canal. The canal was adorned with colorful houses.

The restaurant was also located near the statue of the Little Mermaid. The statue reclines on a rock in the harbor. It is a bronze work by Edvard Ekiksen, a Danish sculptor. Carl Jacobsen, the magnate of the Carlsberg Brewery commissioned the Little Mermaid in honor of Hans Christian Andersen, a famous Copenhagen author.

At the end of the evening, Nils drove us back to the ship. Other passengers returned to the ship by taxi. As we stepped out of the car, Nils and his boys hugged us. Several shipmates asked, "How do I know those people." You meet people when you travel, and as I've said, "Get up, get out and travel."

The butlers were concerned about mother because she didn't leave the cabin all day. They came to check on her, and she told them she wanted to rest for the day. Once, I returned to the ship and caught up with her, we dressed for dinner and shared a table with another couple.

The final night on board was special because several new friends lined up at the top of the stairs. There were two sets of stairs, that lead to the main dining room. I asked the band to play 'Hello Dolly.' The conductor said we'll play that next. No, you don't understand, we need you to play it now! The band began to play as each group kicked from the left to right side down the stairs. We were having the time of our life. Mother was so embarrassed, that she lowered her head. I had ordered a birthday cake for her. Everyone in the dining room celebrated Mother's birthday with a song and a large birthday cake. I was so delighted we shared time together. It will always remain in my mind as the most memorable experience. I felt very blessed to have shared quality time with her in Senegal and on the twelve-night cruise.

After I returned home, my friend Bob Deadmon introduced me to the editor-in-chief of a magazine. The editor asked me to write travel articles and include photos of my experiences. Several months later, an editor from that magazine, began working for a weekly newspaper. He called and asked me to contribute a weekly travel and restaurant column. He also suggested that I didn't have to write the columns, just put my name on them. No, I wanted to write the column. It was a very exciting time for me because I had to produce two articles per week in a timely fashion. I also recalled the editor called to tell me that I hadn't sent in my columns.

"Just give me a half-hour."

I banged the articles out in no time flat. I worked with that newspaper for four years.

My review of Le Perigord Restaurant brought Sidney Poitier and James Earl Jones in for an evening. Georges Briguet, the owner, was so delighted. He called and told me how the two men laughed and enjoyed the evening.

Two other reviews ended with these clever buttons:

"I have never seen sun-dried ravioli before."

"I asked the DJ to lower the music and he lent a deaf ear."

Reviewing restaurants for my weekly column was very special. My friend Eric Copage once commented, "They treat you like a King."

"What else should I expect?"

Savoy magazine, asked me to write a three-hundred-word article featuring twenty-four hours in a destination. My article featured a stop-over in Thailand. They loved and published it, and said they didn't have to make any changes.

I frequently wrote articles for *Upscale* magazine, until I did not receive my check. So, I called Sheila Bronner, the owner, to inform her. She said, " You shouldn't call me."

I told her, "I wouldn't call you if you paid the bill."

Well, that was the end of that relationship.

I moved my office to 49th Street and Madison Avenue. A very strange thing happened one day: I chained and locked my bike in front of my office building at 49th Street and Madison, knowing that I would use it later in the day. When I was ready to leave my office for the day, I couldn't find my keys and couldn't imagine what happened to them.

Then, it occurred to me that I might have left them in the lock downstairs. As I stepped out of the office building, I was shocked to see my bike standing next to a pole where I locked it. The chain was loosely tossed over it, but the lock was nowhere to be found. My keys were laying on the sidewalk next to the bike. The thief had taken my good lock. I was a bit insulted because they didn't take my bike. I burst out laughing, then rod to a bike shop to replace the lock. I asked for the price of several locks. The first lock cost $45.00 and the second cost $5.00. I bought the $5.00 lock.

Well, I said to myself, "Next time the thief won't be tempted by either my bike or the lock." I sent a note to *The New York Times* for their 'Dairy' page, and they printed the incident. Only in New York kids.

My office was conveniently located to everything. I kept a tuxedo in the office for formal occasions and there were many. One day a friend told me, he was surprised that I popped out of Le Grenouille Restaurant dressed to the nines, then hopped on my bike.

I had the best view of Le Cirque Restaurant, from my office window. It was located in the Hemsley Palace. I frequently lunched in that restaurant.

Many tourist offices were conveniently nearby. The Italian Tourist Office always invited me to their Christmas Party where they had the best view of the lighting of the Christmas tree in the Plaza. Fortunately, knowing New York as I do, I avoided the Christmas crowd, because all the streets were blocked off. So, I entered the subway at 47th St and Sixth Avenue. and walked up to 50th St, then entered the basement of 30 Rockefeller. There was a passage leading to 630 Fifth Avenue, where the Italian Tourist was located. No fool like a New Yorker. The Italian Tourist office always offered several delicious Italian dishes and lots of sparkling Prosecco throughout the evening.

CHAPTER TWENTY-THREE

TV Shows

B ob Deadmon also asked if I'd like to host a weekly local television show.

"Yes, yes, yes," I quickly responded.

I jumped at the chance to have my own TV show. I had been a guest on many local and national TV shows, but never a producer or host. I had no idea what goes into hosting and producing a show or what the hell I was getting into. My first show in 1997 was taped in the studio. The original name was, 'Travel Tips'. It was a half-hour talking heads travel show. Being a host is a different responsibility. I arrived at the studio without any music or guests. So with no guest, I had to perform a 28-minute monologue. I reviewed the tape several years later and was impressed because it was very informative. I was proud of myself for creating that moment in TV land.

Well, moving forward, I immediately signed up for several production classes at MNN Studios. I wanted to learn how to produce and edit a show. During my first class, the instructor asked me to identify various gadgets, such as the Lavalier mic, which I called a 'Clip On'. Mistake! Whenever I was a guest on a variety of national TV shows, the production people hooked me up and I didn't have to think about anything, except to stimulate and keep the conversation going. Suddenly, I was thrust into technology and was forced to learn, quickly. I was on my own.

Producing a weekly television show is very demanding. It's taught me to be disciplined and it allowed my creative juices to flow. Editing is my favorite part of the production because I'm in complete control. It's where I control the destiny of the guest. I always look for the best sound bites that help to tell the story in the shortest amount of time.

When I first began producing my show, I had no idea of how many hours and how much videotape footage would be consumed for a half-hour travel show. Editing is a time-consuming process that one has to love. Editing Southerners is very difficult because they never close their mouths when they talk. Which makes it difficult to edit their speech. 'Bless their hearts. Editing is also the most creative process, similar to designing dresses. The difference is, that I'm doing it with images and sound. If you could only see what goes on in the editing room. I recall a guest continued to talk without breathing, so I yelled, "Shut that Bitch up." It's all meant in fun.

My experience in TV land has been immeasurable, because of the knowledge I've gained. I've learned how to operate a camera, visualize images, edit and select audio tracks, and record voice-overs at MNN Studio in New York City. It's been one of the most stimulating experiences of my life.

The editing studio at MNN is like a sitcom. One day a very large size producer asked a very thin producer if he wanted a piece of him.

"I'm on a diet," the thin producer responded.

On another occasion, another very large size producer wore a horizontal stripe shirt and asked me if it makes him look fat.

"But you are fat, my friend."

There are so many characters and lots of laughs that the public is not privy to.

Helen Gurley Brown, the international editor-in-chief of *Cosmopolitan* magazine, was a guest on my show and commented that she has known me since I was a pup.

I responded, "I was never a pup."

Then she asked, "How did you learn to host? You are attentive even when the camera isn't on you." I told her that I listen because I'm interested in what my guests have to say. I have always been interested in people. We talked about travel and her new book, 'I'm Wild Again.'

She said, "Jon dear, you are a superb interviewer. Thanks for your charm. All my love and admiration."

Another guest once asked if my show was a "Black" show.

"Is Time Warner Black?" I asked.

They certainly wouldn't ask David Letterman if his show was "White."

I was a food and travel writer for a newspaper for four years. So, I covered a lot of territories. I wrote a review on Patsy's restaurant. Sol, the chef was impressed and loved the article. I often invited the last guest and two of the production people out for a drink after taping my *GlobeTrotter TV* show. On one occasion, we walked to Patsy's restaurant and I ordered a round of drinks for my guests. After we finished the first round, I asked for the check. The bartender said. "No bill, have another." So, we took him up on the invitation.

Sol came out of the kitchen and greeted me:

"Jon I know you're hungry, so I want you guys to sit down at a table. I'm going to prepare something special for you."

As we were patiently waiting to place our drink orders, the entire restaurant staff fawned over us, as if we were royalty. Tony Bennett happened to be sitting on the opposite side of the room and called a waiter over because he wanted to know who I was.

I also produce and host The Taste of New York TV, which features a variety of NYC restaurants. I want my audience to taste the cuisine from a variety of countries. I have always said, "New York is an eclectic, international town with a variety of restaurants, with offerings from around the world. You can taste the food, even if you can't travel."

Our most unusual day was taping four restaurants in the Waldorf Astoria Hotel. We taped a segment in a French, a Japanese, a Steak, and a Continental Restaurant. Nat Wood, the cameraman, called the next day to say, he was so tired at the end of the day, that he just sat on his toilet and fell asleep.

One of my favorite Taste of New York TV Shows was taped at The Leopard at des Artistes Restaurant. Gianfranco Sorrentino, is the owner and the best host. The restaurant serves the freshest and the most appetizing dishes from Southern Italy.

Gianfranco shared a little history of the restaurant: "The des Artistes building was originally a hotel for starving artists. Their rooms were upstairs. And they came downstairs to this space. which they called the canteen, to prepare their meals. Then returned to their rooms. The building was sold in the '20s and converted into a residential building. The guy who took over this space, created the first Café des Artistes. He asked Chandler Christie, the most acclaimed artist, at that time, to paint something on the walls for a little money and some food. Well, Chandler took about ten years from 1904 until 1914 to finish painting those beautiful naked nymphs, that you see today. Also, history says that when they first open the restaurant, the ladies used to come and complain, because they said their husbands or boyfriends used to look more at the murals than at them. History also said the restaurant used to hang tablecloths to cover the mural, so they wouldn't be a distraction."

Another funny story: When I opened the restaurant about twelve years ago, I received a reservation from a lady who was 102 years old. I wanted to give her the first table by the door because I thought perhaps at 102 years, she would prefer not to walk. When she arrived on the arm of a gentleman, she refused the offering of the table near the front door. She said NO! Then pointed to a table in a corner, and said I want that table. So of course, we sat her there. We prepared a special cake with 102 candles, everyone came out and sang, Happy Birthday, even the chef. Then suddenly the gentleman who had accompanied her, said, "You see that painting of the lady in the corner, it's my mother." She was that 102-year-old lady.

After talking about many destinations around the world. I had to travel to all those places I talked about, so I changed the name from 'Travel Tips' to 'GlobeTrotter TV' in 2000. I felt my message was bigger than just sitting in the studio. GlobeTrotter TV is a half hour weekly lifestyle travel show that features many destinations around the world.

CHAPTER TWENTY-FOUR

Travel for

GlobeTrotter TV

While preparing for an international trip for GlobeTrotter TV.
A friend once said, "You are going on a work vacation."
I responded, "Don't you dare use that word, VACATION, again."

Traveling for work is not a vacation. It's not as much fun as most people think. Perhaps, I make *GlobeTrotter TV* look easy but believe me, many hours are spent taping, producing, and hosting the show.

David Fasano, my videographer/ director, and I travel with eight pieces of luggage: two video cameras, two tripods, a monopod, a drone, electronic equipment, two backpacks, lights, and two personal bags. A funny thing happened while checking in at New York – JFK, an airline ticket agent, weighed our baggage and told us one of our bags was over-weight, so we open the bag and began stuffing items from that bag into the Tripod bag.

She weighed again and said, "It's still overweight."

Then suggested we pay $100.00 for the extra weight. She asked us to think about it. We simultaneously looked at each other and thought about it for a moment, then picked up the tripod bag and headed to the TSA to board the plane.

On another occasion, we arrived at JFK and another ticket agent informed us that one of our bags was overweight, so I open the bag, took out my shoes, and put them under my arms.

She was so frustrated and said, "Never mind."

We were permitted to board the plane. You gotta have a sense of humor when you travel.

We hit the road running the minute we arrive because I'm always thinking of the next thing to feature and how to edit it in the show. I never really get a chance to relax. I wear different color pants each day because I don't have time to take notes. That's my way of identifying each destination when I return to the studio.

To create a show, I have to review the video, sort it out and then import it into the computer, place it on the timeline, edit it, and add graphics, music, voice-over, and transitions. Then the show is finally exported in the proper format. The last step is to upload the show to the control room for airing. To produce a show also requires lots of patience. The process can take a week for a single show.

I recall wrapping up a day of taping, *GlobeTrotter TV*, when someone asked if the show will air the next day.

"Are you kidding me?"

GlobeTrotter TV's first international trip was on the magic carpet to Tunisia. It was a very long flight, especially since there are no direct flights from New York. Tunisia is an exotic destination. Located on the northeastern tip of Africa, its embraced by the Mediterranean Sea. The entire country is the size of Florida. Tunis is the capital, and it's a bustling metropolis that offers a path into its rich history of spectacular Roman and Venetian historical sites, such as Carthage and the Roman Mosaics in the Bardo Museum.

I loved the location of our hotel because it's a short walk to Sidi Bou Said. Sidi Bou Said is a seventeenth-century Andalusian Village, that's perched on top of a hill. The village has a labyrinth of narrow winding cobblestone streets and white-washed buildings. The buildings are embellished with decorative Mediterranean blue shutters. The doors are adorned with cerise color bougainvillea. There were a variety of cafes to rest my weary feet and have a glass of mint tea. I loved browsing through the galleries and small shops that featured antiques, leather and silver items, and handicrafts. I especially loved Sidi Chebaane Café. The cafe is washed in white paint and accented with large Mediterranean blue umbrellas. The café also offered the best view of a modern marina and the bay of Tunis.

Tunis held its Third International Film Festival. It was dedicated to women producers and directors. The all-star-studded event invited a variety of International Stars and producers from around the world. Guests arrived from China, Chile, Europe, Tunisia, Canada, the United States, France, Iran, and a variety of other countries. Our first formal dinner was shared with Eileen McGonigle, and actress Claudia Cardinale, she was dressed from head to toe in Armani. I was most impressed with a group of performers from China. The group had a variety of disabilities, such as loss of hearing or sight, but that did not prevent them from performing. Those who couldn't hear responded to the bass vibration from the floor. They were very creative and synchronized. Their visual performance was very much like the Busby Berkley Films of the 1940s. I was invited to six movie screenings per day. It was a dizzying experience. While interviewing the producers, one of them asked if I liked her film. I was polite and made favorable comments because there was no way I could remember which film. A young woman producer from Iran, won the best film of the year. Her film featured a story of a traditional Iranian family, where the father had the last word regarding his daughter's love relations.

Claudia Cardinale said, "I'm the only actress who was born in Tunisia. I'm making a movie here. It's incredible to be here again because people love me. I've been traveling around town and everyone calls out, "Claudia come here." Movies are a terrific inspiration for everyone. Young people need to discover movies from around the world."

The very next day we were off for a long drive through the desert to Tozeur. There were bays of salt mines along the side of the dusty dirt roads. In a far distance, voluminous mountains with graduating shades of dusty rose colors reflected the sunset. Camel crossing signs were quite common because herds of camels grazed along the roadside. We occasionally stopped for a refreshing beverage to cool ourselves from the hot sun and dust from the road.

The city of Tozeur is known for its elaborate brick facades and a towering minaret. It's also known for fantastic markets, where one can find carpets, ceramics, footwear, and of course dates. Dates are a specialty of Tozeur. Tozeur even has a date museum (Eden Palm Museum) where I explored the history of dates. Did you know there are 250 varieties of dates? The translucent date is the Queen of dates and it's undeniably the most prestigious. Its name means "The fingers of life." It's also the most exported Tunisian variety. It was introduced in Tunisia in 1600 B.C. from Southern Algeria. The museum also featured products made from the date fruit, such as jams and bread. There were by-products made from the tree and leaves, such as baskets, furniture, and mats.

I love dates and Tunisian cuisine. A young agile man climbed a tall palm tree and chopped off a branch of fresh dates, just for me. Did you know that a strand of dates is very heavy? I know this because I tried to lift one. Those dates were the most delicious and the BESTEST I've ever tasted. There is nothing like a fresh Tunisian date.

David and I had just finished taping. While walking along the street, a gentleman stepped out of his shop and yelled, "Goodbye Jon" Obviously I made an impression on him. Then again, they don't see other Black TV hosts walking down their streets. Tunisians are very welcoming and friendly.

We continued our journey along, long winding dirt roads through the desert. I spotted olive farmers and families harvesting olives from a tree. We casually stopped to help. I was offered an Afro-comb to comb through leaves to harvest the olives on the tree. The olives dropped from the tree branches onto a large net, where the olives would later be transported to an Olive Mill. It was the most fun experience, especially while wearing my white cashmere sweater. David asked me to taste an olive. I put one in my mouth, then he asked, "How did it taste." I responded, "Bitter."

Tunisia exports minerals and garments. Olive oil is the third-largest industry. Tunisia is one of the world's largest olive oil producers.

There are seventy-million olive trees in Tunisia. It's against the law to destroy an olive tree. Figures released recently by the Tunisian Olive Oil board show that about 70 percent of the country's oil is exported. Olive oil production plays a key role in the Mediterranean country's economy, employing more than 300,000 farmers and providing an income to an estimated one million Tunisians.

Once we arrived at the Mahjoub Olive Oil Mill, Mr. Mahjoub gave us a tour, to help us understand the process of making the first and second cold press virgin olive oil. He said, "We make the oil when the olives are half-green, half-dark." His family has been making olive oil for more than a century. The hand-picked olives are then crushed at a slow speed to keep the temperature cool. "This process is very important to avoid giving heat to the paste." By keeping the olives cold, the Mahjoubs' seek to preserve their antioxidant qualities, something consumers are looking for more and more these days. Their golden olive oil is branded organic. "The velocity of the crushing machine is very important. Our machine is made for bigger velocity, but we change it all the time to have this cold product."

But what makes this Tunisian olive mill unique is that the oil and water separate, not in a heated centrifuge, but by gravity. The oil is lighter than water, so it rises to the top and is then ladled, by hand, into barrels. The Mahjoubs' slower, more labor-intensive process fits in with the family's traditional approach. Abdelwaheb Mahjoub said that 15 years ago, his family met to consider the future of their business, whether to go mass market or concentrate on niche. They chose a niche. The mill just crushes the olives, and nothing is added. The color of the first press is a rich leaf green. I tasted the first and second press and it reminded me of Castrol from my early childhood. But, it's awfully tasty, when I dip a piece of bread in the oil. The mill only exports the first cold press Virgin Olive Oil. Tunisians buy the second press for cooking because its consistency is heartier. He only uses the first cold press in his home. Now, I have a greater appreciation of what goes into making olive oil.

The local bread baked in a tandoor oven is the best, especially with a little olive oil. After all, Tunisia is also known for its bread and olive oil.

Majid and Onsa Mahjoub Recipe

Ingredients

- Harissa (hot chili paste)
- 3 ounces mild and hot dried chilies, such as anchos, New Mexican and guajillos
- 1 red bell pepper, roasted
- 1 clove garlic
- ¼ teaspoon salt
- 1 teaspoon ground coriander
- 1 teaspoon ground caraway seed
- 1 teaspoon fine sea salt
- Olive oil

Preparation

Stem, seed, and break up chilies. Place in a bowl and cover with boiling water. Cover and let stand 30 minutes. Drain; wrap in cheesecloth and press out excess moisture. Repeat the process with the red bell pepper. Crush garlic clove with 1/4 teaspoon salt in a bowl.

In a food processor or blender grind chilies with red bell pepper, garlic/salt mixture, coriander, caraway, and salt. Drizzle in enough oil to make a thick paste. Pack the mixture in a small dry jar. Cover Harissa with a thin layer of oil. Cover and refrigerate.

Harissa will keep 2 to 3 weeks in the refrigerator with a thin layer of oil.

Serving size — about ½ cup

Les Moulins Mahjoub M'Hamsa Salad

Ingredients

- 1 ¹/₃ cup of M'Hamsa Couscous
- 1 large onion, Julienne
- 2 fresh tomatoes, small dice
- 1 green pepper, small dice
- 1 preserved lemon, rind only, small dice
- 1 cucumber, small dice
- 1 tsp. sun-dried capers
- 2 Tb extra virgin olive oil
- 1 tsp. dried mint, or 1 Tablespoon fresh mint
- 1 tsp. white wine vinegar

*(Do not add salt, the salt from the capers
should be plenty of seasoning)*

Preparation

Put about 2 quarts of water into a saucepan and bring to a boil. Add a pinch of salt. Pour the M'Hamsa Couscous into the saucepan and gently stir to ensure that the grains are evenly distributed. Turn down the heat and cook uncovered over low heat for 7-8 minutes until the couscous is "al dente." Turn off the heat and drain the water. Add two tablespoons of extra virgin olive oil and gently stir it into the couscous. Pour the couscous into a large bowl to cool on the counter. When the couscous is cold, add the julienne onion, diced tomatoes, green pepper, preserved lemon, cucumber, mint, and vinegar. Mix gently with a wooden spoon and put into the refrigerator to chill for half an hour.

Serve as an accompaniment to grilled fish or meats.

I returned home and gifted my mother a bottle of Mahjoub's Olive Oil. Several weeks later, I asked, how she used it.

"I fried chicken," she replied.

"That was the best olive oil and it should've only been used with an eye-dropper," I commented.

"Well, you'll get me another bottle next time."

I did return to Tunisia and bought another bottle for her.

I have traveled throughout Tunisia, from the mountains to the sea, through the desert, and visited historic sites. Tunisia is filled with excitement, history, great cuisine, and friendly people.

Those are only a few words to describe Tunisia.

CHAPTER TWENTY-FIVE

Defining Moments

A defining moment for me was landing on my back in the hospital with bacterial pneumonia after a rugged travel schedule around the world. I knew I was going to pull through and make my life fuller, bigger and better. I created a routine every day, to keep my mind and body healthy, and not feel sorry for myself. I knew I was going to pull through with flying colors. I began writing my first travel book while lying in the hospital. One of the volunteers came around and asked if I wanted her to read to me. She had a thick European accent.

I said, "With that accent, no thanks."

I began decorating my room, by turning the bed diagonally towards the window, so I'd have a better view. The nurse came in, then ran out to tell the doctor what I had done. The doctor told her to leave me alone.

Someone sent a beautiful basket of flowers, I soon discovered I was allergic to the flowers, so I offered them to another patient. One of my friends asked if they could bring me something, I requested fried chicken, which was something I would normally, never eat, especially from a fast-food restaurant, but it was certainly better than the hospital food. Now, let's talk about the hospital food. I requested to see the dietician to whom I complained about the mystery food that I didn't recognize. It was not worthy of putting in my mouth. So, she began sending me lots of chocolate-flavored Ensure. That was the best thing in the hospital.

The attendant who changes the bed linen was standing in the doorway of another room complaining about me,

He said, "He thinks he's in a hotel."

I was standing behind him and he didn't know it, suddenly he turned around and was thoroughly embarrassed. I asked him to change my linen.

He said, "We only change the sheets when they are soil."

I walked him over to my bed and said, "Take a look at this, there is blood on my sheets from the nurses sticking me to take blood.

I would say, "this is soiled." Then he changed the sheets.

I recovered after a month in the hospital. No more sticking me with needles. I couldn't wait to get the hell out of there and get back to work. I checked myself out and then hopped in a taxi to take me to my studio, where I began working on my goals because nothing was going to stop me now. I was determined to follow my dream, without wasting a moment. I couldn't wait to travel again and allow my life to evolve.

David and I were in Parati, a lovely Colonial town in the State of Rio de Janeiro. We had just finished taping a show. He accidentally left the camera on. Later, when I looked at the tape and saw myself limping away from the camera. I knew for sure, that I needed a knee replacement.

At first, I thought I was too young for the operation. But, after careful consideration, I asked my friend, Vanessa Groce, for a reference to a specialist, because she had the operation and trusted her doctor. She suggested Doctor Amar Ranawat, at the Hospital for Special Surgery. He specializes in knee replacement surgery. The next Defining Moment was getting a knee replacement. I followed her advice and made an appointment. The operations were seamless. The next day after the operation, the doctor asked me to walk down the hall. He gave me a choice of a short walk or a long walk, naturally, I chose the long walk. I spent two nights in the hospital, The food was equivalent to a five-star restaurant. The Hospital of Special Surgery is the best place for knee surgery. The post-op visits were seamless. I called Dr. Ranawat a butcher because he performs six knee operations on Tuesdays and Thursdays.

I chose a Rehab facility in the West Village, after being released from the hospital. The facility was more like an old folk home, rather than a Rebab. All the old ladies wanted to have dinner with me, and I politely told them that I have a lot of reading to do. Fortunately, I had a private room. My friends Maybelle and Neal Webster, brought me a copy of Michelle Obama's book, 'Becoming'. The book was a page-turner and I was anxious to finish it. I kept myself busy reading and reflecting on my life, especially the things I wanted to accomplish. I checked myself out on the fifth day and returned home, where I received personal therapy. I had a lot of time to think and reflect on my life, and what I wanted to achieve. I couldn't wait to travel again.

I was off and running within a few weeks. I returned to the TV studio to produce my *GlobeTrotter TV* shows. Several months later I visited Sicily, where I climbed to the top of Mt. Etna and toasted with a glass of Firrriato full-body red wine. I had the best view of the volcano and the craters. David used a drone to capture the site from above.

When I returned home, I sent Dr. Ranawat one of my travel books, where I shared my experience of climbing to the top of Mt. Etna with amazement and no pain. I told my ten-year-old nephews that I no longer have knees, and they laughed. I look forward to a long and fruitful life.

Archbishop Desmond Tutu

I met Archbishop Desmond Tutu and his wife Leah at the airport in Aruba. Upon arrival, he sighed, "It is so HOT!" I laughed and thought to myself, "What else should he expect? After all, we are in the tropics." His wife looked resplendent in her colorful boubou (a native African dress). "I love your Boubou, Mrs. Tutu," I whispered in-ear, and she smiled appreciatively.

Archbishop Tutu was consecrated Bishop of Lesotho in 1976. He became General Secretary of the South African Council of Churches in

1978. The government confiscated his passport in reprisal for his call for an international boycott of South Africa in 1980. Archbishop Tutu is well-respected around the world for his struggles against apartheid in South Africa. It was a struggle to gain equal rights for all Black people. Tutu is opposed to all forms of violence.

The next evening, he opened his speech with: "God was nailed to the cross without arms. The reason God didn't have arms was that we are his arms and have to be his partner and an instrument on this earth to help God do his work." Tutu was a powerful, riveting, inspiring speaker that got everyone's undivided attention; you could hear a pin drop.

I spoke with him regarding winning the 1984 Nobel Peace Prize in recognition of his nonviolent campaign to limit International Trade and Investment activities in South Africa. He used his prize money to establish the Southern African Refugee Scholarship Fund, enabling disadvantaged students to further their studies.

I have visited South Africa on three occasions and I have toured the black township of Soweto, which is located west of Johannesburg. No trip to Soweto is complete without visiting Mandela's original home, which is now a museum. The guide told us that Winnie always kept her floor spotless because they never knew when someone would throw a bomb or shoot through the windows. It was an unsettled time.

It was a different time when I visit. Because, there was a contrast between the palatial, modern homes of Archbishop Tutu and Winnie Mandela. Soweto is a peaceful neighborhood today, but it wasn't always that way. During the 1970s student riots, Hector Peterson was among some 30,000 students who took to the streets of Soweto protesting a government edict that all classes were to be taught in Afrikaans — the language of the white minority. Thirteen-year-old Hector was the first student that was shot and killed by a policeman's bullet in the square. Peter Magubane, a young photographer, captured that moment of Hector being carried away in the arms of a young man, while his seventeen-year-old sister walked by his side. At the end of that day, there were officially twenty-three dead, although locals say it was more than two hundred. Hundreds more were injured as the protest spread throughout the country.

Archbishop Tutu told me that winning the Nobel Peace Prize helped South Africans maintain their hope and struggle against apartheid, because suddenly the rest of the world cared, especially after seeing the photo of Hector Peterson that was carried by the wire services and got the attention of the world. That photo also helped to end the attempt to impose Afrikaans on Black students and helped in the battle to end apartheid. It was a noble struggle and for the most part, it was a non-violent struggle. He added that he felt his honor was a warm tribute to his people.

A Hector Peterson Museum was erected on the square where the riot took place on that horrific day. The museum also displays other photographs, films, and artifacts depicting that inhumane period. Bricks lined the floor inside the museum, each brick represented a student who lost their lives on that faithful day.

South Africa was reborn in 1994 and got its freedom and democracy with the election of Nelson Mandela. After retiring as Archbishop in 1996, he became Chairman of the Truth and Reconciliation Commission in South Africa, presiding over the traumatic revelation of the secrets of apartheid. The Committee was established to create mending and healing of the races, to get people to confess to the atrocities during the Apartheid period.

When the ANC (African National Congress) was formed in the late fifties, America was going through the same integration problems as South Africa. Nelson Mandela was the president of the organization that spoke out about the injustices of his country.

I empathize with their struggle during apartheid because I was exposed to bigotry during my younger years in Sanford, Florida, where Blacks and Whites were segregated in toilets, buses, restaurants, and neighborhoods. Also, Colored people weren't allowed to try on shoes or clothing in stores. It was an awful period in American history. There were vile lynchings and cross burnings throughout the South. We were fighting for the same equality and justice.

I asked Bishop Tutu if winning the 1984 Nobel Peace Prize changed his life, and he told me it certainly opened doors that weren't previously available. For instance, he had been desperately trying to get an invitation to the White House to meet with President Reagan

Jon and Bishop Desmond Tutu

regarding the constructive engagement policy, which he thought was a disaster. But he had no luck, until he received an announcement from Oslo, that he had won the Nobel Peace Prize. Then he received an invitation immediately. All the things he had previously been preaching hadn't been taken seriously; suddenly, winning made him appear as almost an Oracle.

When asked what was his most defining moment, he took a moment to respond, "To be loved for yourself, not because of your achievements or for being good or bad, but for being you. That seems especially important in the Black community when everything seemed to conspire to prove that you were not valuable, that you were worthless, that you were regarded as a non-entity." He told me that when he began to understand the fundamentals of the Christian faith—that each of us was created in the image of God and that God invests in every one of us as an extraordinary infinite worth—that was his defining moment.

Then I asked what was it like growing up in South Africa? "White kids were privileged, while Black children were disregarded very much like the disparity between Blacks and Whites in America. When the people from the township went into town to work in the homes of the Whites, they saw the disparity. There were separate entrances at the post office and so on. It was a difficult time, but they lived through it.

We didn't spend too much time thinking about the conditions, because we were too busy living our lives. Everything was very segregated. Blacks lived in locations characterized as ghettos. The township didn't have lights, running water, or toilets."

I toured Soweto, where there were shacks as well as modern homes like his. Certainly, things haven't changed for those people who live in the shacks. Those same people have probably lived in shacks for generations. They wake up in their ghettos and go to work in a white person's house, which has all the amenities.

Archbishop Tutu recalled going into town, where White folks lived. White boys sometimes taunted him with racial slurs. But what was quite extraordinary to me, was the fact that he didn't go around moaning, with a heavy burden on his shoulders; he just lived life, a deprived life as it was. He didn't go around feeling sorry for himself, but he noticed certain things.

Going into town, he looked at the beautiful schools that White children attended. Then he saw young Black children scavenging through rubbish bins because White children were getting government supplies that they didn't need. They would throw away what they didn't want because they preferred what their mommies had prepared for them. The Black children were not getting the basic amenities that were needed for school. That was indelibly impressed on his mind— the kind of existence that Black people had in South Africa.

"South Africa has changed for some Black people, but others are too poor to notice. The poor man has nothing to compare it with. That was the most fundamental change that could ever happen to anyone, anywhere. As it happens, even when material circumstances for people changed, it didn't happen for everyone. We don't have magical ways to turn a wilderness into a garden or turn a land of oppression and injustice suddenly into a paradise. For example, slavery was abolished in the United States many years ago, but just look around and you'll see, that there is still contrast in many places between the Whites and Blacks, nothing has changed. Things could be a great deal better in South Africa, but then again, things could be a great deal worse."

I asked if he felt the Black people of South Africa would ever forgive Whites for the pain and degradation they cause during apartheid.

"They have; otherwise we wouldn't be living with White people now. That's why South Africa can build and go forward."

I was surprised at how patient people can be. They have not yet said to hell with Nelson Mandela and Desmond Tutu and all those people who talk about reconciliation; they have not gone on a rampage. They wake up from poverty and go to the affluent to work. At the end of the day, they leave the affluence to return home. You would think that they would say they have had it up to their eyebrows and were not going to take it anymore. They have not done that. They have continued their patience. That is why we keep saying to White people, that it's in their own interest, it is not being altruistic, to help the transformation happen.

It's in their own interest that there is a better distribution of the resources of South Africa. It's in their own interest that they should be narrowing the gap between the poor and the rich, the haves and the have-nots. It's not altruism—it's the best form of self-interest. They may find that if they don't do that of their own free will, someday they could lose everything they have.

Tutu told me that he was most inspired by listening to the people who have suffered grievously, people who should be consumed by bitterness and anger and hatred. They are actually being magnanimous and generous and forgiving.

Mandela pursued his dream, that someday all men would be free. However, he knew it was against the law to fight and contradict the White system. He was incarcerated for twenty- seven years, most of those years were spent on Robben Island. Robben Island is a thirty-minute ferry ride off the coast of Cape Town. But what he wanted most for his country was to end the apartheid and free his Black countrymen. In his heart, he knew that all men should be free and treated equally.

I visited Robben Island on two occasions. Former prisoners now work as guides. They shared their stories of ill-humane conditions and horrendous treatment from the prison guards. They tell of many events where the cruel prison guards brutally beat them and force them to eat their own feces. Somehow, that man survived and lived to tell his story. There wasn't a dry eye in the house as he reflected on his life on Robben Island.

I passed Mandela's small cell and couldn't imagine having spent most of his twenty-seven years sleeping in that small quarter. Day after day chopping granite in the quarry under the bright sun. However, Mandela found time to read books and write his autobiography, although the prison confiscated his first manuscript. Mandela never lost his perspective and steadfastly focused on his goal.

My first recollection of hearing Mandel's name was through his association with the ANC and his fight for equality and freedom for the Blacks in South Africa. Here in the United States during the 1960s, African Americans were going through the same Black Power struggle. Blacks were in the majority in South Africa, yet unable to vote and share freedom with the rest of the country. Blacks were not allowed to walk on the same sidewalk as Whites.

When Mandela returned to civilian life in 1992, he wasn't bitter; he opened his heart to forgive, but will never forget his past. In 1994, his countrymen held him in the highest esteem and elevated him to the pinnacle of his life as the President of South Africa.

I complimented Tutu at the end of our meeting by saying, with age comes wisdom and knowledge, and Thank God you are gifted with both. He told me that if someone is inspired to follow in his footsteps, they must believe that human beings are fundamentally good. "Human beings are not made for hatred; they are made for love. Human beings are not made for nursing grudges, but for forgiving. And if we give people the opportunity and we say, here are the alternatives, I believe that most people would much rather be good than be bad."

I have visited South Africa several times since Apartheid and experienced its growth as a new country. What an inspiration.

CHAPTER TWENTY-SIX

Kyle & Kaleb

Mother's grandchildren gifted her with four great-grandchildren: Xavier Jr., Colette, Kyle, and Kaleb.

When my twin grand-nephews, Kyle and Kaleb were three years old, one of them asked me to bounce him on my knee, then the other one wanted to bounce. I told them I'll give them one minute and that's it. I was always firm with them and I didn't take any crap.

I decided to give my mother a 90th Birthday party. I invited Carolyn and Carolyn Jr., Kelly, (Carolyn's daughters) Kyle, and Kaleb (Kelly's twins). Mother was beyond delighted to have four generations sharing her special day. I cooked a beautiful fresh salmon steak, corn on the cob, and mashed potatoes, complimented with a salad. We presented mother with a large birthday cake and lots of colorful balloons. After Kyle finished his dinner, he looked up at me and said, "Thanks, Uncle Jon, that was the best dinner ever." I was so moved by his kind thoughts and the fact that he loved his dinner. He was only five-year-old, it brought me to tears.

Mom with Kaleb, 2003

Kyle and Kaleb asked, "When can we travel with you?"

"When you get a little older," I responded.

I bought several books when they were ten years old. I want them to read and discover our history and the world beyond. I also thought it's best to advance them with books for twelve-year-olds. So they could be ahead of their class. I also told them they have a lot to learn about the life, the world, and our history. The first book was Barack Obama. They were familiar with him and his presidency.

The second book was Harriet Tubman. I asked if they knew anything about Miss Tubman.

Kyle said, "Yeah, she rode on the back of a bus."

I laughed and said, "No, that was Rosa Parks."

Miss Tubman lead the Underground Railroad. And if there was a bus, she would have taken it, instead of walking barefoot from the south. Then they asked if I was a friend of Miss Tubman. "How is that possible, since she lead the Underground Railroad about 175 years ago."

Their third book was Frida Kahlo, a Mexican artist. I wanted them to get familiar with other cultures and artists. They enjoyed reading about Miss Kahlo. There was a query at the end of each book, so I tested them on what they had read.

One of the defiant ten-year-old twin nephews said, "The one thing we don't like about you, is that you make us read."

I responded, "Years from now, you will re-think your words and realize how fortunate you were to have me care about your education

Mother's 90th birthday with Kyle and Kaleb, 2015

Kyle and Kaleb Grant, my grand-nephews, 2020

because when I was ten years old, I didn't have anyone to volunteer to help me read."

I also informed them that they are special because they are not living during the time of Slavery and Jim Crow, because our ancestors were not allowed to learn to read or write. If a slave was caught reading, they were whipped or possibly killed. Then I explained that reading is a gift that they should cherish.

I reminded them that the Slaveholders in the South felt that if the Slaves learned to read, they would have an uprising and the Slave owners would lose their position as the Superiority class.

I'm always busy working on something. I work eight days a week and they responded,

"There aren't eight days."

I asked them to count the hours that I spend working. As they continue to grow, they have become wiser and smarter, thank God. Hopefully, I will be an inspiration for them when they grow up.

CHAPTER TWENTY-SEVEN

Recognizing Dementia

Mother in Israel, 2003

Several years after my mother returned from her pilgrimage to Israel, I noticed she had stepped up in age and all of her friends had passed away. I began to notice a change in Mother's behavior shortly after her 90th Birthday Party. At first, it was subtle and could have easily been missed, if I didn't know her well. She was becoming forgetful. One evening, while I was at the TV studio editing, someone rushed over to me and said, "Your mother is downstairs."

"My Mother?"

I was totally surprised because she had never come to the TV studio before. I instantly knew something was wrong. I ran downstairs to see what was going on. Mother said she couldn't find her house keys. She went to Carolyn's house, but no one was there, so she came to the studio to find me. I looked in her purse and low-and-behold were her keys.

I said, "Wait two minutes, while I collect my things and turn off the computer. I'll ride with you to make sure you get home in one piece."

There was one problem: I had no idea how to get to her house by car because I had only taken public transportation. And I don't know how to drive, so I could not offer any driving assistance.

After crossing the Queensboro Bridge, she drove against traffic, I knew we were in trouble, and it was obvious she was lost. I prayed for us to arrive in one piece. I also prayed that she would stop driving before she killed someone or herself. Fortunately, we arrived safely at her home. I swore never to ride with her again. I didn't want to force her to give up driving, because I knew she would resist. I waited for her to give up it up on her own. Following the Queensboro Bridge incident, she wrecked two cars and eventually stopped driving.

I also knew something was wrong when she missed a payment for the telephone bill. It wasn't for the lack of money. She had always been financially diligent. She never let a bill go beyond the payment date. The telephone company threatened to turn her phone off. That was the second sign that got my attention. Something was not quite right. She was not herself.

I recall her sitting next to the stove and didn't realize the food was burning. When I discovered that this happened more than once, I immediately removed the knobs, so she couldn't use the stove or mistakenly leave the gas on. I was afraid for her life.

There were many tell-tale signs. One day, I arrived at her home, only to find that she had walked out of her house and was on her way to the back driveway to look for her house. It was difficult to get her to return because she resisted any suggestions. Joan Perry, one of her neighbors, tricked her and walked her back to her home, by saying she came out of another. Then, on another occasion, while I was at her home, the doorbell rang. I opened the door and two policemen were standing there. They said there was a report your mother was wandering the streets. I quickly walked to her bedroom and fortunately, she was sleeping.

It was painfully clear she could no longer handle her affairs, so I arranged a meeting with an attorney. We prepared a will, so no details or wishes would be overlooked. I became Power of Attorney (POA) to manage her bills and make decisions on her behalf. That was a difficult role to assume because it confirmed Mother's diminished mental capacity. She had dementia and it was crucial for advanced planning to be in place before it was too late. Throughout her life, Mother was a healthy, beautiful, strong, and independent woman with an infectiously warm smile. However, we have to remember as our parents step up in age, their mental faculties depreciate, but we have to continue to give them undying love, patience, and support.

I wasn't as patient as I could have been at the beginning of her decline. I often got upset and reminded her of something she did wrong. She would throw her hand up in the air, wave, and say, "So, help me God, I didn't do that!" I told her I was going to call her Mother to give her a spanking.

Then I'd ask, "Are you afraid."

"No!" she replied.

Her mother passed away many years ago, but I loved to tease her. Then I laughed because she was seriously not afraid. Patience is a virtue. My friend, Lorraine Curry, taught me the importance of having patience.

Lorraine said, "Whenever your mother does something strange, don't reprimand her, put a little humor in it and be patient."

On another occasion, I arrived at her home and discovered the sink and toilet were clogged. I called a Roto-Rooter plumber. He used a large machine to clear the sewage drain. After he opened the drain, he pulled out the strangest thing and showed it to me.

"Oh, my God, that's my mother's wig!" I laughed.

It was the roots from a bush in her garden.

I knew I needed help. I contacted a caregiving service for people with dementia, but they made several suggestions that I did not like. For instance, they suggested I place mother in a care facility and sign her home over to them to cover the costs. I couldn't let that happen. Mother worked too damn hard to buy her home and I was not going to let anyone take it away from her. I had to carefully figure out a solution. Several doctors also suggested placing her in a nursing home. I think that would have killed her. I wanted her to be in her home, in a familiar environment, with people who loved her. I spent weekends with her to ensure her that she was loved and protected. Yvette Taylor, a neighbor, was the first person to help out that summer. That took a lot of pressure off my shoulders. Then, I had to find a permanent caregiver for five days a week.

I searched high and low and found a young lady, but she was unreliable and often called at the last minute to say she couldn't come in. That annoyed the hell out of me because it screwed up my schedule. One day, I ventured into the garage and found a basket of summer T-shirts. I asked her to wash and fold them.

"You are always giving me more work!" she screamed.

"The machine does the washing, all you have to do is fold them and put them away," I responded.

She also decided she wanted more money. That occurred two days before my trip to Malaysia. I grabbed her by the seat of her pants and literally threw her out the front door.

Then I thought, "What the hell am I going to do now?"

Suddenly a bright light entered my head: I walked to the Senior Citizen Recreation Center and asked if they knew of someone who could take care of my mother. Low-and-behold, they recommended Denice Royes, who happened to be available right away. Bingo. Denice was my saving grace.

Carolyn and her daughters live in Brooklyn, but rarely came to visit and never called, which contributed to mother not remembering them. On one or two occasions during Carolyn's visit, Mother addressed Carolyn as, "Miss", or she just stared at her granddaughters without much to say. My friend, Kiko, called Carolyn, "Cruella," because she thought Carolyn was cruel for not contributing to the care of our mother. I took the responsibility of taking care of her needs and did not consider it a burden. I loved my Mother and am not saying Carolyn did not, but I was the one, that cared for her.

I was fortunate and blessed to find four young ladies to help with mother: Denice Royes, Lisa Royes, Opal Williams, and Yvette Taylor. Those ladies showed patience, loved, and took special care of her. They were a "God send" and I don't know what I would have done without them.

Denice, mother's helper, 2015

When Denise found a better job. She introduced me to her sister Lisa and took over after Denise. She was with us for three years until her husband insisted that she come to Florida to live with him. It's amazing how lucky I was to have had such caring ladies. Lisa introduced me to Opal. Opal was a dream come true. She was very patient and understood that terrible disability. Mother was fond of her.

Mom on her porch, 2016

I often called mother, "Pussy Cat", out of affection, like Sophia, Dorothy's mother in the Golden Girls. "Don't call me that," she would say.

Sometimes mother didn't recognize me.

"Who are you?" she'd ask.

"I'm Jon, your only son."

There were several occasions when she didn't want to get out of bed.

She'd say, "I can't."

I told her, "Don't use that word, because you can do anything you decide to do.

'Can' is the operative word."

Then, she would blurt it out again. I had to use several tricks, like yelling, "Fire!" to get her moving. Several times, I told her the day light is brighter in the living room, then walked her to the bathroom to wash her face and brush her teeth. Then, she was ready for the day. I often told her a guest was waiting to see her. She loved having guests and a companion to watch TV with, although watching television quickly became an effort, because she couldn't concentrate.

Often in the late afternoon, she'd suddenly want to go home. Opal reminded her that she was at home, "Just look at your nightgown. You wouldn't walk down the street in your night clothes, would you?"

302

Then it registered and she calmed down.

Once upon a time, mother had a terrific hobby. She spent hours crocheting beautiful bed coverings and throws. Not only were they colorful, but very practical. Her gifts were shared with friends in Florida, Connecticut, and New York. However, without the ability to concentrate, she had to give it up.

I bought a beautiful rich maroon color leather reclining chair to comfort her and a large screen TV to amuse her. I was never sure if she ever watched TV, or if she still could comprehend, but that didn't matter. The most important thing was she was comfortable and had some form of entertainment. It broke my heart to see her in that state.

Opal occasionally noted that Mother took three showers a day, forgetting she had taken the first. Opal allowed her to shower again if that's what she wanted to do. Mother never had a problem eating and she loved dark purple grapes. I bought six pounds a week for her to nibble on. She'd often finish dinner, and then say she didn't have anything to eat. That's when Opal offered her something refreshing like grapes. She constantly looked in the refrigerator to find something to eat. Thank God she never lost her appetite.

It was interesting to watch mother take her pills out of the glass, count them, put them back in the glass and repeat this until I thought, I would lose my mind. Finally, she swallowed the pills. Otherwise, Opal crushed them and mixed them in apple sauce.

Whenever mother was left alone, for a moment, she would find something to occupy her time. I guess she was used to doing things for herself and thought she could still do so. She put grapes in a pot of water on the stove to cook. She also put ready-made Jell-O and cheese in a pot and even poured orange juice in a pot to cook. She wanted to cook any and everything she found in the cabinets or refrigerator. Fortunately, the knobs were removed from the stove and hidden away to prevent an accident. Even without her wits, she was still smart. She tried to get around the missing stove knobs by using a knife to turn on the stove.

As dementia progressed, mother didn't sleep very well. I was told that, in the middle of the night, she moved furniture to the center of the room. I jokingly called her the "Santini Brothers", a moving company.

We kept the basement stairway door locked because on one occasion she miss-stepped and fell to the bottom of the stairs and landed on her head. Fortunately, I was there and called 911 for an ambulance to take her to the hospital. Thank God, she only broke a finger and bruised her head. Fortunately, it wasn't more serious.

Sometimes during our conversations, she didn't have a normal reaction. She just stared off into space or talked about something obscure and nonsensical. Of course, I had no idea what the hell she was talking about, so I humored her and pretend to understand to prevent combativeness.

Opal, was mother's helper for several years. On one occasion she asked, "Is she crooked?" When a person has dementia, the only way to handle the situation is with a sense of humor. She would have never responded that way when she was in her right mind.

One day, I told my mother that one of my dress designs from my former career as a fashion designer was being exhibited in the Museum Fashion Institute of Technology. I looked at her face and there was no expression. I don't know if it registered.

I often teased her by telling her, "You're going back to Africa. Your people are waiting for you."

"I've never been to Africa," she responded.

Then I showed her a photo of her in Dakar, Senegal, to prove my point.

She often took items from her armoire, neatly folded them, and then refolded them to place them back on the shelf. She was always very neat and tidy and still remembered the experience. There were good days and bad

Mother in Senegal

days in terms of her memory. She remained strong and feisty, but as time passed she continued to dissipate.

One Sunday morning, I called Mother to come to breakfast. Suddenly, I heard a thump on the floor. Mother cried out because she had fallen and couldn't get up; like the commercial where the old lady falls and says, "I've fallen and can't get up." Mother was a large size woman. So, I ran to ask several neighbors to help get her up. That's when we realized it was a serious fall. I called 911. The ambulance took her to the hospital where they discovered she had broken her tibia bone. She underwent a leg operation and after a few days of observation in the hospital, she was discharged and sent to a rehabilitation center.

The rehabilitation center was like a "death sentence, it was hell." I don't know why it was called a rehabilitation center, because nothing about it signified rehabilitation. Mother shared a room with another lady. Her room was on a floor, where there were 57 patients with only three nurses on the floor. How could she get proper service? Fortunately, I had Opal there to assist.

Occasionally, I arrived early to find my mother in a zombie-like state after being drugged. The nurses just tucked her in a corner in the dining room and didn't care whether she ate or not. And the food was horrible, horrible. Everything looked like mystery meat.

The nurses lined the patients up against the wall in their wheelchairs after breakfast. It appeared as if they were preparing to execute them. Most of the patients didn't have visitors to check on them. The patients looked as if they were in a mental institution. On one occasion I asked the nurse to get Mother out of bed.

"I need three people to lift her."

"So, what's the problem? Get them." I quipped.

That nursing home was so depressing.

One day, I was departing the building, when the receptionist asked if I was a patient!

"No, I'm escaping."

That didn't sit well with the nursing home. While walking to the bus stop and talking on my phone. Suddenly, a guard from the nursing home followed me and asked if I was a patient.

"Are you kidding me? Get away from me!"

I think she was trying to capture another patient. I couldn't believe the ridiculousness.

I couldn't wait to check mother out of that miserable place. She returned home and she was happy because Opal and I were there to assist her. There was a lot of love in her home. I arranged for in-home care, which included a nurse, therapist, doctor, podiatrist, and of course Miss Opal. Mother was fond of Opal and it gave her comfort of having someone around that she knew. The four ladies that took care of my mother, allowed her to continue to have her dignity.

Mother's fall was traumatic and the beginning of her downfall. She lost her energy and ability and desire to do things for herself. The wheelchair was her only mode of mobility. We tried everything to get her motivated again. The therapist wasn't very helpful. He told me, she would never walk again and suggested I return her to that awful rehabilitation center. Needless to say, I didn't agree with him. I believed she would improve. It was a wait-and-see-what-happens situation. I hired help for seven days a week to make sure she was taken care of.

Within a short time, she proved the therapist wrong, she did walk again, for a short time. Mother had strength in her hands and arms. She gave a firm grasp to let you know she was still there. She fed herself and was in good spirits. Mother looked radiant and her face glowed with Opal Williams help, mother's best buddy.

In the beginning stage of her dementia, I often informed her of my travel plans and she would continue to ask me again and again when and where I was going. I learned to keep it simple and solved that problem by not telling her. Mother never said, "I love you," or "I'm proud of you." However, the words weren't necessary, because she showed love with action and support. She was my best friend.

I published another book, *Jon Haggins, the GlobeTrotter.* I dedicated it to my mother. I read the dedication to her:

"This book is dedicated lovingly to my mother, Willie Mae Haggins. Through her struggles, perseverance, and determinations she has remained strong."

I don't know if she comprehended the dedication, but it didn't matter as long as she looked good and smiled.

Mother continued to descend into the abyss. Her decline was rapid after she fell and broke her tibia. Cousin, Debbie Davidson-Gibbs from Maryland visited her.

Debbie asked her, how are you doing?

"I'm well taken care of."

Then, she grabbed Debbie's hand for reassurance. It made me proud to know she felt confident and appreciated all that was done for her. I often thought, what would happen to mother if something happened to me during one of my international trips. I wanted to out-live her because I know if anything happened to me, Carolyn and her daughters would immediately lock her in a nursing home and that would have finished her off.

Unfortunately, mother was housebound during her final years, because there are four steps down to the sidewalk. She often sat on her porch with Opal and Denice to observe the friendly squirrel, the birds, and people with babies as they passed. At the end of her life, she was not able to walk. She arrived at the dinner table in the wheelchair. She never lost her appetite. One of my last memories was of her sitting at the dining table. She dropped her head on the back of my hand as if to give up. She was weak and tired. I think she was ready to go. Later, she refused to get out of bed for a few days.

My final remembrance was when I said goodbye before I left for Ireland. I reached down as she lay in bed, kissed her on her forehead, and said, "I loved you." I asked her to please wait for me until I return from Ireland in a few days. She simply stared up at me as to say, "I won't make it."

While in Dublin, Ireland, I received a call from Sharon Alcidas, a neighbor: "I have some unfortunate and sad news, your mother quietly passed away tonight and the ambulance is here."

Mother passed away on the evening of September 7th, 2018. My first thought was: I was hoping she would have hung in for two more weeks to celebrate her 93rd birthday on September 21st. I returned to New York the next afternoon to make funeral arrangements. It was a very stressful time; a time that no family is ever prepared for, but it's the natural course of life that we must face.

Thank God, my mother lived to see her great-grandchildren and the election of a Black President. I was blessed to have such a loving Mother and Grandad, who spirited me through my fears, successes, and my dreams.

I recently had a dream, that my mother returned with a brilliant smile. She was happy. I only had one mother, and I have to respect and appreciate her for all that she was. Mother will be remembered as a generous loving friend. I miss her humor, style, flair, friendship, generosity, independence, and discipline. I think about her every moment, every day. I see her face, her eyes, and smile and I know she is at peace; no more memory loss, no more pain, and suffering. She is in a better place, but she is dearly missed.

The passing of Grandad and Mother was so devastating for me. I miss them every day and every moment. Even though they are no longer with me, they were the foundation that made me who I am today. The love and devotion they shared with me are irreplaceable. They were a fountain of water that flowed through my veins and made me who and what I am. They were my rock and wanted me to be the very best I can be —to reach for the stars. They were also so proud of me as I was of them. They inspired me to pursue my life with freedom. They also told me I can do anything and become whatever I desired, there are no limits. I have been fortunate to have traveled the world. I say, "If I die today, I will have lived."

After Mother passed away, I mourned in a personal way of remembering her for her joy. I was so proud of her accomplishment.

I will always remember how important my Mother and Grandad were to me for the love they shared with me. I was blessed to have two remarkable inspiring people in my life, who gave me a better life than they had. Because of them, I am a better person.

After my mother's death, I got back on the road or plane and continued to travel the world. I have traveled all my life, but not as frantically as I have for my *GlobeTrotter Television*. I have always looked beyond the horizon of my couch, because I know there's a great big world out there, that's waiting to be discovered. After all, the world is a discovery. I love to get up, get out and travel.

Travel in Malaysia

Globetrotter TV has given me enormous opportunities to get acquainted with different cultures. It's as if a flower has bloomed in the garden and it permeates my world. I often visit places that the general public is not knowledgeable of, such as Zacatecas. When I asked several friends if they had ever heard of Zacatecas. They think it's a venereal disease. No, it's a wonderful, magical colonial town just north of Mexico City, or Gozo, off the coast of Malta in the middle of the Mediterranean. Whenever I say Gozo, people say what, where?

There is nothing better than writing and learning about people and places around the world. As a travel and food writer, TV host, and radio personality, I look beyond the horizon of the couch. Fortunately, I have traveled with wondering eyes to five of seven continents, Asia, South Pacific, Africa, India, Europe, and North and South America. I have explored many cultures and had fun while doing it. There's a great big world out there that's waiting to be discovered. I know it's not possible to see the entire world in a lifetime, but I will die trying.

I always seek goals, even during COVID-19. I scheduled at least three to five 'To Do' lists each day. This book was one of the most important projects I worked on. I dedicated several hours a day and kept on schedule to finish. Dedication and passion is the most important thing in life.

I continue to breathe and live and take one day at a time because life is short, so we have to live it to the fullest and cherish each moment. Dedication and passion is the most important thing in life.

I miss my Mother's majestic smile. She was my best friend.

CHAPTER TWENTY-EIGHT

Reflecting

I returned to Sanford in 2009, because I wanted to see if the town had changed. Yes, the town had changed, a little, but remained very still. The home I lived in was no longer there, and neither was the large white clapboard house where I spent much of my time. Both had been demolished, but the gigantic oak tree I used to climb still stood proud. The large ditch next to our house was covered up. The dirt road where I played stickball, was paved. As a child, the St. John River was larger than life, but upon my return, it appeared much smaller than I remembered. My elementary school is now a museum. Sanford is now integrated. What was originally the downtown, has become a historic district with a variety of outdoor cafes. The segregated movie house that I used to go to is now a cultural center. There was even a library and a museum. I certainly don't recall ever having either when I was a child.

I lived in Coney Island for nine years as a boy. That seems like a lifetime ago. But the memories lingered from my early childhood, where I continued to dream of making a better world for myself. I look back and thank God, I left that small town of Sanford. I can't imagine living in that small town now. I question myself, "What would have become of me, had I not been inspired to leave Sanford and Coney Island."

Thoughts

I have had an active and stimulating life. My usual day begins with a visit to the New York City Chelsea Recreational Center, where I participate in Dana Brown's, George Giraldo, and LeSharn's water aerobics classes. We stretch to popular soul music for forty-five-minute and the last fifteen minutes are devoted to a game of volleyball. Volleyball allows us to stretch even more, and let me not forget, lots of laughs. A group of us indulge in a Volley Ball game at the end of Dana's and LeSharn's class. LeSharn also enjoys a game of Volley Ball. LeSharn, George, and Dana are the best water aerobics teachers because they have lots of enthusiasm, which is what one would expect from a teacher. Nothing could be more invigorating than exercising in the pool, bright and early in the morning. I thoroughly enjoy their classes, because they make me feel like a kid again.

Never Too Late to Learn

I took swimming lessons in my early teens, having only learned the backstroke. Unfortunately, I never practice, because of my fear of drowning. There were three occasions when I almost drowned. On one occasion, I walked out on a sand bar in Rio de Janeiro, and upon returning to shore, the bottom dropped out and I panicked. I was going down for the third time while trying to think of the word for help in Portuguese. Finally, I yelled, "Help." Someone rushed over and saved me. A similar incident happened in Hawaii, but luckily, I talked myself out of panicking and rescued myself.

Another frightening incident happened when I jumped off a boat in Sharm El Sheikh, into the Red Sea and attempted to snorkel a thousand feet to shore. After I had snorkeled five hundred feet, suddenly a young man swam over to me and asked:

"Do you know you're over one-thousand feet of water?"

Well, that did it for me. I panicked and quickly took off the goggles. He asked if I was alright. I managed to return to the boat and then drank twelve bottles of coke. I promised myself that I would not try that again.

After several terrifying swimming incidents, I joined a New York City recreational facility at age forty-nine. The Romanesque-style building was originally built as a bathhouse at the turn of the century. New York City spent six million dollars renovating the building and its facilities.

After observing several athletic, stylized swimmers, I began timing their movement through the water. Their strokes had a rhythm and count, as in dance. I began counting and stroking across the width of the pool, while my friends swam the length.

A young man who had been observing me for weeks suggested that I swim the length of the pool. He assured me that he would swim with me to give me moral support. I emphatically stated, "No way." The water on the other end of the pool was fourteen feet deep. After several days of encouragement, he convinced me to charge ahead. I foolishly believed him, so I set out with a brisk backstroke up the length of the pool. When I arrived at the opposite end, he was still standing in the shallow end.

Two days later, as I was floating on my back, suddenly my entire body began to submerge and I panicked for a moment. It was like the commercial, where the little old lady falls on the floor and yells, "I've fallen and I can't get up." I called out for help. Everyone including the lifeguard thought I was joking. He looked at me and said, "Yeah, right." Something suddenly came over me. I relaxed and surfaced, then floated away, then realized I had just saved myself. From that day forward, I've never been afraid of deep water. Except while snorkeling in Sharm El Sheikh.

I always wanted to learn to swim properly, so I recently began taking swimming lessons at the Chelsea Recreational Center in Chelsea. George Giraldo, teaches a learn-to-swim class. I practice swimming the width of the pool for an hour per day and then take lessons for another hour, twice per week. Always trying to perfect my stroke and my kick.

Unfortunately, I was used to holding my breath, while swimming seventy-five feet, the length of the pool at the bottom of the pool. Old habits are hard to break. But, I needed to BREATHE while doing the crawl. My favorite thing to do is a casual backstroke across the pool. I recall the first day, George asked everyone to swim the length of the pool. I thought I was doing fine. I also thought I had reached the length of the pool, only to discover, that I had only swam three-quarters of the pool. But, you know what? I keep trying to achieve my goal of being the best damn swimmer I can be. With each stroke, I gain confidence in the water.

George often screams, "BREATHE, BREATHE." It has taken me a while to understand and coordinate my kicking and breathing. There is so much going on at one time. However, I will continue to improve my freestyle to perfect my swimming. My favorite thing I like to do is a cool backstroke, where I can relax and take my time. I am committed to learning from George, and one day, I will be as good a swimmer as George.

I have always said, "It's never too late to learn to swim or do anything in life."

Let me not forget George's Salsa Class, where I learned fantastic Broadway dance combinations. His classes are invigorating, and boy, do I sweat.

I also take several computer classes with Sara Skwira, such as photography, where I learn the functions of the camera. I got to understand lighting and color balance, in in-order to take the best damn photographs. Sara's Adobe Premiere class is where I learned to edit videos for *GlobeTrotter TV* and Illustrator for graphic design. It's a perfect way to start my day. Love, love, love it. Wow, what a full schedule.

I feel very fortunate to have lots of friends such as Kevin Dickens,

Erich McCall, Norma Jean Darden, and Phyllis Bishop. They invite me to Broadway openings, lots of movie screenings, and events. No one could be busier than I. I also meet friends for lunch or dinner and drinks at the end of the day. I'm busy.

Several friends often invite me to their homes for the weekend, such as Roseanne and John Forde in Asbury Park, Candy Levine in Fairfield, Ct., Carolyn McGonigle in Boca Raton, and Kiko Morgan in Chicago. I love visiting. I recall someone in Florida suggested I buy a place there.

"Why would I want to do that, when I can stay with you?" I responded.

Norma Jean Darden and I decided to support New York City restaurant during COVID-19. We dressed up and dined in a variety of restaurants to experience different cultures. I have always said, "If you can't travel, you can dine out." We have documented some of them with photos on:

Linkedin.com/in/jonhaggins

Facebook.com/jonhaggins.9

Another thing I believe: when you have an appointment with someone, make sure you arrive on time and don't keep them waiting, because it's disrespectful. Time is money and respect, and that's how you respect the other person's time.

However, through every obstacle I have lived my life with pride and determination, making "can't" an incomprehensible word. I feel like a bowling pin that gets knocked down and quickly stands up to face the challenge of every day. My greatest reward is to live each day to the fullest.

I continue to think positively about all the possibilities in life. I set goals every day and try to accomplish them. I always think that tomorrow will be a better day. I'm in touch with the present and don't look back, because I'm going for the brass ring.

I have always looked beyond the horizon of my couch, because I know there's a great big world out there, that's waiting to be discovered. I have traveled with wondering eyes to five of seven continents. After all, the WORLD is a discovery. I love to get up, get out and travel, and have fun while doing it.

Throughout my life, no matter what profession I ventured into, and boy I've had a few, I approached each, with commitment and passion. I believe if you don't have passion for whatever you do, then you shouldn't do it.

Several people told me that I re-invented myself and I respond, "No, I have evolved," I tell them that, I just continued to live and grow. Another person asked when was I going to retire.

"From what?"

I like what I'm doing and haven't figured out the next step yet. One can always apply what one has learned in the past and apply it to the present.

I have also had the most inspiring experiences visiting other cultures, history, cuisine, and people. Travel makes life worth living. Nothing is better than being there and sharing the experience.

I continue to travel around the world with an open mind and accept other customs and traditions. Throughout the many countries where I have traveled, my imagination continued to be challenged and my cultural scope broadened—that's what travel is all about.

As I step up in age with great remembrances of how sweet life is. I continue to enjoy life to the fullest.

I celebrated my 78th Birthday party at the legendary, The Leopard at des Artistes, one of my favorite restaurants. I invited 19 friends. Gianfranco and Paula Sorrentino, the owners, designed an extraordinary menu. First, we toasted my 78th Birthday with a glass of bubbling Prosecco. There were five divine-tasting dishes and a lovely salad. The main course included a choice of lamb chops, and boy, do I love lamb chops or a fish dish. To top off the celebration, the waiters brought out an enormous, delicious Birthday cake then everyone sang Happy Birthday. It was a memorable night.

Top left: Gianfranco Sorrentino and I, 2022. Top right/bottom left/bottom right: Jon's birthday party at The Leopard at des Artistes Restaurant, 2021.

To my surprise, several guests brought gifts. Rosanne and John Forde presented me with an envelope filled with seventy-eight dollars. I was puzzled at first until I found out that each dollar represented a year of my life. That was a pleasant surprise. I called Roseanne and John to thank them, I said, "Next year, you only have to bring a dollar, because you already gave me 78 dollars."

Life is like fine wine, that's been aged. As I grow older and wiser, everything becomes more focused. I have lived my life with pride, dignity, and determination making "can't" an incomprehensible word. I feel like a bowling pin that gets knocked down and quickly stands up to face the challenge of another day.

My greatest reward is to live each day to the fullest through each obstacle. However, through every obstacle, I made my life a 'Yes I Can' experience. I continue to breathe and live and take a day at a time, because life is short, and we must cherish each precious day. Life is also like a flower that blossoms and becomes more beautiful each day.

I set goals each day and do my best to accomplish them. I continue to think positively about all the possibilities in life.

Several people have said, "I re-invented myself,"

I respond, "No, I have evolved."

I always think that tomorrow will be a better day because I'm going for the brass ring.

Blessings to all and may you have a fruitful life.

I have traveled to five of seven continents.

*The people in all those countries have always called me an American,
only here in America am I called an African American.*

*I have lived through being referred to as
Colored, Negro, Black, and African American.*

*No matter what you call me, I know who and what I am.
I have perseverance and determination.*

*I am inspired.
I am a man with a dream, thanks to my forefathers and mothers.*

I hope my family's story is an invaluable inspiration
that inspires you to explore your family's history
and discover what you're made of.
I want you to live out your dream and think positively about life.
I hope my book will also inspire you
to achieve a long, fruitful, and successful life.

My Grandad said, "Go out there and spread your wings."

Travel is in my blood.
To travel is to live.
To travel is to breathe.
To travel is freedom.

When a good American dies, they don't go to heaven, they go to Paris.

— Oscar Wilde

I wanted to fly around the world for my *GlobeTrotter TV* Show, but couldn't during COVID-19, so I decided to write this book about me and my family. The process was lethargic and inspiring. It is my greatest hope that *Just Being Jon* will inspire you to achieve your goals.

APPENDIX

Commercial and academic honors came to me just as my fashion future narrowed.

The Schomburg Center for Research in Black Culture at 515 Malcolm X Blvd, NYC 10037 has my archive of sixteen boxes of my fashion editorial:

http://archives.nypl.org/scm/23942

BLACK FASHION SUPPORT

Eleanor Lambert
Empress of Seventh Avenue

Eleanor Lambert was an avid supporter of black fashion models, designers, and publications. She hired black models for high-profile fashion shows such as the 1959 Moscow Exhibition and the 1973 Versailles Fashion Show, which she organized. She selected her client Stephen Burrows as one of the five designers to represent American fashion at Versailles. Lambert wrote about the designer Jon Haggins in 1972 in her syndicated newspaper column, citing him as the "first black fashion designer to make a name on Seventh Avenue." In 1961, Lambert's client Pauline Trigère hired model Beverly Valdes, making her the first black Seventh Avenue fit model.

The Original *NY Times* Article

𝕿𝖍𝖊 𝕹𝖊𝖜 𝖄𝖔𝖗𝖐 𝕿𝖎𝖒𝖊𝖘

At Show's End He Married the Model

By Nan Ickererngill
September 22, 1970

As a fashion show, yesterday afternoon's event wasn't particularly unusual. A beautiful setting on the terrace of a Tudor City penthouse. Taped ballet music. Models flitting like butterflies to show the fluidity of Jon Haggins newest resort and spring designs. And, in the end, a beautiful bride in all her starry-eyed glory.

As a wedding, it was something more unorthodox. After all, fashion shows generally end with a bride. But weddings — real ones-don't usually begin with a fashion show.

According to the designer, combining the events saved him from being nervous on two separate occasions. And it necessitated only one set of invitations.

Familiar Dress

If I meant that most of the 200 wedding guests were strangers (mainly press people covering the show) while the bride's dress was very familiar (since he designed it), Mr. Haggins didn't seem to mind. Neither did the former June Murphy.

She thought it was "a fantastic idea," even though modeling in, and acting as coordinator for the show meant she hadn't had time to decide on her going away outfit. Miss Murphy made her first appearance in a long red one-shoulder dress. She made her second appearance in the wedding dress — a purple print silk chiffon with a matching trailing scarf binding her braided hair — walking demurely on the arm of the designer. Mr. Haggins wore a purple tucked shirt and a purple velvet bow tie with the black suit he didn't design.

Almost Inaudible

They were married by an associate minister of the community church of New York (Unitarian). The service, which was almost inaudible, seemed both joyous and solemn, despite its unusual prelude.

There was nothing solemn about the clothes. The whole collection of 36 dresses could, it was claimed, fit in one small bag-and pop right out again, fresh as ever.

There was certainly plenty of movement in the clothes, even in those rare moments when the models were still. There was quite a bit of bareness, too, generally in the back. There was some cleavage, but the only time breasts were bared was when a model danced energetically or, on one occasion when a pin gave way to the top that barely covered anything ceased to do so.

Cloaks accompanied many of the dresses, pants a few. Scarves flowed from the wrist or where ever the sleeve happened to end. Most of the styles were purple or black, with an occasional peachy pink and the one red dress worn by the bride.

Mr. Haggins met his bride when she modeled in his last collection in May. According to the bridegroom, they argued about the wedding dress, but in the end, his ideas prevailed. He didn't want her to look like every other bride, and she didn't.

The couple, rode their bicycles to City hall last week to get their license and went in carrying the front wheels so no one could steal their vehicles.

Mr. Haggins borrowed the apartment of Blair Walliser, president of the Communication Capital Corporation (which finances radio and television stations) and former director of radio soap operas in Chicago for the show and wedding.

Mr. Haggins said he wished they could keep the penthouse, but until they find what they want, they will occupy his rather small quarters. At least they won't have too much trouble over closet space. They both wear the same size pants.

The New York Times

A Fashion Show With a
Surprise Ending: A Wedding

AS TOLD TO JACLYN PEISER

February 7, 2017

Fashion designer Jon Haggins married his model June Murphy at one of his fashion shows in 1970.
Bill Cunningham, far left in white jacket, was on hand to photograph the event.
JACK MANNING/THE NEW YORK TIMES

Fashion designer Jon Haggins married his model June Murphy at one of his fashion shows in 1970. Bill Cunningham, far left in a white jacket, was on hand to photograph the event.

Jon Haggins, now 72, was a fashion designer in New York City in the 1970s and '80s. Known for making a statement, Mr. Haggins invited guests to a fashion show in September 1970, promising a wedding at the end. Mr. Haggins retired from fashion and is now the host of the travel show *GlobeTrotter TV*. This interview has been edited and condensed.

This was over in Tudor City, on a friend's terrace, which holds 200 people. It was just an incredible day. The wind took her veiling and wrapped it around the two of us. The sun was right, the weather was right and it was a great time.

I thought it was a cheap way to have a wedding, honestly. And it was really different. The guests were trying to guess, "Which model is he going to marry?" as the models kept coming out.

I met June when she came into the studio to collect her money from doing a show. It was just something magical when she walked in. They say you shouldn't flirt with your employees. But this was just something that happened. I was deeply in love with her.

June didn't want a typical wedding and she didn't want a typical dress. She wanted something very special and didn't want any of the dresses I had designed previously. So, we did a special dress for her that didn't look like a typical wedding dress.

The sides were open all the way down to the waist. A cowl front and a cowl back. It draped like a handkerchief and it was a slim, easygoing dress. She's wearing a long scarf, and a florist that I know painted the butterfly on it, and it just flowed down the back.

We were together for about six months before getting married. I just felt it was time to do it. I was 27.

We were married a year and a half. We just had different visions. It was a bitter divorce. It was a very special time in my life and I wish it had lasted.

I still have a little thing here [points to his heart] for her. It's something I never quite got over.

Jaclyn Peiser is a news assistant and contributing reporter for *The New York Times*, where she also writes wedding announcements.

Women's Wear Daily
Lost and Found

They were the 'IT' boys and girls of fashion...then they disappeared. Where are they now?

HOT...THEN NOT. WHAT'S A BOY OR GIRL wonder to do? Lack of funds, backers pulling out, a so-so season or two, plain old disillusionment—The reasons for dropping out of the spotlight may vary, but one thing's for sure: There IS life after fashion.

It's not difficult to see why Jon Haggins was a favorite of the fashion pack. He had charm, good looks, and enough talent to win raves for his groovy clothes. Sixties features in *WWD* showed him roller skating about town with a model decked out in his skimpy halter dress, and whooping it up at a disco with two models dressed in pants and bar tops. He even turned his 1970 wedding to June Murphy into a post-fashion show fete. But shortly after, he closed up shop, blaming money woes. Haggins went back in and out of business for the next several years and also worked for larger corporations such as Leslie Fay to make ends meet. Finally, he wanted out.

"Stores were taking clothes on consignment, returning merchandise that they didn't sell, and I couldn't survive that way," he said. When I resigned from my last fashion job, I just said, "I quit and I left." Haggins found a new life as. Travel and food writer and host of a weekly travel show on cable. His current career as a professional Globetrotter suits him. "I'm a gypsy," he says. "I have to sew new pages in my passport. It's like the bible."

I love meeting people and learning about their history and culture and of course their cuisine. As I continue to expand my horizon, I have searched many corners of the world to discover a tolerance for many things. I feel very fortunate that I have had the opportunity to travel around the world for *GlobeTrotter TV* to five of seven continents.

Corey from NPR Radio called and invited me to contribute travel features for his show. Being a contributor was one of the best experiences of my life. NPR is a national radio station that reaches twenty-five million listeners. I shared travel experiences with my audience and showed them how to stretch their dollar when traveling. One of my fans called and told me she heard my broadcast on NPR while she was shopping in a mall in Washington State. That was certainly rewarding. It was a terrific gig that only lasted six months because a new host reigned over the show. I could feel her vibes through my headset. Unfortunately, that was the end of my gig at NPR.

BET-TV also called me to audition as a travel person. They gave me a script. There was no way I could remember the text. The teleprompter was a large TV screen up on the left side of the camera. I began reading the text, suddenly the control room sped it up.

I yelled, "Why don't you listen to what I'm saying."

Then they slowed down the text, and that didn't work either, because it was too slow. Normally the teleprompter is located on top of the camera. That was a total disaster. The text read as if I were a travel agent giving tips to the audience on where they can go if they only have $100.00. How the hell do I know. I'm not a travel agent. That position was not for me. I'm not fond of auditions, but I'm very comfortable hosting *GlobeTrotter TV*.

I have contributed to several publications and have written several travel books with color photos and aromatic recipes to whet your appetite and allow you to dream of those far away destinations. Fashion was my first love; however, travel has always been my passion.

I was exiting a restaurant in India, when an Asian woman approached me and asked,

"What part of Africa are you from?"

The Today Show on NBC-TV called and asked, where would I like to tape my travel segment, I suggested Le Périgord.

The TV anchors lead into the segment was:

"If you hate your job, get ready to get sick, because, Jon Haggins travels around the world for a living and he is in his favorite restaurant, Le Périgord."

I have received three B-free Speech awards for *GlobeTrotter TV* for the Best Entertainment/Variety Show in 2016, 2018, and 2021 and an MNN-TV Award in 2017.

I was surprised each time the Moderator announced my name. I had not written an acceptance speech, because I didn't expect to win. The minute the host announced my name, I got up from my seat and walked to the stage, and stood in front of the microphone, then I looked out into the audience and said, "I love BCAT," which was the former name of the Brooklyn Cable station. However, they had changed the name to "BRIC." Everyone laughed.

Then I announced, "I have just written *Chasing Wild ASS.*"

The entire audience laughed again. I smiled and said, "That's not funny, because that's the name of my travel book. The book is filled with lots of color photos and recipes to whet your appetite and allow you to dream of those far-away destinations. I accept this award with honor and would like to thank, Lorraine Curry, David Fasano, and many others. I truly enjoy traveling around the world meeting people and sharing their culture."

On another occasion, I was in La Marche, Italy, photographing the buffet table when a young man rushed in and said, "They want you in the auditorium, now!" As I entered the auditorium, the moderator asked me to come on stage. To my surprise, he presented me with an award for show that I featured on Italy. I was totally surprised and delighted.

Another highlight for me was a month-long retrospective exhibition of my fashion designs in the Johnson Museum at Cornell University in Ithaca, New York.

The Smithsonian Museum in Washington, D.C. invited me as a guest speaker. My message stretched far beyond fabrics, thimbles, and buttons. I use my creativity and rely on a positive attitude, which has helped me survive against all odds, maneuvering through many rocks in the hardest of places.

The Smithsonian National Museum of African American History and Culture honored me for my contribution to the Fashion Industry.

I have had many unbelievable experiences around the world and captured most of them on video for my *GlobeTrotter TV* show. I have also contributed articles to several publications and written several travel books with color photos and aromatic recipes to whet your appetite to allow you to dream of those far-away destinations.

Jon Haggins the GlobeTrotter is a journey onto itself. If you've ever had a desire to see the world, the color photos will take you there as you turn the pages. You will explore Egypt, Thailand, Malaysia, Vietnam, the Caribbean, France, Corsica, The Aegean Sea, Greece and Turkey, Italy, Portugal, Canada, Alaska, Mexico, Sweden, Brazil, and many more.

Let me not forget the history, culture, and aromatic recipes that will whet your appetite for the taste and flavors from around the world. No matter where we are in the world, food makes us feel like home.

I am proud to be an American, to experience other cultures, and to get acquainted with other people and their customs. This is only a brief sampling of my worldly experience. For more travel experiences and recipes, you have to read my:

1. *Chasing Wild ASS* travel book

Oooooh, it's not what you're thinking. *Chasing Wild ASS* is a narrative of my travels around the world. I have interspersed photos and aromatic recipes that will whet your appetite and allow you to dream, discover, rediscover and understand the pleasures of traveling to a variety of those far-away destinations.

2. *Jon Haggins the GlobeTrotter* travel book

Travel Book of the Week: *"The GlobeTrotter"*

POSTED BY: JOHNNY JET

Jon Haggins

THE GLOBETROTTER

Looking for a book to get you into the spirit of traveling? Then check out my buddy Jon Haggins's "The GlobeTrotter."

From Amazon: "The GlobeTrotter is a journey onto itself. If you've ever had a desire to see the world, the color photos will take you there as you turn the pages. You will explore Egypt, Thailand, Malaysia, Vietnam, the Caribbean, France, Corsica, The Aegean Sea, Greece & Turkey, Italy, Portugal, Canada, Alaska, Mexico, Sweden, Brazil, and many more. Let me not forget the history, culture and the aromatic recipes that will whet your appetite for the taste and flavors from around the world. No matter where we are in the world, food makes us feel like home."

My wife and I traveled with Jon to Lake Como in Italy, and he's a great guy to travel with in person, so I'm sure in his book will be great to travel with virtually.

Grab it: Grab "The GlobeTrotter" Jon Haggins on Amazon (currently on Kindle only, for free).

The cover of *Jon Haggins the GlobeTrotter* is whimsical, and it gets you in the spirit for traveling.

You have to read my travel books for more adventures: *Chasing Wild ASS* — travel book and *Jon Haggins the GlobeTrotter*.

Both books are available on Amazon.com

You will discover many stories and places that I've traveled to. However, I have only included a sampling in this book.

I am often asked, what is my favorite place to visit.

"Wherever I am at the moment."

ACKNOWLEDGEMENTS

Marie Brown
She said, "You tell great stories, why don't you write them down and share them with everyone.

Brigitte Jackson-Buckley
You lifted my words off these pages and made them fly.

Neal Webster
Your energy, time, and dedication helped me visualize the pages of this book.

Maybelle Webster
You are brilliant. You made my vintage photos come to life with your beautiful restorations bow@webmadphotography.com

Eric Copage
You taught me how to paint a picture with words.

Beth Grossman
Thanks for introducing me to Brigitte Jackson-Buckley.

Vickie Swisher — Studio 20/20
You are a creative genius. Thank you for designing this book.

Cover photo: Bo Zaunders

ABOUT THE AUTHOR

JON HAGGINS is the producer and host of *GlobeTrotter TV*; a half-hour weekly lifestyle travel show that airs in two-million NYC homes on Spectrum HD channels 1993 and 56. Jon Haggins *GlobeTrotter TV* received three Brooklyn B-Free Speech Best Entertainment/ Variety Show Awards in 2016, 2018, and 2021 and let me not forget an MNN-TV Award in 2017. *GlobeTrotter TV* also received an award from the Italian Tourist Office and an award from Beaujolais, France.

The Smithsonian Museum in DC invited Jon as a guest speaker. Jon was also a national spokesperson for Proctor and Gamble's Ultra Detergents. And let's not forget his voice for FOX-TV's public service announcement, "It's Ten PM. Do you know where your children are?" He was also a contributor on NPR Radio with 25 million listeners across the country.

His first love was fashion; however, travel has always been his passion. Jon started as a fashion designer, just fresh out of FIT in New York City. Many celebrities such as Debbie Allen, Helen Gurley Brown, Sheryl Lee Ralph, Kaity Tong, Felicia Rashad, Diahann Carroll, Diana Ross, Lynn Redgrave, and Sybil Burton rushed in and purchased his fashions.

The Museum of the Fashion Institute of Technology, Cornell University, and the Museum of the City of New York have exhibited some of his designs. Smithsonian National Museum of African Art also has a collection of his designs.

Jon was the darling of the fashion editors in the late 1960s and early 1970s. His fashions were featured in many national publications such as *Vogue, Harper's Bazaar, NY Times, The Daily News, Town & Country, Women's Wear Daily, Essence, Ebony,* the *Chicago Tribune, New York* magazine, and *Cosmopolitan* magazine where is fashion graced eight covers and eighty-five inside pages. Jon was also a guest on numerous radio and television shows such as *Good Day New York* — FOX TV, *Here & Now* ABC-TV, CNN — *Daybreak, Geraldo, Elsa Klench* — CNN, *Today Show, Regis Philbin, Midday Live,* Joan Hamburg WOR & ABC Radio, and etc.

Jon's designs have also appeared on several soap operas such as, *As the World Turns* and *One Life to Live, Love Boat* as well as the *Debbie Allen Special* and *Star Search* with Ed McMahon. He also designed special projects for Clairol, Revlon, Seagram, Procter & Gamble, and Chesebrough Ponds.

He has written numerous food and travel articles for a variety of newspapers and magazines and authored four books:

- *The African American Travel Guide: To Hot, Exotic, and Fun-Filled Places.* Tips on how to get it together to travel.
- *Yes, I Can.* Anything is possible, all you have to have is a dream.
- *Chasing Wild Ass.* A narrative of his travels around the world with recipes.
- *Jon Haggins The GlobeTrotter.* Another narrative of his travels and recipes.

Made in USA - North Chelmsford, MA
1325053_9780981507620
08.02.2022 1615